BOB LANG'S

THE COMPLETE

Kitchen Cabinetmaker

revised edition

MW01014785

BOB LANG'S

THE COMPLETE

Kitchen Cabinetmaker

revised edition

Shop Drawings and Professional Methods for Designing and Constructing Every Kind of Kitchen and Built-In Cabinet

ROBERT W. LANG

FOX CHAPEL
PUBLISHING

© 2006, 2014 by Robert W. Lang and Fox Chapel Publishing Company, Inc., 903 Square Street, Mount Joy, PA 17552.

Bob Lang's The Complete Kitchen Cabinetmaker, Revised Edition (2014) is a revised edition of *Bob Lang's The Complete Kitchen Cabinetmaker* (2006), originally published by Cambium Press and Fox Chapel Publishing Company, Inc. This version published in 2014 by Fox Chapel Publishing Company, Inc. Revisions to the original book include the addition of color photographs and a new introduction. The patterns contained herein are copyrighted by the author. Readers may make copies of these patterns for personal use. The patterns themselves, however, are not to be duplicated for resale or distribution under any circumstances. Any such copying is a violation of copyright law.

ISBN 978-1-56523-803-9

Library of Congress Cataloging-in-Publication Data

Lang, Robert W., 1953-

  Bob Lang's the complete kitchen cabinetmaker / Bob Lang. -- Revised ed.

     pages cm

Includes index.

ISBN 978-1-56523-803-9

1. Kitchen cabinets. 2. Cabinetwork. I. Title. II. Title: Complete kitchen cabinetmaker.

TT197.5.K57 L36 2014

684.1'6--dc23

2014009236

To learn more about the other great books from Fox Chapel Publishing, or to find a retailer near you, call toll-free 800-457-9112 or visit us at *www.FoxChapelPublishing.com*.

We are always looking for talented authors. To submit an idea, please send a brief inquiry to acquisitions@foxchapelpublishing.com.

Printed in Singapore
Sixth printing

CONTENTS

INTRODUCTION

A little more than ten years ago I had this idea to write a book about building cabinets. I didn't know it at the time, but I was at the point where my career was about to change from full-time cabinetmaker/part-time author to full-time author/part-time cabinetmaker. After thirty years of earning my living making things out of wood, I was ready for a change. I thought there was a need for a book written from the point of view of someone who had been exposed to different methods and techniques.

In my woodworking career I cycled through a number of jobs in shops large and small, intermixed with owning my own shop. My resume from that time may look like I'm the type of guy who can't hold a job, but those years gave me a broad base of experience. I wanted to distill the best practices from those years and adapt them into techniques that could be used successfully in a typical, minimally equipped shop. I also wanted to include details and options for face frame cabinets, frameless cabinets, and what I typically build, cabinets that utilize the best features of both styles.

What I had in mind was the sort of book I needed when I was starting out, a reference that would lay out sensible options for construction and a way to manage a project from conception to completion. The woodworking part of a typical kitchen project is relatively simple; the difference between satisfaction and frustration is usually found in how the numerous choices and steps of the project are handled. The risks are higher if you are doing this work for your own home as opposed to doing this work for someone else.

Things can still go wrong when you're not your own customer, but eventually you get to walk away. If you have to live with the results of a poorly planned project (or with a family who had to go for far too long without a working kitchen), what might have been a rewarding experience can turn ugly and stay ugly. That sort of thing can be avoided, and avoiding disaster is what this book is all about. There are a lot of parts in a typical kitchen, and the sequence of making them and putting them together along with keeping track of them all is a big job.

The success of the first edition of this book was a bit of a surprise, and it has been gratifying as an author to hear from readers who found it helpful. In the fast-changing world of publishing, not many books have the staying power to last through several printings. It's surprising how similar the process of putting a book together is to a large cabinet project. There are a lot of little pieces to fit together, and the goal in each case, at least for me, is to put together something of quality that will last a long time.

There is a real satisfaction to be found in taking an idea and a pile of lumber and turning it into something useful and enduring. There are practical benefits to be found in making cabinets. You can have a kitchen far nicer than you could otherwise afford and much better suited to your own needs when you build your own. If you're considering cabinetmaking as a career or as a serious hobby, a kitchen or other cabinet project is a good way to get a taste of it while filling a need and to get equipped with the basic tools and machinery.

The real benefits are far beyond the practical ones—at least they are for me. Being able to see physical evidence of a day's work is a far cry from what most of us do these days. Parts become boxes and boxes become cabinets and before long an empty room is transformed. That's a satisfying experience, and the satisfaction carries on and grows every time you enter that room. When we build, we build in parts of ourselves and we find that the project also helps to build us. Physical evidence that we did something of lasting value is hard to come by in the information age.

No book introduction is worth a hoot without some thank-you's. First of all, I want to thank all of the people I worked with in shops and on job sites. Every one of them has been a teacher in one way or another, and our shared experience enabled me to leave behind things I am proud to say I made, or helped to make. Second of all, I want to thank all of the readers who have supported my work since my first book was published in 2001. As I tell students in my classes and readers I meet in person, "guys like you make it possible for guys like me" and it is deeply appreciated.

Last but not least is a special thanks to my friend Dale Barnard. He and I first met when he stepped forward to help my research for *Shop Drawings for Greene & Greene Furniture*. In this book, the photos of finished cabinets are Dale's work, and once again I am grateful for his help.

Robert W. Lang

—Robert W. Lang
Maineville, Ohio
March 2014

Fitting the space. *The line between fine furniture and fine cabinetry isn't always clearly defined. The visual elements are the same, but the "built-in" nature of cabinets requires some different techniques and attitudes. Much of cabinetwork remains unseen when the project is finished, but what happens behind the facade is critical. In this built-in, several individual cabinets fit together, and in the course of installing them, they all need to fit the allotted space. Accurate measurements and a few tricks make it possible.*

GALLERY

Variety within a style.
Custom cabinets can be adapted visually to suit the character of the home and the home's residents. On the practical side, variations of details define zones in the room, tailored to suit the task at hand. Color and consistency tie a variety of everyday activities into an inviting space. The central island is a good example of "right-sizing." It is big enough to provide additional work and storage space without being so big that it dominates the entire room.

Purpose built and a purposeful look. *The large sink makes the function of this area clear, while the custom cabinets make it an integral part of these cabinets. The extended stiles anchor the sink to the room and to adjacent cabinets.*

A common front. *These cabinets share a single face frame. The reversed arch on the lower rail ties the cabinets to the space. In the upper cabinets, small drawers and open shelves define the corner.*

Fitting function in style. *Several of these cabinets have been designed to fit specific appliances, yet the common design elements ensure that nothing looks out of place. The contrast between the spectacular veneer on the panels and the simpler grain of the frames helps define each space.*

A graceful transition. *Cabinets placed back-to-back are transformed by a single end panel into a peninsula that separates the kitchen from the dining area. The vertical divider on the counter shields the working parts of the kitchen from view.*

Design challenges and solutions. Seen from the dining area, the effectiveness of the vertical divider is evident. If you look closely, you can also see that the upper cabinets have been custom made to fit around the exposed ceiling beam.

A place for everything. This view shows cabinets made for specific tasks. A sink is placed in the corner, lower cabinets accommodate pastry preparation, and a small refrigerator is tucked away.

New cabinets with an authentic look. *In this restored bungalow kitchen, the cabinets look as if they have always been there, but they are brand new. Period construction details and the right hardware aid in creating an authentic look while up-to-date appliances and granite counters fit right in. This small kitchen combines function and charm in a way that wouldn't be possible with stock cabinets. Attention to every detail makes the difference.*

Making the most of a small space. *The back door and window above the sink provide natural light, and the white paint and linoleum floor help to make this small space warm and inviting.*

A matter of scale. *In this large kitchen, wide vertical elements at the ends of the island match the scale of the cabinets to the scale of the room. This and the taller, narrow counter caps define the kitchen as a distinct area.*

Tradition at the toe. *In modern kitchens, the area below the cabinet doors is recessed and known as the "toe-kick." In the early 20th century, the detail matched the baseboard of the room.*

Borrowed from architecture. *Decorative curved brackets, called corbels, serve a functional purpose. In this case they provide support for the heavy, overhanging counter on this island. Here again we see the end panel extend to the floor and baseboard below the doors.*

Taking care of the transitions. *The tall cabinet at the left end of these cabinets is deeper than the counter and base cabinet next to it. This provides an elegant way to move from one cabinet form to another and simplifies installation, as the shallower cabinets butt into the tall one. Notice the recess between the two sets of upper cabinets. This visual break carries around the corner so that the upper cabinet matches the depth of the tall cabinet. Slight misalignments between the cabinets can be hidden by the recess.*

Details aren't always fussy. *The addition of glass in these upper cabinet doors turns this run of cabinets into a visual opportunity. The stiles (vertical elements) of the doors and the long horizontal edges of the drawers feature a small bead. This easily added detail gives visual interest to simple inset doors and drawers.*

Adapting an elegant style. *These cabinets feature several design elements of California architects Charles and Henry Greene, who worked in the early 1900s. The sculpted handles, cloud-lift shapes on the rails, and ebony pegs were all signature features, adapted here in a thoroughly modern kitchen. Posts on the outer corners define the wall cabinets.*

Beauty and function combined. *Details usually found only in fine furniture are combined with the functional elements a working kitchen needs. In these cabinets, as in the upper cabinets, posts define transitions between cabinets, and behind the outer face, several individual boxes make construction and installation manageable. Careful planning at the outset leads to success when the job is finished.*

1. TWO KINDS OF CABINET

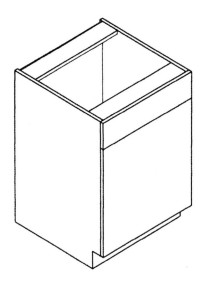

European 32mm, or frameless, base cabinet with overlay doors and drawer

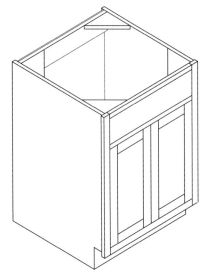

Face frame base cabinet with inset doors and drawer

Figure 1. Basic definitions*: A European 32mm, or frameless, cabinet with overlay doors and drawer, top, and a traditional face frame cabinet with inset doors and drawers, bottom.*

European Frameless vs. Face-Frame Cabinets

One of the biggest decisions the cabinetmaker will face is whether to build traditional face-frame cabinets, or European frameless cabinets, also known as 32mm cabinets. This choice will affect nearly every aspect of the project, and also introduces a third option, building hybrid cabinets using the best aspects of each method (**Figure 1 & 2**).

Both choices use boxes that are mainly constructed of plywood. The differences lie in how the finished face of the cabinet is constructed, how the parts are prepared for assembly, and the type of hardware used to swing the doors and move the drawers in and out of the cabinet.

When European cabinets were introduced to the United States about 30 years ago, nearly every element was different than what was commonly used. Today, the great American melting pot has worked on cabinet design, and it is rare to see a cabinet made in one style that doesn't contain at least one element of the other.

Differences in Construction, not Appearance

People think that appearance is the biggest difference between the two styles, mainly because we think of the visible parts of face-frame cabinets as being constructed of wood, and European cabinets as being of plastic laminate. Visualize the door of a face-frame cabinet, and an oak raised panel, stile-and-rail door likely comes to mind. Think about European cabinets and the image will likely be that of a hospital laboratory: a row of uniform white plastic doors with brushed-chrome wire pulls.

The truth is, you can build in either style and achieve the finished look that you want. You can also mix the elements to achieve the look that satisfies your eye, the construction method that suits your building style and the tools you have available, and your budget. Big decisions should be informed decisions, and you should have a thorough understanding of both styles before you can intelligently choose which one, or which parts of each one, are right for you.

32mm Center to Center

When the 32mm system was developed, Europe was still being rebuilt after World War II, and German design was heavily influenced by the Bauhaus dictum "form follows function." The cabinetmaking system that was developed provided a method to efficiently produce an inexpensive, standardized, yet flexible product.

The notable feature of the system was line-bored rows of precisely spaced and located holes that could be used for many purposes: locating hinges, drawer slides, and other hardware, as well as dowels to hold the cabinets together. The "32mm" name came from the spacing of the holes, and that was a function of the machines developed for drilling them. 32mm wasn't chosen because it met perfectly a predetermined set of design goals, it was simply as close as the German engineers of that time could place two drilling heads next to each other.

Overlay and Inset

The other, major feature of 32mm Eurostyle cabinets was the absence of a solid wood frame — the face frame — around the front of the cabinet. These cabinets are known as frameless because the front edge of the plywood box is covered with a finished band and is exposed to view. In traditional 32mm cabinetry, the doors and drawer fronts overlay nearly the entire face of the cabinet. Except for the gaps between them, the doors

European Frameless vs. Face-Frame Cabinets

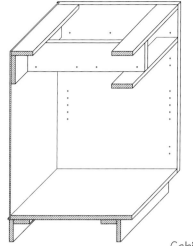

European or 32mm system cabinets consist of boxes with an open front side, reinforced by horizontal rails. Their side panels have rows of holes for assembly fasteners, drawer slides, and door hinges.

Cabinets sit on a separate base.

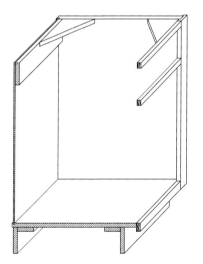

Face frame or traditional cabinets consist of boxes reinforced by corner blocks, with a solid-wood frame attached to the open front side.

The doors and drawer fronts added to the front of the cabinet determine its looks and style. Either kind of cabinet can deliver any finished look.

Both kinds of cabinet are made from panels of ¾ inch plywood, particleboard, or medium-density fiberboard, with a ¼ inch back panel. These sheet materials may be surfaced with wood veneer, Melamine, plastic laminate, stainless steel, or paint.

Figure 2. Cutaway views of European 32mm cabinet, top, and traditional face-frame cabinet, bottom.

Door hinges, drawer slides and shelf
supports plug into 5mm system holes.

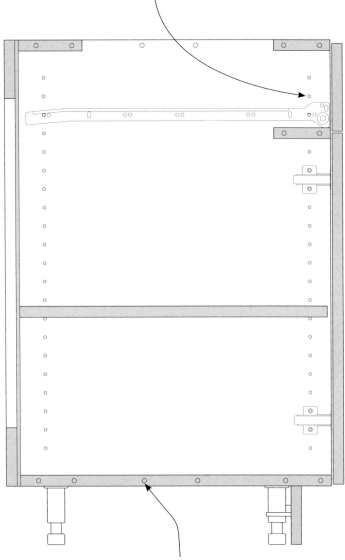

8mm assembly holes are used for
dowels to join cabinet components.

Figure 3. *Typical hole layout for frameless cabinets. The 5mm system holes locate hardware such as drawer slides and hinges, the 8mm assembly holes are for the dowels that hold the case together. Boring all the system holes allows the standard cabinet end panel to be used in any number of configurations.*

and drawers are the only visible parts of the cabinets when viewed from the front.

This clean, modern look has great appeal to many, but others find it too stark and sterile. Functionally, it increases access to the inside of the case, and makes it easier to get things in and out of the cabinets. Structurally, the front of the cabinet isn't as strong as a face-frame cabinet, but unless the cabinetmaker has gone too far in using cheap material, or has pressed the limits of width to their maximum, frameless cabinets are stronger than they need to be.

The doors and drawer fronts don't have to be overlaying the front of the cabinet, they can be inset, that is, they can fit within their openings. This brings the edges of the cabinet into the picture as a design element, and changes the appearance significantly.

With either method, all of the doors and drawer fronts, as well as all of the other parts, need to be made as precisely as possible. With overlay doors, the gaps between the doors and drawer fronts are crucial to the appearance of the finished product. They need to be a uniform size, and they need to form uniform lines and square corners. The hinges and drawer faces are adjustable for position, but the hinge adjustment can't make an obtuse corner square, or a short door taller.

Standard practice is to set these gaps at ⅛ inch (about 3mm) or less between doors in overlay cabinets, or between the door and the cabinet in inset doors. People will say that overlay cabinets are easier to make than inset, because the doors don't have to fit inside the openings. The truth is, either way you do it, you have to get the cabinet openings and doors square and the right size, or they won't work or look right.

Don't make the half-overlay mistake — Europeans will make fun of you if you do.

In face-frame cabinets there are times when the edges of the doors overlay their openings by ⅜ inch or ½ inch. Misguided souls, trying to adopt the frameless 32mm system, often try to impose this form, usually as a method for building cabinets without working carefully. The existence of half-overlay hinges is taken as confirmation that this is an acceptable method. In fact, half-overlay hinges are for the purpose of hanging two doors from one vertical cabinet component.

If you try to build a frameless project with half-overlay hinges everywhere, you will be introducing all kinds of complications and variations to a relatively simple and elegant system, and the finished product won't look right, because you won't be able to achieve uniform gaps between the doors and drawers.

32mm in a Nutshell

As the 32mm system matured, several parameters were developed:

• System holes are a vertical line of 5mm diameter holes, 32mm from center to center, bored on the inside of the cabinet side. The line is 37mm back from the front edge of the cabinet, and a second line of holes is close to the back of the cabinet. The distance between the two rows is ideally some multiple of 32mm.

• Assembly holes are at 90 degrees to the system holes, near the top and bottom of the cabinet sides, and at other locations where a fixed shelf or divider may occur. These holes are 8mm in diameter, and are spaced in multiples of 32mm. There are fewer assembly holes, and they are used for dowels that hold the cabinet components together.

• Different types of cabinets can be made from components with the same boring patterns. Drawer slides and door hinges are engineered to go in the same holes, simplifying the production process.

• Cabinet components are standardized as much as possible, and most of the work is completed before the cabinets are assembled. Raw edges of plywood are covered, hardware is attached, and the components, if wood, are finished before they are assembled.

Because of this standardization, parts need to be made with precision. Many new machines, and refinements of old ones, were developed to handle these processes quickly and accurately. However, these expensive machines are not necessary to produce quality work. A careful worker can produce high-quality work efficiently with minimal investment in tools.

The drawing on the facing page (**Figure 3**) illustrates a typical side-section from a European-style 32mm base cabinet. Note how the vertical system holes are utilized in three different ways: the hinges plug into holes in the front row, the shelf is supported by pins in both rows, and the drawer slide is screwed into holes in the front and back rows. The bottom of the cabinet is attached to the sides with six dowels, and the front and back top rails, as well as the rail below the drawer, are attached to the cabinet side with dowels.

Designed-in Flexibility and Efficiency

This cabinet could also have doors that extend to the top of the cabinet, eliminating the drawer using the same group of holes. Or, the doors could be eliminated and a stack of drawers could take their place. The two sides of this cabinet could be part of a huge number of parts that are cut to size and

OVERLAY:
the doors and drawer fronts cover and overlap their openings.

INSET:
the doors and drawer fronts fit inside their openings.

RAILS:
Frame, door and cabinet parts that go side to side.

STILES:
Frame and door parts that go up and down.

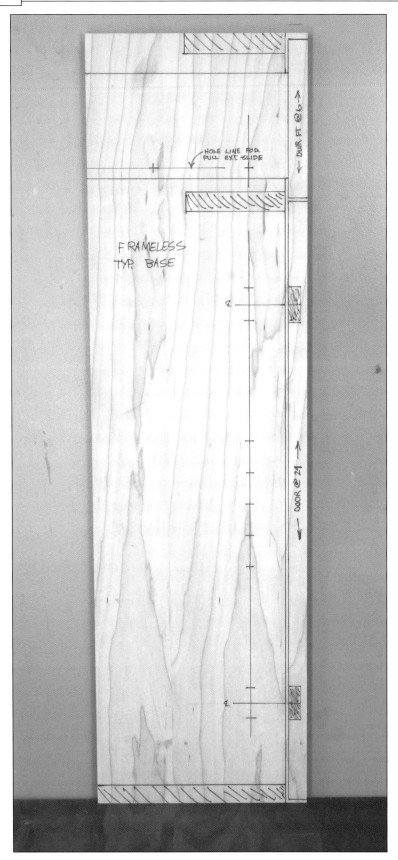

have their edges banded, the holes bored, and even make their way through the spray booth if they are veneered, easily handled as flat parts taking up a minimum amount of shop space. Even the mounting plates for the door hinges, and the drawer slides are attached while the sides are flat parts. It doesn't become a cabinet until just before it goes out the door to be delivered.

If the planning is done correctly, and the right machinery is in place, this is an incredibly efficient process, especially when compared to the way that a lot of people made traditional face frame cabinets. Finished doors and drawer boxes arrive at an assembly station where a complete box has just arrived, the doors and drawers and put in place, some minor adjustments made, and the cabinet is complete and ready to be delivered.

Efficiency Isn't Everything

People tend to focus on the holes and the hardware when examining the 32mm system, but these are not some kind of fairy dust that magically makes the system work. In fact, the system of holes can actually produce serious bottlenecks, especially if you want to build a variation that requires deviating from the standard pattern. In a manufacturing environment, drilling all of those holes is a one- or two-step process, because of the equipment that is used. In a small shop that has to drill these holes one at a time, the process is a slow and tedious one.

The real keys to the efficiencies of frameless cabinets are the thorough planning, the precision of making the component parts, and the concept of bringing each part as close to completion as possible before assembling the cabinet box. If you can come close to these three goals, you can build anything in an efficient, cost-effective manner. If you are building cabinets professionally, you might even make a profit.

Figure 4. Euro story board—*This full size layout for a frameless cabinet shows the location and size of all parts and hardware mounting holes for a typical base cabinet.*

Many cabinetmakers, especially those building traditional face-frame cabinets, don't plan very well, don't work as precisely as they can, and as a result tend to assemble complete boxes or face frames first, then completely assemble the other major component based on what size the other component ended up. Once the cabinets and face frames are together as a unit, measurements are taken, cut-lists are figured for doors and drawers, and these pieces are started. In a small shop, this can be a nightmare because all the machines and benches are surrounded by completely assembled boxes that won't be heading out the door anytime soon.

For me, the decision on which style to build is based on aesthetic and financial decisions, not on faith that one system is stronger, or the other is faster. Nice cabinets can be made with either method, and as we take a closer look at each, and at some hybrid methods, we will find some methods to build either style as efficiently and pleasantly as possible.

The Rise and Fall of Line-boring

If you take a close look at a cabinet made with system holes, you will quickly realize that most of the holes are not being used, and likely never will be. As the 32mm system evolved, boring machines were developed with enough drill heads to bore all of the holes for a cabinet side at one time. At first glance, this seems like a good idea: the part goes in the machine, the operator hits a button, and the boring is complete. But a more complicated machine requires more setup and maintenance. In a commercial shop using the 32mm system and line-boring machines, it made sense to drill holes that might be needed, but likely wouldn't, than it did to stop and reset the machine.

The result of this was a lot of wear and tear on tooling, a lot of particleboard dust gener-

Figure 5. **Hinge plate jig**—*A shop made jig will locate the holes for hinge plates in the same location in each cabinet.*

ated, and cabinets with interiors that looked like they had been strafed by machine-gun fire. It was also a Herculean engineering task, trying to place the line of holes in just the right spot, so that any possible variation of drawers and doors could be accommodated, and in trying to make custom work fit the system.

The small, under-equipped shop may have been at a disadvantage for speed, but could produce a more attractive product, drilling and using only the holes that really did something. And the economics of being under-equipped can bring about some very efficient practical solutions. As we get further in to the specifics of building European-style cabinets, we will look at some low cost methods for locating the holes we want where we want them, without a tremendous capital investment in machinery.

Ironically, in the last few years, line-boring machines have been replaced with Computer Numerically Controlled (CNC) machinery. Where the goal was once to twist the design to fit the boring pattern, the boring pattern can now be easily adjusted to fit the design. The large manufacturers with millions of dollars in machinery are finally catching up with the little guy with a few simple jigs, like the ones shown here.

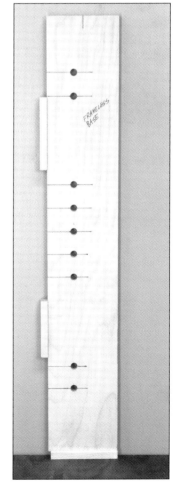

Figure 6. **Shelf pin jig**— *This jig locates the holes for pins for adjustable shelves.*

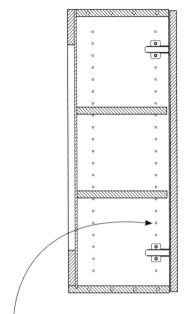

Typical 32mm system holes are on center on the cabinet opening, 37 mm back from the front edge of the cabinet side. Locations for hinge plates, drawer slides and shelf supports all depend on the 32mm system.

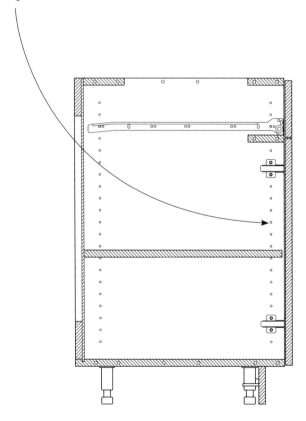

Figure 7. Many holes — *In a manufacturing environment, all system holes are bored to simplify the production process and avoid the necessity to make decisions.*

Working the System in a Small Shop

Three of the four advantages to the 32mm system have nothing to do with the system of line-bored holes — they are attitudes and ways of working that can be used no matter how you build your boxes and hang your doors. I think they are so important, that I have given each of them — planning, precision, and doing as much as possible before assembly — a good deal of space in this book. For now, let's take a close look at the parts of the 32mm system that a small shop or one-man band can successfully adopt, and some that should be avoided.

Dowel construction is only efficient if you buy into the entire process: multi-head boring machines, dowel inserting and gluing machines, and case clamps. I have seen commercial shops that were incredibly efficient at sizing parts and line-boring holes, but were very slow in assembling cabinets because the cabinetmaker putting the boxes together had to manually put glue in each hole, and place each dowel by hand. If you add in drilling all of the dowel holes one at a time by hand, you will feel like you will never be done. Pick a method from the chapter on "Building Boxes: Joint Decisions" **(page 52)** instead, and avoid a major bottleneck in the production process.

Instead of trying to apply the system as a whole, find ways to make the individual parts of the system work for you. Other than the coincidence of being 37mm back from the front edge, the holes for door hinge plates and drawer slides don't need to have anything in common. Use the jigs shown in **Figure 5 & 6, page 13**, and you can locate the hinge plates for all of your doors in the same location on every cabinet, without measuring and laying out each and every one **(Figure 7)**.

Plan your hinges so that they are the same distance in from the corner of the door (I use 3⁄8 inch) no matter what size the door is. If you then set, or make your jig for drilling the hinge plates to work from that, you only have to do layout or measuring work when you change door heights, like when you go from wall cabinets to base cabinets. If you have a different overlay on the top and the bottom of the door, as you will in a base cabinet, the distance from the inside edge of the cabinet to the center line of the hinge plates will be different at the top and bottom. Rather than measure every one, make the jig to reflect this, and you will have saved yourself hours of layout time, and eliminated numerous chances for a mathematical, measuring, or layout error.

Locating hole positions for drawer slides can work the same way. Find a convenient, consistent distance to set the drawer slide from the bottom of the cabinet, (or the top of an intermediate rail, like the top drawer in a typical base cabinet) to the bottom of the slide (I use 1⁄2 inch). Make or set your drawer-slide jig to hit this distance, and you can now drill mounting holes for all of the drawer slides on the job.

These jigs and holes can be set up to use either #6 x 5⁄8 inch bugle-head screws, or for 5mm Euro screws. I prefer the 5mm Euro screws, as I believe that they hold better than the wood screws, but I frequently use the wood screws. I suggest trying both, and using your personal preference.

Because we have placed the hinge plates and drawer slides where we want them to be, rather than on the grid, we can also put the holes for the shelf supports where we want them to be, and we can only drill the ones that are likely to be used. I also prefer to drill the shelf support holes at 1⁄4 inch diameter, instead of 5mm. I am a worrier about shelves, and don't think the European 5mm shelf pins look strong enough. I know that

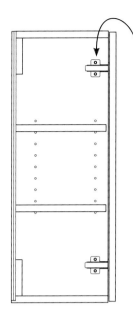

Holes for hinge plates are still located 37mm back from the front edge of the cabinet side, but are placed so that hinge cup holes in doors are drilled a constant distance from the top and bottom of each door.

Holes for drawer slides are located to set all drawer slides a consistent distance up from the top edge of the rail or cabinet bottom.

Holes for shelf supports are still centered vertically on the cabinet opening, but no longer need to be 37mm back from the front edge. The only holes drilled are the ones that are likely to be used.

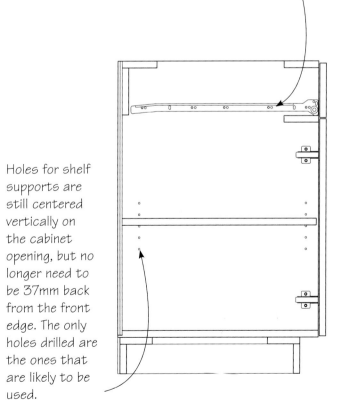

Figure 8. Fewer Holes — *In a small shop only the holes that will be used are bored. This means less work, and a more attractive cabinet, but it does require decisions by the cabinetmaker.*

they have been used millions of times successfully, but I still don't trust them. So I use ¼ inch shelf pins instead. **(Figure 8)**

The actual plywood boxes can be assembled in the same way whether the finished cabinets are frameless or contain face frames. There is a separate chapter on "joints for cases" **(Page 52)**, and the chapters on assembling will cover the minor differences that might occur in some situations. For now, let's look at what makes a face-frame cabinet, and what needs to be considered and decided before building. **(Figure 9 & 10)**

Traditional Face-Frame Cabinets

Face-frame cabinets are often referred to as traditional. The use of this term makes it sound like we have been building cabinets this way for centuries, that perhaps the founding fathers had kitchens with 36-inch high countertops and 3 inch x 4 inch toe-kicks. In fact, the traditional way of making cabinets is a rather recent development, as is the concept of kitchen cabinets entirely.

The modern kitchen only began to take its present form around the turn of the 20th century, with standard sizes of cabinets and appliances evolving in the 1920s and 1930s. It wasn't until the post-World War II era that the forms we consider as having been used forever became entrenched. Before standards were established, most kitchens had very few cabinets. What cabinets there were resembled freestanding pieces of furniture, and often were called furniture-like names such as dressers and presses. The style and dimensions of these reflected the taste, skills, and judgment of the local cabinetmaker.

Even during the building boom of the 1950s, most new American kitchens were

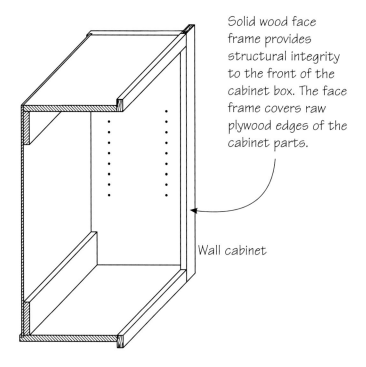

Solid wood face frame provides structural integrity to the front of the cabinet box. The face frame covers raw plywood edges of the cabinet parts.

Wall cabinet

Corner blocks secure and square joints between cabinet sides and face frame.

Edge of face frame is not flush with cabinet sides, this means blocking will be required for the drawer slides.

Base cabinet

Figure 9. Face frame — *Cutaway view shows typical face frame cabinet construction for base and wall cabinets.*

cobbled together on-site, and the standards that were followed were a mixture of what fit with the sink and appliances, and what the carpenter doing the work preferred.

The point is, we aren't dealing with anything sacred when it comes to how we build face-frame cabinets. We are using methods and materials that have evolved over the years, and continue to change.

The big difference, of course, is the presence of the face frame, a solid wood framework that is attached, as one might expect, to the face of the cabinet. The members of the frame are usually between 1½ inches and 2 inches wide, but they can also be narrower or wider in some circumstances. This solid wood frame adds strength to the front of the cabinet, and helps to keep the box behind it from racking. It also covers the raw plywood edges.

With frameless cabinets, the front edges of the plywood parts form the face of the cabinet. These edges are covered cosmetically, but if you cover them using ¾ inch square solid wood, you will also stiffen the face of a frameless cabinet. Plastic laminate on the edges will also be stiffer than edges banded with a more flexible plastic material. If frameless cabinets are designed, built, and installed properly, the difference in strength at the front of the cabinet will not be significant.

The sum of all this is, you can make a perfectly sturdy and strong cabinet using the so-called traditional face-frame method, or using the so-called European frameless method. Although there are no meaningful differences in strength, there are differences in appearance. In the drawings on the next few pages, we'll take a closer look at the differences in appearance between face-frame and frameless cabinets, and between overlay and inset doors and drawer fronts.

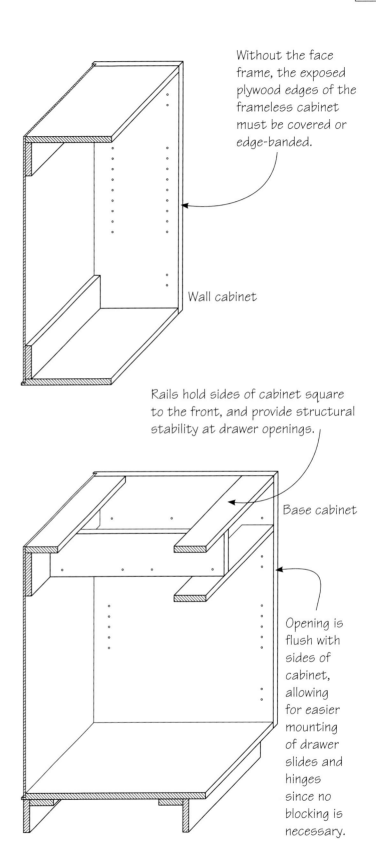

Without the face frame, the exposed plywood edges of the frameless cabinet must be covered or edge-banded.

Wall cabinet

Rails hold sides of cabinet square to the front, and provide structural stability at drawer openings.

Base cabinet

Opening is flush with sides of cabinet, allowing for easier mounting of drawer slides and hinges since no blocking is necessary.

Figure 10. European 32mm — *Cutaway view shows typical European 32mm, or frameless, cabinet construction.*

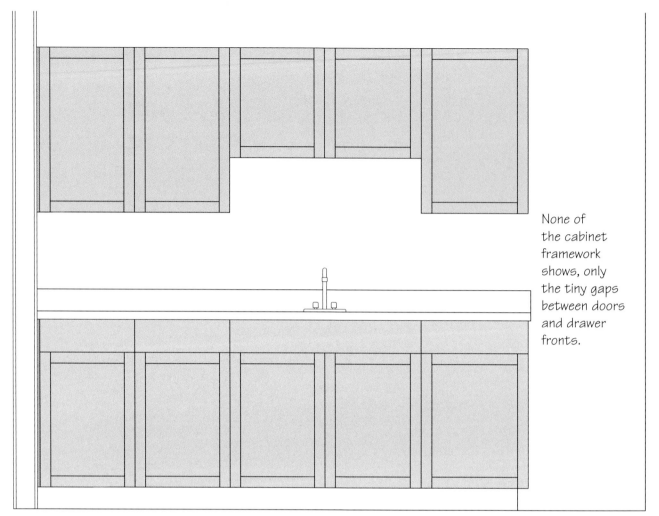

None of the cabinet framework shows, only the tiny gaps between doors and drawer fronts.

Figure 11. A traditional look can be achieved with frameless construction by using wood frame-and-panel doors and end panels, with full overlay hinges.

Frameless Cabinets with Full Overlay Doors

Frameless cabinets can be made to have a traditional look with the addition of stile and rail doors, as seen in the elevation drawing above.

To most people, face-frame cabinets look better, and the general perception is that they must be of higher quality. Quality, however, is a function of the materials used and the skills of the maker, not the type or style of cabinets.

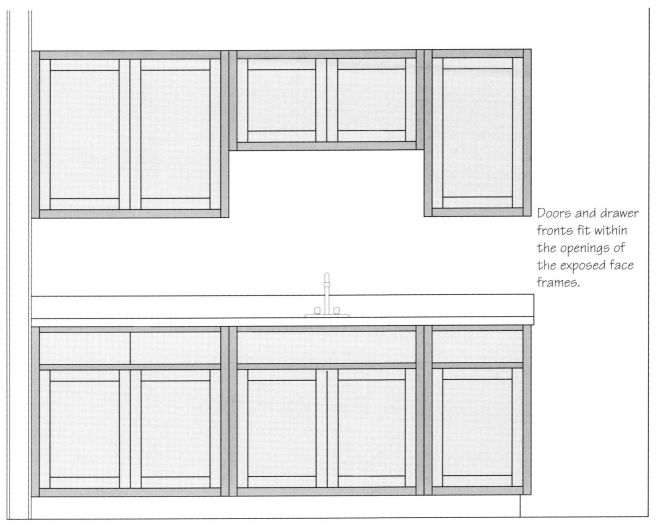

Doors and drawer
fronts fit within
the openings of
the exposed face
frames.

Figure 12. *Face-frame cabinets with inset doors have a more traditional and formal look.*

Face Frame Cabinets
with Inset Doors

The nicest-looking face-frame cabinets will have inset doors and drawers, as seen here. Many cabinetmakers shy away from making inset doors because they are afraid to hang the doors on butt hinges. Many makers won't build cabinets with inset doors for this reason, and few professionals actually have much experience at all with using them.

It really isn't that difficult, you can make jigs and efficiently make mortises for butt hinges almost as quickly as you can bore holes for Euro hinges. And butt hinges offer some real advantages over other types of hinges.

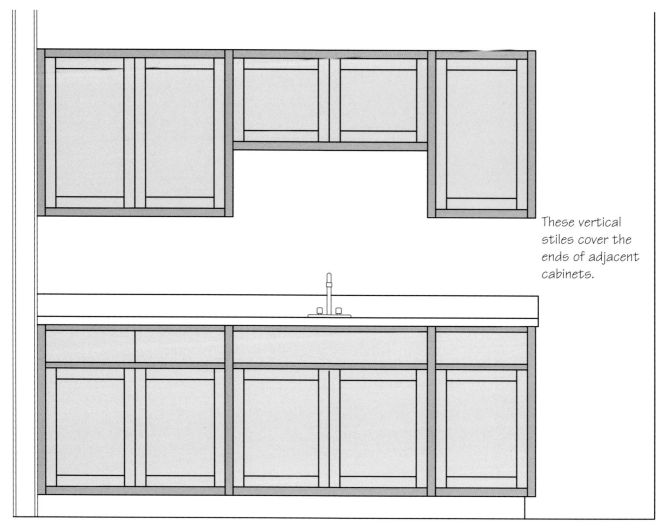

These vertical stiles cover the ends of adjacent cabinets.

Figure 13. *Face-frame components can be added to frameless cabinet boxes giving a traditional look with simple construction and installation.*

Butt hinges will open as far as someone wants to open them, unlike concealed hinges that have built-in stops. People expect that their cabinet doors will open like the doors in their house, and many concealed hinges fail after being pushed to their limits over a period of many years. Quality butt hinges can last for hundreds of years.

European-style concealed hinges can be used with inset doors in face frame cabinets without much trouble. You won't be able to see the hinge barrel when the cabinet door is closed, the door won't open as far, and you will see what appears to be a big robotic arm every time you open the door, but it is an alternative for the faint of heart. In the chapter on hanging doors **(page 175)** we will go step-by-step through both methods.

Hybrid Cabinets

The same appearance can be achieved by building smaller boxes, and using a common face frame across the fronts. This hybrid method, after being installed, will look more like one cabinet built in place than the previous examples. Building an entire elevation as one big cabinet is an option, but I don't recommend it. I haven't made a giant cabinet since the hernia surgery. The boxes in the drawing on page 19 are built as individual units, each with a distinct face frame. When the boxes are installed, the frames look wider where the cabinets butt against each other, and there will be a visible line where the two cabinet stiles come together. This method is so commonly used that its appearance won't usually be objectionable.

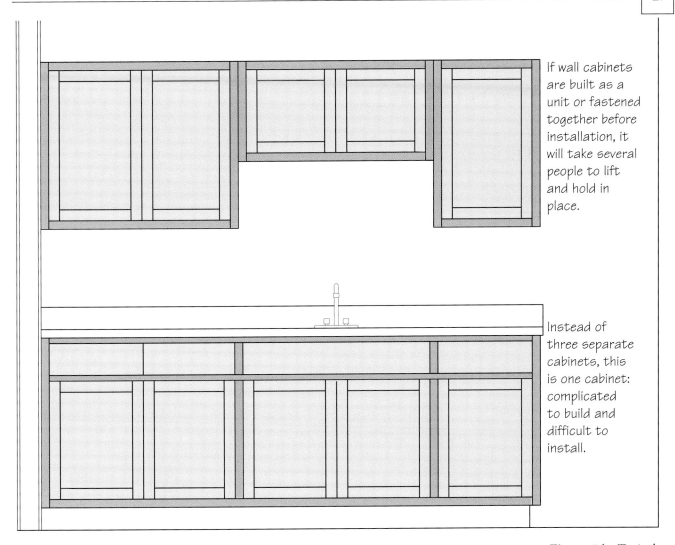

If wall cabinets are built as a unit or fastened together before installation, it will take several people to lift and hold in place.

Instead of three separate cabinets, this is one cabinet: complicated to build and difficult to install.

Figure 14. Typical site-built cabinets look nice, but are difficult to move and install.

Building the cabinets as distinct boxes is an idea borrowed from the European modular concept, and from the manufacturers of factory-built face-frame cabinets.

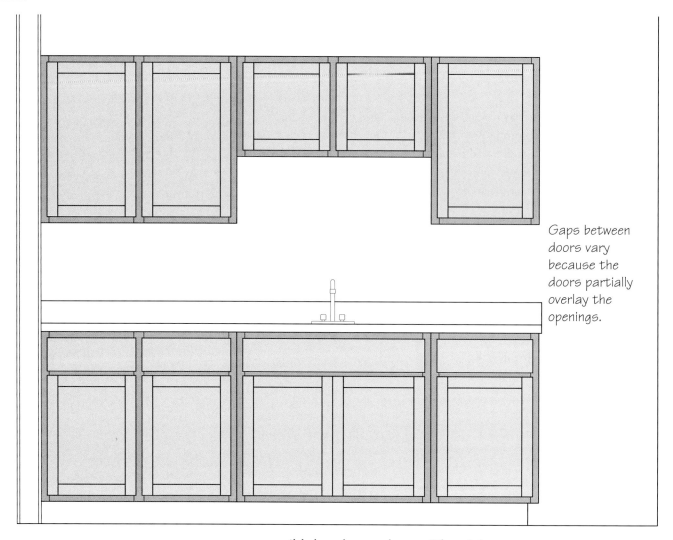

Gaps between doors vary because the doors partially overlay the openings.

Old-Time Cabinets

The old-time method was to build an entire elevation as a single cabinet. Some would argue that it looks better, but there are many disadvantages to this approach.

The first problem is in fabrication. If you are building modular cabinets, you don't have to deal with vertical dividers inside the cabinets. The places where vertical dividers would occur are now cabinet ends. Making the dividers as dividers introduces the need for another method of producing joints, likely a dado across the width of the long cabinet bottom. It also complicates joints in components that would normally go entirely across the cabinet horizontally, such as the

rail below the top drawer. These joints can be difficult to lay out and cut, and will also be harder to assemble. At the very least, they break the rhythm of building the same consistent box.

The second issue is that of size and weight. One big cabinet is harder to move than two or three smaller ones. This may seem minor, but if you are working by yourself, it is a major issue. It will also be harder to level the big cabinet during installation, and a long wall cabinet will need several people to hoist it into position. There is some slight savings in material costs, but this is outweighed by the difficulties imposed by size and weight.

Figure 15. When overlay doors are used on face-frame cabinets, the gaps between the doors are not uniform, resulting in a clumsy appearance.

Face Frame Cabinets
with Overlay Doors

Lipped doors and overlay doors on face-frame cabinets are a common combination, but they don't look as well as cabinets with inset doors. Both of these sit on the outside of the face frame; with overlay doors, the entire thickness of the door is outside the box, while lipped doors have a rabbet around the perimeter, so that part of the thickness of the door is inside the opening, and part is outside. Lipped doors have a slight advantage in that they keep dust from getting inside the cabinet. This might be an issue if you heat with coal or wood, or otherwise live in an extremely dusty environment, but other than that, I would avoid them.

It is quite difficult to get a uniform look to overlay doors on face-frame cabinets. They become a jumble of seemingly randomly placed lines. Though often recommended as being easier for the amateur to build, I think it is an easy route to amateurish-looking work. They are commonly used, and I think people don't object because they are used to seeing them. The hinges used for lipped overlay doors also leave a lot to be desired; they are complicated to install, and don't hold up very well.

Decisions, Decisions

There are many variations among builders in how the face frame relates to the other parts of the cabinet. Are the outer edges of the face-frame stiles flush with the outside of the box, or is the inside face of the cabinet side flush with the inside of the face frame? Is the bottom of the cabinet flush with the bottom edge of the frame, or even with the top of the bottom rail? All of these variations are used, and there are valid arguments for doing them either way or in between. As we look at the specifics of cabinet design, we will see what the differences are.

Because the face frame takes up a bit of space, it can be argued that frameless cabinets make better use of space. I myself used this argument just a few pages back, and while it is true, it isn't important enough to sway your decision on which cabinets to build.

To the beginner looking to make his own kitchen cabinets, I would advise staying out of the kitchen for a while. Build some frameless cabinets for your workshop or garage, and try a face-frame vanity to gain some experience and become familiar with your choices. Try different materials, methods, and hardware before you commit to a major undertaking. The volume of boxes, doors, drawers, and snags along the way in a typical kitchen project will be challenging enough without doing it with methods that don't feel right to you. The information in the following chapters will enable you to do that.

2. THE POWER OF THE LIST

Typical wall cabinet is 12 inches deep, which can be increased. Usually it is 30 inches high, but may be made taller to reach the soffit or ceiling.

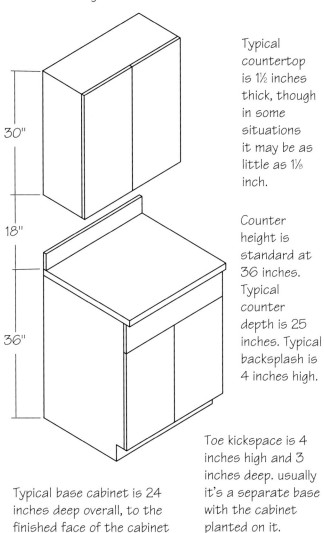

30"

18"

36"

Typical countertop is 1½ inches thick, though in some situations it may be as little as 1⅛ inch.

Counter height is standard at 36 inches. Typical counter depth is 25 inches. Typical backsplash is 4 inches high.

Toe kickspace is 4 inches high and 3 inches deep. usually it's a separate base with the cabinet planted on it.

Typical base cabinet is 24 inches deep overall, to the finished face of the cabinet doors, whether they are inset or overlay.

Figure 16. Typical dimensions for kitchen cabinets, regardless of the method of construction.

Start with the Finish

Painted kitchens have been with us since the late 1890s and early 1900s when the modern kitchen came about. My bias is towards actually seeing the wood, but there is an appeal and an advantage to painting the cabinets. The original reason for paint was that it was more sanitary than a clear finish. Modern wood finishes make stained or natural-colored wood just as easy to keep clean as paint, so the decision to paint or not can be based on cost and appearance, not practicality.

What a light colored painted finish will do, especially if the room is small, is make the room appear larger. It will also keep it from being the dark and dreary place it could become if a dark stained wood finish were used. On the other hand, if paint is used in a larger room, it starts to look stark and institutional, more like a hospital than a home. The other advantage to paint is that the wood used doesn't need to all match or even be the same species. You can use less expensive raw materials, and lower your budget.

Natural finishes — that is, a clear coating on the wood, rather than a stain — will have the same effect on a small room, and also work well in larger rooms. The color and texture of the wood grain and figure add interest to the expanse, rather than make it overwhelming. A natural finish will also age gracefully, darkening and mellowing over time, developing a wonderful patina. Most hardwood species will darken over time, some more than others, so consider what the appearance will be in a few years if your sample seems a bit too light.

Beware of the Dark Side

While my preference is for a natural finish, that shouldn't be enough reason to keep you from staining the wood if that is what you prefer. I would stay away from really dark stains, especially if the room is small, because it will feel even smaller than it really is.

Make a sample board of the wood species, stain, and finish you want to use. Make it big enough to see from several feet away. If you're on the fence between a few choices, make a sample for each, set them in your room, and look at them over a period of several days. Look at them at different times, under both natural and artificial light. This is the best way to judge what color you want. You don't want to finish the job and have someone you love say, "Hmmm, I didn't think it would be that dark."

Do you really need to make this decision before you start to build? You might be saying, and in all likelihood you're thinking, "I'll just get going and let the wife decide while I'm making the boxes." You need to know before you start for several good reasons. The first is monetary. Different finishes can have quite an impact on your material costs. You need to have one eye on the finish samples, and the other on your checkbook if you hope to stay close to your budget.

Different finishes, or details, can impact how you put your cabinets together, and what methods you use. If you're going to paint, you can nail the face frames onto the plywood, fill the holes, and no one will ever know. If you're using oak, and a medium to dark stain, you can do the same thing. If you're using maple or cherry, you will want to carefully match all the exposed parts for color if you're going to use a natural finish. If you're staining, you can be more flexible in your wood selection. The point is, you need to know where you're going before you take the first step. It's much easier to change your mind, or let your wife change hers, before you have a thousand dollars of plywood cut.

Details, like solid wood raised panels, or flat veneered panels, will also affect the bottom line, the amount of labor you need to do, and the finished appearance of the room. The chapters on construction review many

different options. Study them, and picture yourself both building them and living with them. Design and plan what works for you before you start.

The Bottom Line

Most people who contemplate a large do-it-yourself project have two motivations; they want higher quality than what they can afford to purchase, and they want the satisfaction of accomplishing something that not just anyone is willing and able to do. If you plan thoroughly, keep track of which of these two paths you are following, and make a sacrifice now and then to the other path, you will likely be successful.

If on the other hand you jump in without looking, chase after satisfying your sense of accomplishment when you should be watching your budget, you will likely end up frustrated and miserable. You could easily spend $20,000 on equipment and tooling to build $10,000 worth of cabinets, and when you're done, you could very well decide that woodworking and cabinetmaking aren't that much fun after all.

If you're really interested in pursuing it as an avocation or even a vocation, then your investment in time, equipment, and learning could be the best investment you will ever make. If you've read this far, it's likely that no one will be able to talk you out of doing this. Since I can't talk you out of it, I may as well show you how to do it.

Lists, Lists, and More Lists

There are many, many pieces and parts that go in to a typical kitchen. Each one has a cost in dollars, and an associated cost in the labor required to make it. Some alternatives

A light colored finish makes a small room appear larger.

Dark colored paint and stain makes a small room appear even smaller.

you may be able to dismiss out of hand, but most you need to compare to at least one alternative in order to make an intelligent decision. I'm not a list-making person (I have a lengthy list of reasons why), but I begin every sizable project with a fresh legal pad, and start making lists.

If you don't have a lot of woodworking experience, keep a legal pad handy as you read this book, and make two lists. The first would be of your skills. On one side of the page list the things you are comfortable doing and on the other the skills you need to acquire. Most of the skills required to successfully build a kitchen are more tedious than demanding, and can be picked up through practice.

The second list should be of tools and equipment: what you own, what you'd like to buy, and what you can really afford to buy. If you're feeling overwhelmed, don't be afraid to ask for help. If you have some woodworking friends, talk with them about sharing tools and time. Look around for local resources, there is likely a woodworking club or school nearby where you may find some help, and there are some excellent resources on the Internet. It would also be a good idea to practice, either on something smaller than an entire kitchen, or by helping out on someone else's project.

A small project is also a good way to practice dealing with all the lists and details you will need to complete a major one. You will need to create two budgets, one for money, and a second one for time. The first is lengthy, but simple. The second is more difficult to create, but just as important.

If neither budget can be stretched, I try to show alternatives that will save you time or money, or both. As you read along, look at the alternatives presented, and make note of which ones you prefer, and which ones you would like to try.

> Choose your finish before you start to build. This decision affects not only the materials you buy, but also how you build the boxes.

The Mother of All Lists

In order to set your budget, you need to know exactly what it is you will be building. Once you have created your cabinet layout, you can calculate the material and hardware you will need, and what your total costs will be.

The starting point is called a cabinet schedule, and an example is found on **page 28.** You can do this on an accountant's columnar pad, or you can do it as a computer spreadsheet. This is a list of each cabinet to be built, along with some details about it. As you progress in your planning, this information will be used to generate other needed information about each cabinet, cutting and purchasing lists for solid wood and sheet goods, and schedules for hardware and accessories.

If you're still on the fence about certain details, say types of doors, or types of drawer slides, make a separate column for each of your choices. You should also add columns to enter the dollar amounts of each item, such as hinges and pulls, and the cost per cabinet of each of these. Once you have your list of cabinets done, you will know how many doors and drawers you will be making, and you can accurately price your hardware. You will also know how much of the total cost any one item is. You may be agonizing over a decision that would change the total price very little.

Let's go through the spreadsheet example, and I'll explain the terminology that I use.

The first item is the cabinet number, which will refer to this cabinet's location in the room. The letters N and B let me know that this is on the north wall of the room, and that it is a base cabinet. I always start my numbering with the cabinet on the left end of the elevation, and continue numerically. When I turn the corner, the N becomes an E (for east) and I start over at number 1. I usually list all of the base cabinets in the room, then all of the wall cabinets; floor-to-ceiling cabinets are numbered with the base cabinets, but detailed at the end of the cabinet schedule. I always start the numbering for each type of cabinets at each elevation at 1.

I number the cabinets this way so that when I'm comparing the cabinet to the elevation drawing, it's easy to locate the exact one I'm looking for. When the cabinets are delivered, they can be placed close to where they are to be installed without referring to the drawing. Some people will assign cabinets numbers that don't directly refer to their location, but when your helper asks, "Where do you want WB3?" you can let him know it's on the right side of the west wall without having to stop and look at your drawing.

The columns marked "elevation" and "cabinet type" may duplicate information contained in the cabinet number, and if they do, I can keep them hidden in my spreadsheet program unless I have a good reason to show them, like two elevations on the south wall, or an odd type of cabinet make it necessary. If a cabinet is different from the norm in any way, like a blind corner wall cabinet, or a sink base cabinet, it is noted here.

Of the three columns that give the dimensions, the depth and height will normally be constant throughout the elevation. If that's the case I will also hide these columns. If there is an unusual situation, like a cabinet that isn't as deep as the others to accommodate some obstruction in the building, or a place where the countertop changes height, I will show them.

The next two columns tell how many doors are on the cabinets, and the type and location of the hinges. If I'm only using one kind of hinge on all the doors, I mark the hinge column "standard." When different types of hinges are used, I designate them in this column. The "L" in parentheses in the hinge

type column let's me know that the single door is hinged on the left side. It might seem odd that cabinet "N-B-2" doesn't have a door, but if I read across, I see that it has four drawers.

The number of hinges may seem like a silly column to add as most doors get two hinges, but I may have wall cabinets that are taller than normal that get three hinges per door, or a pantry cabinet that gets five hinges per door. By having a separate column for this I can keep track, and when it comes time to buy the hardware, I can let the spreadsheet program do the addition, and I know in an instant if I qualify for the quantity discount for buying fifty hinges.

Pulls are usually the same throughout the job, but in case they aren't, I add this column to locate the odd ones. The next column tracks the number of pulls I need for all the doors. Like the other hardware columns, it can be used to calculate the total amount I need to purchase, and I can add a column or columns to track the cost, or the cost of options.

The columns for drawers, drawer slides, and drawer pulls function in the same manner. I know at a glance how many there are, where they are, and what they cost. If I'm considering the cost of full-extension drawer slides versus bottom-mount three-quarter extension slides, I can simply add two more columns and compare them.

The columns in the spreadsheet schedule for "left end" and "right end" refer to the sides of the cabinet box. Different cabinet-makers use some different terms for cabinet parts, but these are generally accepted. I use the term "finished end" if that end will be exposed to view. In reality, it can be finished in a few different ways. Generally speaking a finished end is at the end of an elevation, and is always completely visible. If I specify it as "finished," with no quali-

> The cabinet schedule is a list of each box to be built including dimensions, hardware details, and many construction details.

The cabinet number tells you right away which cabinet it is and where it goes in the room.

fier, then I know that it is always exposed to view. The note stating it as "raised panel" reminds me of this.

A finished end may also be next to an appliance or another cabinet, and only part of it may be exposed. In this case, the finished end won't be a raised panel; instead it will be veneered plywood. The first wall cabinet on the north elevation (N-W-1) will have a small portion of its lower right end exposed next to the built-in microwave. It makes no sense to make this as a solid wood raised panel, but the exposed plywood portion should be finished to match the other exposed surfaces. A base cabinet adjacent to a dishwasher or range may have the first few inches back from the front edge exposed when the appliance door is opened. Again, this area should be finished, but the designation keeps me from putting a lot of effort in to making the whole side perfect when only the front few inches will ever be seen once the appliances are installed.

The term "wall" when used in the schedules to refer to a cabinet end means that the end will never be seen. Again, different cabinetmakers use different terms, and these terms may also vary by region. I have worked in shops where this condition was referred to as "raw" and also as "unfinished." Use whatever terminology you're comfortable with. I don't like the way "raw" sounds,

and "unfinished" can get confusing. You could have a circumstance where a "finished" end gets finish applied in the field, or an "unfinished" end needs to be sprayed with lacquer. Cabinetmaking is confusing enough without discussing unfinished finished ends, or, "Did Jerry finish the unfinished end on this cabinet?"

The Architectural Woodwork Institute (AWI) refers to surfaces as "exposed," "semi-exposed," and "unexposed." Exposed is defined as being visible when cabinet doors are closed. Semi-exposed refers mainly to cabinet interiors, the general definition being what is visible when the cabinet doors are open. Unexposed refers to parts of cabinets that are never visible after installation. The Wood Institute of California (WIC) uses the same basic definitions, but substitutes the term "concealed" for unexposed. It would probably be better to use these terms, but I learned to refer to the ends as finished and wall. The idea is to use terms that will make clear your intentions, and be consistent in using them.

I use the notes column to keep track of extra pieces that need to be added to the cabinet, or to unusual conditions that may need to be worked around. The accessories column lists items like lazy susans or pullouts that might be added in.

Figure 17. Cabinet schedule

cabinet number	elevation	cabinet type	depth	width	height	doors	hinges	# hinges	pulls	#pulls
N-B-1	north	base	24	32	34.5	2	std	4	std	
N-B-2	north	base	24	20	34.5	0	std	0	std	
N-B-3	north	base	24	16	34.5	1	std (L)	2	std	
N-W-1	north	wall	12	32	30	2	std	4	std	2

This is the basic format that I use, and while it may seem overly complicated, this schedule a central location for most of the information about the project. By formatting it as a computer spreadsheet, I can add columns for labor hours or other factors to prepare an accurate cost estimate. If I only want to look at information on one part of the job, say doors and drawer fronts, I can hide all the columns I don't want to use, or copy and paste the information to another worksheet.

Cutting Lists and Shopping Lists

At this point, I use the cabinet schedule as the starting point to generate several other lists that are necessary for a well-organized job. The next stage is to prepare an elevation sheet for each cabinet in the project.

The elevation sheet **(Figure 18)** contains a simple drawing of the individual cabinet, along with two charts. The first chart is a list of other parts that make up the finished cabinet, such as drawer boxes, drawer fronts, and doors. If I am using an applied-finished end panel, or if the cabinet has filler strips that go along with it, I will also list it in this chart.

This list of additional parts helps both to plan the work, and to make certain that the right parts are in the right places when it's time to put everything together. The sizes for all these parts are calculated from the overall cabinet size noted in the drawing.

The second list is a list of the cabinet parts, also calculated from the finished size of the cabinet. This list also depends on many variable factors, so you will need to refer to the detailed construction sections of this book to calculate the sizes according to the details you want to build.

If there are both plywood parts, and solid wood parts in the same cabinet, I will subdivide the cut-list. If the cabinet has a separate wood base, I will include the parts for that as a subcategory of the cut-list.

The drawing can be as simple or as detailed as you care to make it. Years ago, I photocopied pages that contained a blank elevation and blank charts drawn in, such as the ones on the following pages. I would make a blank sheet for base and wall cabinets for each job, filling in dimensions that were common in a category (like the width and length of standard cabinet ends) as much as possible. After copying as many as I needed for each type, I would go through the schedule, calculating the dimensions that varied from cabinet to cabinet, and sketching in the

The cabinet schedule gives you enough information to budget the entire job.

drawers	slides	pulls	#pulls	left end	right end	notes	accessories
1	full ext	std		fin. panel	wall		
4	full ext	std		wall	wall		
1	full ext	std		fin DW	fin. panel	3" fill at wall	
na	na	na	na	finished	finished at bottom next to microwave		

face and any finished end panels that might occur. The drawings would not be in perfect scale, but the relationships of everything on the cabinet's face would be clearly shown, and the exact sizes could be calculated.

These days, I do the basic drawings on a computer CAD program, make the lists of parts in a spreadsheet program, and electronically cut and paste this information onto individual pages. Either way, the important thing is that the information is accurate, and it is in the right place. This can generate a lot of pages, and I like to keep them in a three-ring binder. The binder also includes a folder for receipts and other paperwork that comes in or is generated during the project.

By going through the completed elevation sheets, I can generate the following:

- A detailed list of all the plywood parts for the entire project. From this list I can calculate the amount of plywood I need to purchase.

- A detailed list of all the solid wood parts for the entire project. From this I can calculate how much solid wood I need to purchase.

- A detailed list of miscellaneous wood or plastic parts, edge-banding, trim molding, etc. for the entire project.

- A list of all the hardware, door hinges, shelf pins, drawer slides, pulls, etc. for the entire project.

- A list of all the doors, drawer fronts, and finished end panels for the entire project.

- A list of all the drawer boxes for the entire project.

Finally, I'm ready to order material and start building. Some of these lists may seem redundant, but they are all worth having. If you don't have all of this information, and if you don't have it organized so you can get to it when you need it, you will likely end up doing all of these calculations many more times than if you had simply written it down the first time.

If you get overwhelmed, and decide to have someone else make your door panels, or drawer boxes, you have all the information ready to hand off. If you are doing all of the work yourself, you will appreciate a simple list of parts for drawer boxes, so you can handle that as a smaller subproject.

> Good preparation generates a lot of pages, so trap them in a three-ring binder along with a folder for the receipts that come in during the project.

> Use the sample elevation sheets on the following pages. They will give you all the information you need, and save you a lot of trouble.

Room Layout Checklist

Before you begin to build any cabinets, you need to know exactly what you will be building and where they will go when you are done. The exact size and location of each cabinet needs to be determined, and to do this you will need to make many decisions, and likely a few compromises. You can lay out the room and the cabinets in a scale drawing, or full size on the walls and floor of an empty room, or on long pieces of wood known as story-poles. You may want to generate a nice looking CAD drawing, or a simple sketch on graph paper. The important thing is to make your mistakes and changes early on when you can fix them with the eraser on your pencil or the delete key on your computer.

Putting together a set of kitchen cabinets would be a complicated task if all you had to do were fit the cabinets to each other. In the real world however, the cabinets must work with each other and also fit within the room without interfering with doors, windows, electrical outlets or light switches. Space must be left so appliances can slide in to position when you're finished, and be connected to the appropriate utilities. It can be a lengthy process and dealing with something that was overlooked in the planning stage at the end of the project can be a nightmare. There are few things more frustrating than having to rebuild a cabinet at the end of the project, or living with the results of poor planning. There are few things more satisfying than getting it right the first time, having the installation go smoothly, and walking away from a job done well.

This list will help you avoid common things that are often overlooked during planning. Use it as a guide in the process of planning the room and sizing the individual cabinets. The time you spend planning before you start building will let you build efficiently and with confidence.

• Decide what appliances will be used and have reliable information available from the manufacturer regarding sizes, utility requirements, and installation before beginning your layout. Appliance specifications are available online at most of the manufacturer's websites, or from sites like www.dexpress.com or www.ebuild.com.

• Decide what style of cabinets you will be building, how the ends will be finished, and what type of decorative and functional hardware will be used.

• Note exact locations of doors, windows, soffits, and other architectural elements of the room on your drawing or story pole.

• If working with existing electrical and plumbing locations, make note of the exact locations on an accurate scale drawing or story pole.

• If working in new construction, make sure that electrical, plumbing, and ventilation connections are planned, and that their final locations are where they should be. Be sure that the rough connections are in the right places.

• Start the cabinet layout by locating the appliances and sinks. Cabinets with widths that are dependent on appliance dimensions (like sink bases or over oven wall cabinets) will locate limits of the other cabinets.

• Decide on the configuration of the corner cabinets, and place them in the plan next.

• Remember to allow for clearance of opposing doors and drawers at corners. Place fillers as required, but don't make them too wide.

• Try to divide the spaces between appliances and corners into an equal number of spaces.

• Keep in mind the practical limits of doors, drawers, and shelves. Avoid cabinets that are too wide, too narrow, or otherwise awkward-looking.

Room or Job #	Cabinet #

	Cabinet #
Left End	
Right End	
Drawer Slide	
Door Style	
Hinge	
Drawer Pull	
Door Pull	

Cabinet Size	
Door #	
Drawer Front #	
Drawer Box #	

2	sides	
1	bottom	
4	rails	
1	shelf	
1	filler	
1	end panel	
1	back	

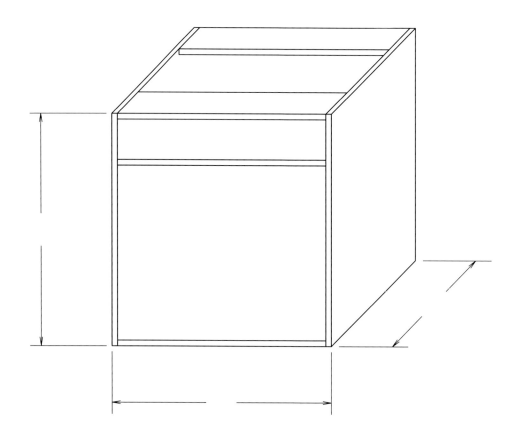

Figure 18. *Blank elevation sheet for base cabinets.*

Kitchen-East	Cabinet # EB1

	Cabinet #EB1
Left End	finished-panel
Right End	wall w/ filler strip
Drawer Slide	full extension
Door Style	inset
Hinge	euro-176 deg.
Drawer Pull	2-brass bail
Door Pull	2-brass knob

Cabinet Size	$30\frac{1}{2} \times 30 \times 24$
Door #EB1A & EB1B	2 @ $\frac{3}{4} \times 14\frac{1}{16} \times 22\frac{3}{4}$
Drawer Front #EB1	$\frac{3}{4} \times 5 \times 28\frac{1}{4}$
Drawer Box #EB1	$2 \times 27\frac{1}{2} \times 20$

2	sides	$\frac{3}{4} \times 24 \times 30\frac{1}{2}$
1	bottom	$\frac{3}{4} \times 24 \times 28\frac{1}{2}$
4	rails	$\frac{3}{4} \times 4 \times 28\frac{1}{2}$
1	shelf	$\frac{3}{4} \times 23\frac{1}{4} \times 28\frac{3}{8}$
1	filler	$\frac{3}{4} \times \frac{3}{4} \times 30\frac{1}{2}$
1	end panel	$\frac{3}{4} \times 24 \times 30\frac{1}{2}$
1	back	$\frac{1}{4} \times 29\frac{1}{2} \times 30$

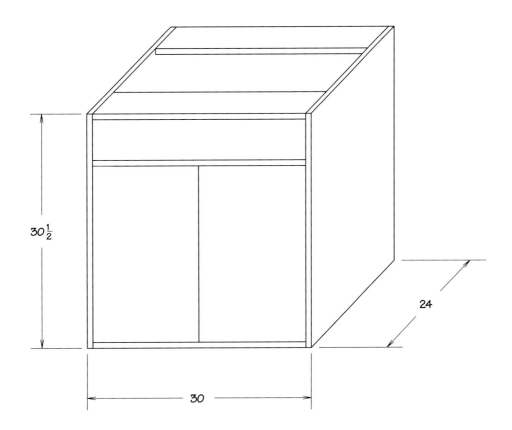

Figure 19. *Sample filled-in elevation sheet for base cabinets.*

Room or Job #	Cabinet #

	Cabinet #
Left End	
Right End	
Door Style	
Hinge	
Door Pull	

Cabinet Size	
Door #	

2	sides	
1	top	
1	bottom	
2	rails	
1	shelf	
1	filler	
1	end panel	
1	back	

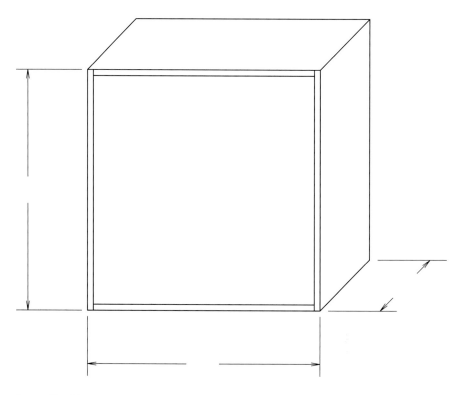

Figure 20. *Blank elevation sheet for wall cabinets.*

Kitchen-East	Cabinet # EW1

	Cabinet # EW1
Left End	finished
Right End	wall w/filler
Door Style	inset
Hinge	euro-176 deg.
Door Pull	brass knob

Cabinet Size	$30 \times 30 \times 12$
Door #EW1A & EW1B	2 @ $\frac{3}{4} \times 14\frac{1}{16} \times 28\frac{1}{4}$

2	sides	$\frac{3}{4} \times 12 \times 30$
1	top	$\frac{3}{4} \times 11\frac{1}{2} \times 28\frac{1}{2}$
1	bottom	$\frac{3}{4} \times 12 \times 28\frac{1}{2}$
2	rails	$\frac{3}{4} \times 4 \times 28\frac{1}{2}$
1	shelf	$\frac{3}{4} \times 11\frac{1}{4} \times 28\frac{1}{4}$
1	filler	$\frac{3}{4} \times \frac{3}{4} \times 30$
1	end panel	$\frac{3}{4} \times 12 \times 30$
1	back	$\frac{1}{4} \times 29\frac{1}{2} \times 29\frac{1}{2}$

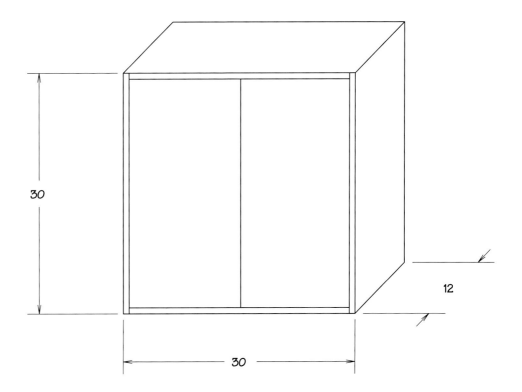

Figure 21. *Sample filled-in elevation sheet for wall cabinets.*

Figure 22a. Door and Panel Schedule

Job Name

Room

Door Type

Panel Style   Molding profile

Cabinet #	Door #	Hinge (L/R)	Hinge Type	Hinge Qty	Thickness	Width	Height

Figure 22b. Door and Panel Cut List

Stile width

Rail width

Base cab. stiles	Door #	Qty	Thickness	Width	Length	Notes
Base cab. rails	Door #	Qty	Thickness	Width	Length	Notes
Wall cab. stiles	Door #	Qty	Thickness	Width	Length	Notes
Wall cab. rails	Door #	Qty	Thickness	Width	Length	Notes
Odd stiles	Door #	Qty	Thickness	Width	Length	Notes
Odd rails	Door #	Qty	Thickness	Width	Length	Notes
Fin. end panel stiles	Cab #/Loc.	Qty	Thickness	Width	Length	Notes
Fin. end panel rails	Cab #/Loc.	Qty	Thickness	Width	Length	Notes
Base cab. door panels	Door #	Qty	Thickness	Width	Length	Notes
Wall cab. door panels	Door #	Qty	Thickness	Width	Length	Notes
Cab. end panels	Cab #/Loc.	Qty	Thickness	Width	Length	Notes

Figure 23a. Drawer Box & Hardware Schedule

Room/Cabinet	Drawer #	Box Ht	Box Width	Box Depth	Slide Type	Slide Len	Frnt Thk	Frnt Wid	Frnt Len

Figure 23b. Drawer Box Cut List

Drawer #	Sides T x W x L	Fronts T x W x L	Backs T x W x L	Bottoms T x W x L

3. CABINET PURPOSES AND VARIATIONS

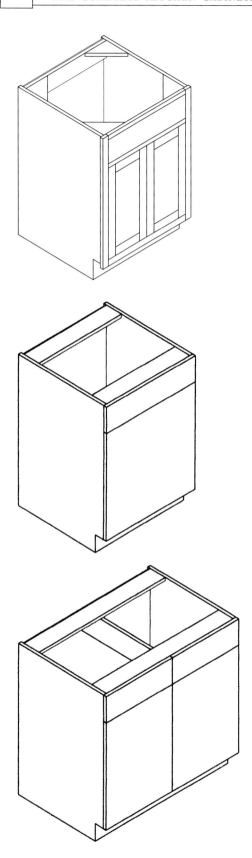

As you complete the room layout checklist **(page 31)** and make the fundamental design decisions, you can get specific with the cabinet layout, and begin planning how many boxes you need, and the specifics of each individual box. You may want to start with function first, as there are choices to be made that will affect the costs of materials and amount of labor required. In most cases, you will want to work on both at the same time, in order to stay within or at least close to your budget.

If you are adept at spreadsheet software, you might want to set up a spreadsheet for your design options, along with your cabinet schedule. That way, if you decide to make a change, or want to see what effect adding a particular functional or decorative item will have on your budget, you can do it without starting from scratch. Before you begin the process of building, you want to be certain of how the finished job will look and function, and the exact sizes of each and every part.

Many of the parameters, such as the depth of base cabinets and heights of countertops, are based on standards that everyone making all of the other parts of your kitchen, such as appliances and sinks, will follow. You certainly have the right to make your kitchen cabinets an odd depth or height, but if you do, you will need to do a considerable amount of adjusting to make things work.

In addition to standard depths and heights, there are some practical limits to items like doors and drawers that will affect your layout and design. These limits are discussed in more detail in the chapters on construction and materials, but at this point you should be watching out for making any cabinet too wide or too narrow. There are both functional and aesthetic reasons for doing this.

Figure 24. In most kitchens, the majority of the base cabinets will have a drawer above one or two doors. A face frame cabinet is shown above, frameless cabinets below.

Most kitchens can tolerate one skinny cabinet: you do need a place to store cookie sheets, and a narrow drawer dedicated to your garlic press and turkey baster isn't really a bad thing. More than one, however, and you will be stuck with unusable spaces. If you go too wide, doors will sag, and drawers won't slide properly. Often, a poor layout will have several cabinets that are too wide, and several that are too narrow.

It is much more pleasing visually if most of the doors and openings are within a few inches of all the others. Your dishwasher will be 24 inches wide, and the wall cabinet above it should be the same size. Your sink base will most likely be 36 inches wide, and will have two doors close to 18 inches wide. If you can keep all of the doors between 12 inches and 18 inches you will have done well with your layout.

In the drawing chapters that follow this section, specific details on laying out and constructing various types of cabinets are given. Most of those details are height-specific, and you need to be able to decide how wide to make things, and how an individual cabinet's place in the room will affect how it is designed and built.

Standard Cabinets

The most common cabinets in the typical kitchen are the 2-door, 1-drawer base cabinet, and the 2-door wall cabinet. Once you have decided whether to build face frame or frameless cabinets, and decided on a style and finish, you should establish parameters for building these typical cabinets. The majority of what you build will be in this form, with the widths varying, and some cabinet ends finished and some hidden. **(Figure 24)**

If you can stay consistent with your methods, and build the odd cabinets as variations of the standard, the entire job — from planning to installation to cooking your first meal — will go smoothly. If you approach each different situation as needing a unique box, you will only frustrate yourself in building, drive your costs up dramatically, and likely end up with an inferior finished product.

Sink-Base Cabinet

The simplest variation is the sink-base cabinet, which looks the same from the outside, but has no drawer, to allow room for the sink. You can just leave the drawer out, and put a false drawer-front above the doors. You may want to get fancy, and have tilt-out trays for storing a sponge where the drawers would normally be. There are some practical considerations, however, that will make the sink installation easier. The front of this cabinet also needs to be sturdy, to support both the weight of the sink itself, and the water in the sink. Often this is ignored, and the sink cabinet is not solid enough across the top front of the cabinet.

These details are covered in the detail drawings on **pages 93 & 112**. You want to keep the construction details as close as possible to a standard base cabinet without making the plumber mad.

Occasionally sink bases will have doors extending the full height of the cabinet instead of the false drawer front. This looks okay in a vanity or other location without cabinets with drawers right next to the full-height door cabinets. There really isn't any practical gain, since the area at the top of the cabinet where the drawer fronts would be contains the sink, and the necessary supports for the front of the sink and countertop.

Cabinets for Cooktops

Cabinets for built-in cooktops are similar to sink bases; there is no functional drawer, and

> Decide how you will build typical base and wall cabinets. Then build the odd cabinets as variations on your standard.

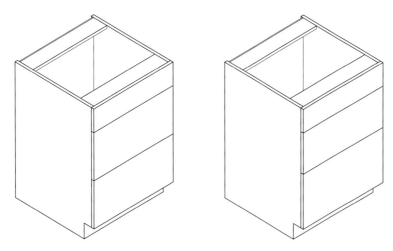

Figure 25. Deep drawers *can be equal (left), or graduated (right). Always keep the top drawer the same height throughout the room.*

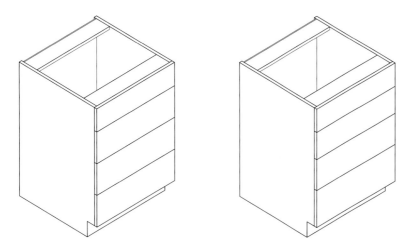

Figure 26. Stacks of smaller drawers *can also be equal (left) or graduated (right).*

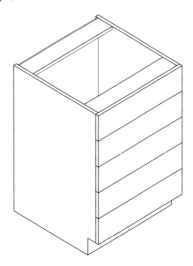

Figure 27. Five drawers *is the practical limit, while keeping the standard-height top drawer.*

the construction is modified to fit the appliance. Since there is no plumbing, a cooktop cabinet can have a pair of drawers tall enough for pots and pans instead of a pair of doors.

Stack of Drawers

Somewhere in the kitchen you will want to have at least one cabinet that is a stack of drawers. The top drawer should be the same height as all of the other cabinets, both to provide a continuous look, and to keep the construction process consistent. Below that, you can have, within reason, as many drawers as you want.

Two large drawers below the top drawer are nice to have near the stove or cooktop for storing pots and pans or other bulky items. In a normal base cabinet, you can have two equal-sized drawers, each about 12 inches high, but you might want to graduate the height — compare the two cabinets shown in the drawings at left. **Figure 25.**

Consider what the drawers will be storing. In many cases, the tall drawers will be too tall, so unless you have a specific need for them, you'll likely be wasting space. Three drawers under the top drawer are more commonly seen, because this configuration is more adaptable. If the drawers are equal in height, they will be about 8 inches tall. They can also be graduated, around 9 inches, 8 inches, and 7 inches below the nominal 6-inch top drawer. **Figure 26.**

If you like to serve seven-course gourmet dinners, and have all the forks and spoons to do that, you might want to have five drawers in a stack, all the same height. This is a little easier to build, since all the drawer boxes and drawer fronts can be the same height, and you won't have any odd-sized parts to deal with. Don't sacrifice usefulness for the sake of expedient construction. It will take a while to build your kitchen, but you will be living with the results for a long time. Think about how you use your kitchen and what you need to store while planning your cabinets. **Figure 27.**

Drawer Width and Height

There is also a practical limit to how wide you can make a drawer and have it function properly. As the drawer gets wider, there is more of a tendency for it to twist on the way in and out. Any deviations in size or parallel, and the problems that can result from those, are amplified as the drawer gets wider. This width also increases the leverage acting on the slide mechanism, and so increases wear and tear on the slide, and the fasteners holding it in the cabinet. Twenty-four inches is a safe width, and 30 inches works most of the time but makes me nervous. Thirty-six inches is possible with the highest-quality slides and careful construction.

Of course, it is possible to err in the opposite direction, and make a drawer that is too narrow to really be of use. Remember that the drawer box fits inside the cabinet, and that the drawer slides and the sides of the drawer box also take up space. For example, in a cabinet with full overlay faces and no face frame, you lose 1½ inches for the cabinet sides, 1 inch for the drawer slides, and another inch for the two sides of the drawer box. For a 12-inch wide drawer front, you end up with 8½ inches for the inside width of the drawer. If it's a face-frame cabinet, you lose an additional 1½ inches. When the drawer front width gets much below 12 inches, it's easy to end up with a drawer that won't hold much more than a single spatula or serving spoon.

Inside Corners

In almost every kitchen, the cabinets will have to turn an inside corner. Even though it doesn't look like a dangerous place, corners are fraught with peril. Drawers in cabinets adjacent to corners need to be sized so that they can open without hitting the drawer front (or the protruding handle on the drawer front) of the cabinet on the other side of the corner.

The inside edge of the drawer front should be out from the corner about 2 or 3 inches. It pays to do a full-size layout of the corner because this distance can vary depending on the style of cabinet, whether it is overlay or inset, and the type of knobs or handles used.

The reason this can be disastrous is that most installations begin in the corner, and if changes need to be made because the drawers interfere with each other, it will affect not only the two cabinets at the corner, but the rest of the cabinets in both directions.

If there is an appliance on one side of the corner, instead of another cabinet, don't assume that you're safe. Many appliances will protrude, at least partially, farther than standard base cabinets, often as part of the door. You don't want to explain to Mrs. Jones (especially if you are Mr. Jones) that she has to choose between not ever opening her dishwasher, and not having a handle on her silverware drawer because you didn't think ahead. In the detail drawings that follow, I show some suggestions for gaining space in the corners. When you lay out the cabinets, start in the corners, make absolutely certain all of the openings will work, and work out from there to the ends of the elevations.

There are also some decisions to be made about what to do with the space behind the drawer fronts and doors at the corners. The

> Drawers collide: inside corners are fraught with peril.

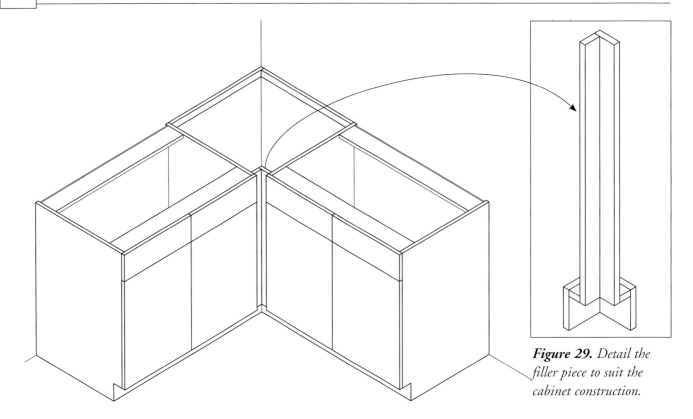

Figure 29. *Detail the filler piece to suit the cabinet construction.*

Figure 28. **Inside corner** — *The simplest way to turn a corner is to use a filler piece between two standard cabinets.*

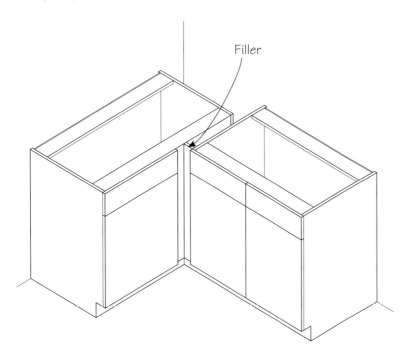

Filler

Figure 30. Inside corner — *A blind corner base makes use of space in the corner but it can be difficult to access the interior of the cabinet.*

easy way out is to leave dead space in the corner, between the two cabinets and under the counter as shown in the drawing above. (**Figure 28**)

You need to make a filler panel that connects the faces of the cabinets and the toe kick, and provides the necessary clearance space. You will also need to run cleats at the height of the top of the cabinets back to the corner to support the countertop. Usually the exposed part of each side of the filler panel is between 2 and 3 inches. Details will depend on the style of cabinets, and how the doors and drawer fronts overlay; the general idea is shown in the drawing above. (**Figure 29**)

Using the corner

Some people hate to waste that space in the corner, and there are ways to utilize it. I have mixed feelings about using it. It seems a shame not to use that area, but it can be difficult to get to it. These feelings can fluctuate depending on the conditions of the room that the corner is in. If either the walls or the floor (or any combination of the two) are out of whack, I would prefer to leave dead space in the corner, and start the cabinet installation at the intersection of the cabinet fronts rather than in, or close to, the corner of the room.

The easiest way to use the corner space is with a blind corner cabinet as shown in the drawing at left **(Figure 30).** The cabinet space in the corner is available, but it isn't easy to get to. If you use a regular shelf, you almost have to crawl inside to get to anything. I like to use a half-moon pullout, which swings out from the corner. Either way, I keep the hidden end of the cabinet away from the wall. The exposed door and drawer opening should be between 18 inches and 24 inches wide. If a pullout is used, size the cabinet and the door opening to accommodate it. A filler panel is usually attached to the front of a blind corner cabinet, and an equal amount of space is left on the face, beside the drawer and door.

A cabinet that spans the corner diagonally is easier to access, and makes better use of the space, especially if there is a turntable or lazy susan inside. A wall and base unit are shown at right **(Figure 31)**. If the access is on the diagonal, the countertop must also have a diagonal at the corner, and the entire cabinet will extend further in to the room.

Some additional structure will be needed so that there will be support for the drawer and drawer slides. If there is to be a lazy susan, make sure that there is room for it in the interior of the cabinet. I like to make the finished face-to-back dimension 24 inches or less. It can be made deeper, but the additional space gained would be difficult to reach, and this is the width that will be going through the doors of the house during delivery.

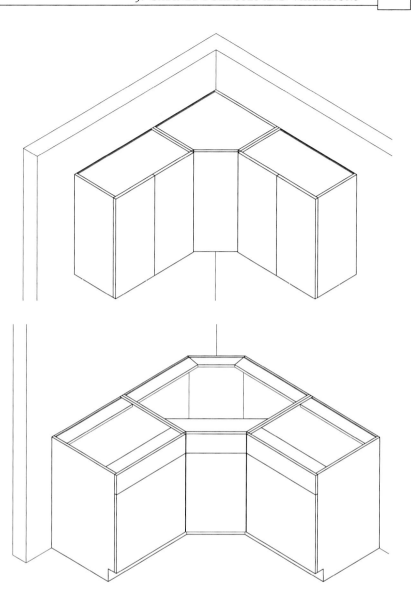

Figure 31. **Angled corner** — *Cabinets that span the corner diagonally make good use of space and are easy to access. Many people like to use a lazy susan here. The wall cabinet is shown at top, with the base unit above, and in plan view below.*

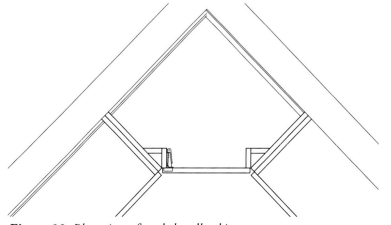

Figure 32. Plan view of angled wall cabinet.

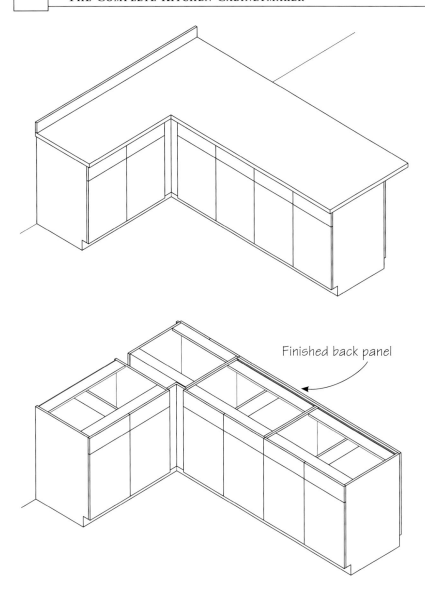

Finished back panel

*Figure 33. **A peninsula** can be created by applying a panel across the backs of several standard base cabinets.*

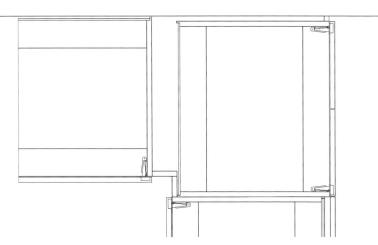

*Figure 34. **Reversing the direction** of the cabinet in the corner provides a storage space on the back of the peninsula (plan view).*

I have seen sink bases placed in corners, but in order to fit the sink, the diagonal front of the cabinet must be wider than would normally be seen in a cabinet of this type. This brings the front of the counter so far in to the room that it makes it nearly impossible for the average person to reach the back corner. It gains some counter space, but it really isn't usable.

Islands and Peninsulas

Islands and peninsulas are popular ways to divide the kitchen space from other areas of the house without closing off the kitchen (and the cook) entirely.

Some cabinetmakers will build large boxes, containing several door openings, or a combination of doors and drawers. The theory is that it saves on materials, looks nicer, and is easier to install. It might save a little on material costs, but these monster cabinets will be more complicated to build, and quite difficult to move. It is much easier to construct separate boxes, and if you want them to appear to be one continuous cabinet, apply a single face frame across several boxes during installation.

Island and peninsula cabinets are standard base cabinets with finished backs. There are three methods of providing a finished back. The simplest method is to build a panel that will span the backs of all the cabinets. This can be fastened from inside the cabinets. You could provide a finished panel for the back of each individual cabinet, but the vertical joints between the backs won't look as good as a continuous panel. This leaves the counter at the same height as the kitchen counters, and the width of the counter can be extended to overhang the back and provide a place to pull up a stool (**Figure 33**).

I think it's a nice touch to reverse the direction of the cabinet directly in the corner, so that there is access to it from the non-kitchen side. If the counter does not overhang, the face of this can contain a drawer above the doors, but if the counter overhangs for seating, it is better to just have two door **(Figure 34).**

Raising the back panel 6 inches creates more of a division between the kitchen and the other room, and will provide a higher and wider counter for eating or serving. It creates more of a visual barrier, so that you can't really see what is on the kitchen counter from the opposite side.

A 2 x 4 stud wall can be used for this — standard base cabinets back up against it, and the eating counter is attached to the top of this low wall. The standard finished height is 42 inches from the finished floor to the top of the counter. This wall can also be constructed from the same material, with the same finish as the cabinets. Since this is not a structural wall, the studs can be made of ¾-inch thick material, either cut from plywood, or of a secondary wood such as poplar or alder. Leave the bottom plate up 1¾ inches as shown **(Figure 35)** and at least parts of the back open below the counter. A 2 x 4 can be screwed to the floor in the proper location, and the entire wall is placed over that, and fastened to it and to the building wall. Then the cabinets can be secured to this. The advantage of the casework wall over the stud wall is twofold — it looks more elegant, and if used for eating will hold up better to being kicked than painted drywall will.

If you don't want to use the elevated counter as an eating or sitting area, you can make the back cabinets as open shelves, or cabinets with doors as seen in **Figure 36**. These cabinets should be securely attached to the floor, and the base cabinets can then be screwed to the back of the taller cabinets.

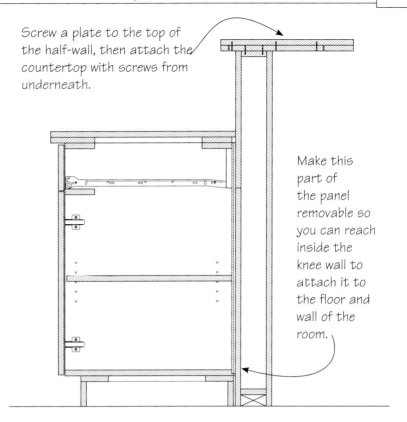

Screw a plate to the top of the half-wall, then attach the countertop with screws from underneath.

Make this part of the panel removable so you can reach inside the knee wall to attach it to the floor and wall of the room.

Figure 35. A counter *that overhangs the knee wall provides a bar area.*

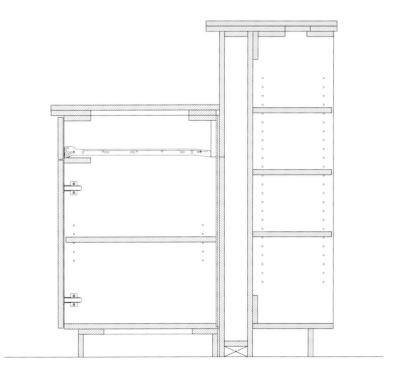

Figure 36. A bookcase *or other cabinet can be placed below the overhanging counter.*

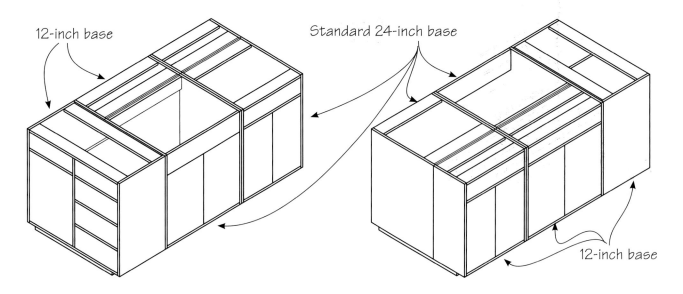

12-inch base

Standard 24-inch base

12-inch base

Figure 37. To make an island, *join two base cabinets back to back with a third cabinet across one end. If one base cabinet is the standard 24 inches deep, make the others half as deep.*

To create an island, two standard base cabinets can be installed back to back, and a finished end panel applied across both cabinets. A separate cabinet can also be used to provide an accessible as well as finished end. One side of these cabinets should be made at half the depth of the standard cabinets, or both sides may be made 18 inches deep, instead of the usual 24 inches **(Figure 37).**

Using two standard-depth cabinets back to back in a peninsula or island is not a good idea. While it will provide a vast expanse of space, the average person won't be able to reach completely across the top. Instead of a convenience, this will become an obstruction, and you will get worn out simply walking around the thing.

If you plan on putting appliances or a sink in the island or peninsula, remember that all of the electrical wiring and plumbing will need to come up through the floor, or out the wall and across the cabinets. If there isn't access from below, consider running the utilities through the base. If you're planning on having a sink, check your local codes about venting the drain. This is often overlooked in planning, and can cause problems at the end of the job.

Islands and peninsulas that are too wide to reach across become an obstruction, not a convenience.

Wall Cabinets

Wall cabinets are mainly the same types as base cabinets, but there are some differences. When you turn a corner, you have basically the same options as with base cabinets, but because the bottoms of wall cabinets are visible, there are some differences in making the corner cabinets.

Again, you want to set some sensible limits for width. Doors should fall within the range of 12 inches to 18 inches if possible. If you have to, you can go up to 24 inches wide for a single door, but this should be the exception rather than the rule. You also want to keep an eye on the distances to be spanned by shelves. Wall cabinet shelves can be loaded up with heavy canned goods, or expensive china and glass. I like to keep shelves under 32 inches if at all possible. Anything wider than that should have some extra support on the front edge.

Usually the doors on wall cabinets will line up vertically with the doors on the base cabinets below them. This provides for a consistent look around the room, but it is one of those things that looks more important in the drawings than it does in real life. You don't want the edge of a wall cabinet door

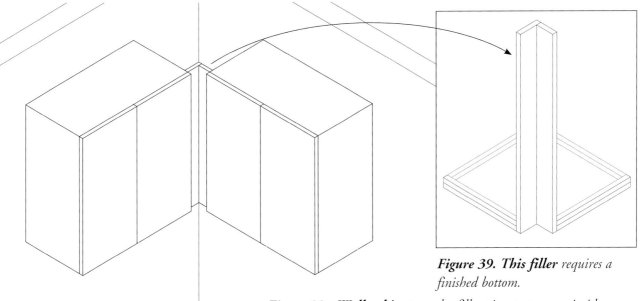

*Figure 39. **This filler** requires a finished bottom.*

Figure 38. ***Wall cabinets*** *need a filler piece to turn an inside corner.*

to be in the center of a door below it, but if it doesn't quite line up, no one will be able to tell because of the difference in depths of the wall and base cabinets.

Corner Wall Cabinets

If you want to leave a dead space in the corner, your filler panel not only connects the faces of the two adjacent cabinets, it also must reach the bottoms, and extend back on this plane to the corner of the walls, as shown in **Figure 38 & 39**. Make these to match the style of the rest of the cabinets. Blind corner cabinets are extended in a similar way to the base cabinets, except that the finished bottom needs to extend all the way into the corner of the room. You should keep the side held away from the wall, however, so that you only have to scribe the bottom. Filler space at the corners is also important in wall cabinets. Keep the edges of the doors 2 inches to 3 inches out from the corner to avoid interference with the adjacent cabinet, and remember that the filler panels also need to extend all the way back to the wall on the bottom **(Figure 38).**

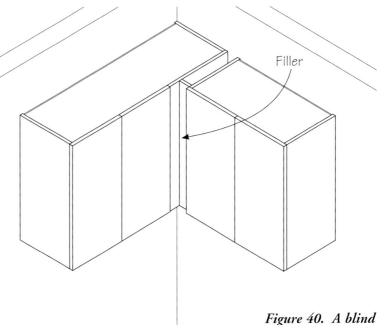

Filler

Figure 40. ***A blind wall cabinet*** *can butt into a second cabinet. The extra space is accessible because the wall cabinets are not as deep as the corresponding base cabinets.*

If you have an angled cabinet across the corner on the base cabinets, you will want to match that with an angled wall cabinet **(Figure 31, page 43)**. The side dimensions of this cabinet will match the depths of the two wall cabinets on the other elevations, and rather than place the back parallel to the opening, as on the base cabinet, there will be two backs at the walls. If you are using European hinges, there are special angled

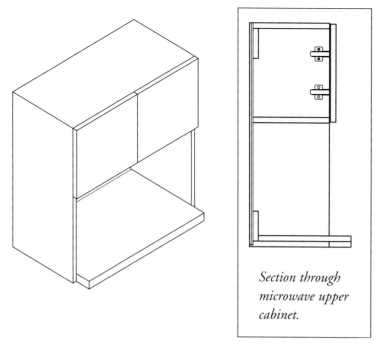

Section through microwave upper cabinet.

Figure 41. Microwaves *are most convenient when placed in cabinets at eye level, not lower down on the countertop.*

hinges that can be used, or you can attach a piece going back into the cabinet at a right angle so the standard hinges can be used **(Figure 32, page 43)**. If you will be using a lazy susan in a corner wall cabinet you should design the cabinet from its dimensions when planning to be sure that there will be room for it.

Appliances

Wall cabinets are often stretched in depth or height to accommodate appliances. You shouldn't place a regular wall cabinet above a range or cook top, but there are vent fans that are made to go above the range, and under a shortened wall cabinet. Often, the duct work for these fans must go through the cabinet on its way out of the room, so when you open the cabinet, the duct for the fan takes up most of the space. After the cabinets are installed, it looks better if a box constructed of the same material as the inside of the cabinet is made to cover the duct.

Microwave

There is also a combination vent hood and microwave oven that goes beneath a short wall cabinet. This cabinet needs to be well made, because the weight of the microwave will be carried by it. Often this cabinet must be surgically altered on installation to allow the ductwork to pass through it, which may compromise its structural integrity. Once again, careful planning will prevent such problems at the end of the job. Make sure the duct will actually enter the correct cabinet, and plan for the duct while building, not while trying to finish the installation.

You can also put a small microwave inside a wall cabinet, in an open area below the doors as seen in **Figure 41.** This puts the microwave at eye level, a much more convenient spot than on the counter. The easiest way to do this is to build the cabinet as a standard-depth wall cabinet with a horizontal divider at the bottom edge of the doors. The shelf that the microwave rests on is inserted into the finished cabinet, not a part of it. The exposed surfaces can be plastic laminate for easy cleaning. Be sure to allow enough space for the microwave, and remember to provide an electrical outlet for it in the wall behind the cabinet. The back can extend all the way to the bottom as shown in the section drawing, or it can stop at the horizontal divider at the bottom of the cabinet doors.

Refrigerator

Refrigerators also pose a problem. The refrigerator usually is a foot or so lower in height than the top of the wall cabinets, so it looks like something is missing if a cabinet isn't there. The problem is if you make a short cabinet the same depth as the other wall cabinets, you won't be able to reach the front of it to open the doors. If you make it deeper, you will be able to reach the doors, but you won't be able to reach or see

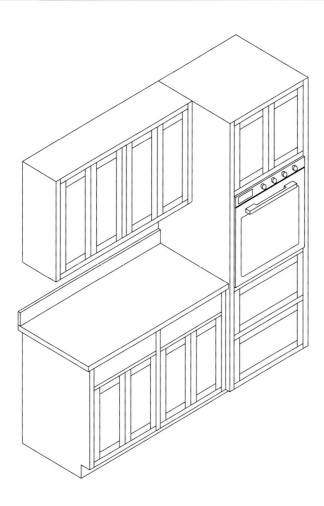

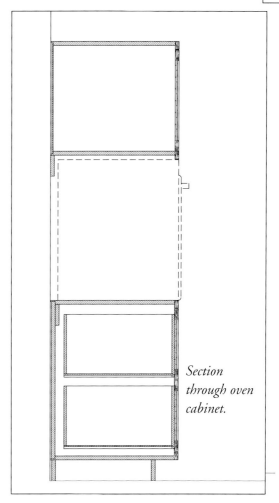

Section through oven cabinet.

the interior beyond the last few inches. The side of the deeper refrigerator cabinet will also have to be finished where it sticks out beyond the other wall cabinets.

The sides of a deep, over-refrigerator cabinet can be extended down to the floor, ostensibly to make the refrigerator appear built-in. This works for high-end refrigerators such as the Sub-Zero, but for other makes it's usually more trouble than it is worth.

The side panels should extend past the front edge of the countertop, so that the counter terminates neatly at this point. This looks nice, but complicates the countertop installation. You also need to be sure that the refrigerator doors will have room to swing past the end panels. Most manufacturer's spec sheets will have a detail of how the door moves at the edge, and this will help you to do a full-size layout to be sure that the panel and the refrigerator door don't interfere with each other. All in all, this is a lot of trouble to go to just to hide the side of the refrigerator.

Ovens

Ovens can also be built into cabinets, and the form of the cabinet is that of a base cabinet, with the ends extending up. It is better to make this cabinet deeper than the countertop, so that the counter dies in to the side of the cabinet. Otherwise, there will be a corner of the counter sticking out at this point that not only looks bad, but tends to be bumped into (**Figure 42**).

This cabinet also needs to be designed from the inside out, setting the size of the openings and spaces from the manufacturer's

Figure 42. **Cabinets for wall ovens** *need to be designed from the manufacturer's specs. The base unit under the oven should have sides that extend upward. The adjacent counter should butt into this extended side.*

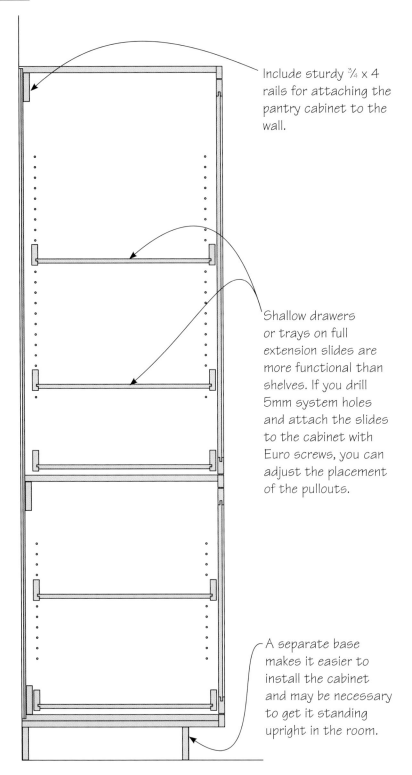

Include sturdy ¾ x 4 rails for attaching the pantry cabinet to the wall.

Shallow drawers or trays on full extension slides are more functional than shelves. If you drill 5mm system holes and attach the slides to the cabinet with Euro screws, you can adjust the placement of the pullouts.

A separate base makes it easier to install the cabinet and may be necessary to get it standing upright in the room.

Figure 43. Pantry cabinets carry a lot of weight and endure heavy use. They need to be especially sturdy and well constructed. Shop-made pull-out trays work as well as expensive pantry hardware and fittings.

requirements to establish the overall size of the cabinet. It is also extremely important to consider what the oven needs to operate safely. Even though it obviously will need electrical power or a gas line, these are often forgotten until the appliance is installed, and someone asks, "Where do I plug this in?" There may also be requirements for venting, structural support, and attaching the appliance that can be missed early on.

The other critical dimension is the height of the cabinet, particularly if the cabinet goes all the way from the floor to the ceiling. You must have room to stand the cabinet up once it is brought into the room where it is to be installed. If there is a soffit that occurs above the cabinets, but not in the rest of the room, you probably will be able to stand up a full height cabinet and slide it under the soffit.

If there is no soffit, the cabinet should sit on a separate base, so that it can be stood erect, then lifted and slid back onto the base. If you're taking this approach, there won't be much room for error. One way to be certain is to draw a scale, or full-size elevation of the side of the cabinet, and take a diagonal measurement from the top front corner to the bottom back corner. If this number is less than the floor to ceiling height, you will have room.

Another solution is to make the box in two pieces, so that the top and bottom may be fabricated separately and then installed to form a complete unit. If one end of this is exposed, the horizontal joint will be hard to disguise. Here is a good place to use an applied end panel for the finished end.

Pantry

Pantry cabinets also go floor to soffit, or floor to ceiling, and the trend is to load them up with as many pullouts in as many forms as is possible. These are helpful in keeping items at the back from being lost behind other stuff. Commercially available pantry pullouts are nice, but this hardware can be costly. A series of pullout trays is nearly as convenient, and not as expensive. Whichever is used, the cabinet itself needs to be well made, and solidly attached to the wall **(Figure 43)**. The doors on pantry cabinets will likely be the largest cabinet doors in the project, and also need some extra attention to be sure they don't sag or warp, and that they are mounted with a sufficient number of hinges.

When you have decided what types of cabinets are to be included in your project, you will be ready to make an accurate room layout, and after determining the exact size of each cabinet, you can easily calculate the size of each of the component parts.

4. Building Boxes: Joints

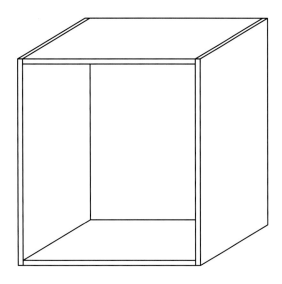

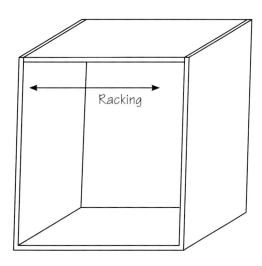

Racking

Figure 44. Racking is the distortion of the cabinet from square due to the actions of some outside force — most commonly gravity over time, but also the sudden trauma of being forced into position during installation.

Regardless of the type of cabinet you decide to build — frameless cabinets, face-frame cabinets, or hybrid cabinets — a rigid box will be the core of each one. This basic box will need to be the proper size, and well made for the project to be successful. In addition to being sized correctly, the various parts and the joints holding them together must be square and solid. If not, every step that follows will be more difficult and less likely to look good and function well in the end. The assembled box should be resistant to the many forces that will act on the joints during construction, installation, and in day-to-day use. A box that is easily racked will be difficult to fit doors and drawers to, and joints that move during construction and installation are likely to fail at some point in use (**Figure 44).**

In actual construction, the use of different materials will make little difference in the completed box. Veneer-core plywood, MDF, and particleboard materials are all in common use, and the choice of one material over the others should be one of personal preference for finished appearance and ease of finishing and fabrication. Technically, the main considerations should be the thickness of the parts, the methods used to hold them together, and not building beyond the reasonable limits of the materials.

Major cabinet components — tops, bottoms and sides — should always be made from ¾-inch thick material. While there will be a slight savings in material costs, material thinner than ¾ inch is more likely to bend or warp, and it is difficult to fasten with screws, nails, or staples without splitting. The back is from a thinner piece of sheet material, generally ¼ inch thick, reinforced with ½ inch or ¾-inch thick rails, which not only reinforce the cabinet, put provide a solid means of attaching the cabinet to the building walls. There is a trend to use ½-inch thick material for backs, and not use rails. This makes for a stronger back, but compromises the overall structural integrity of the cabinet. Half-inch material can be bent by the weight of the cabinet, and is not as secure a method of construction or installation as is using a thinner back with nailing rails (**Figure 45).**

Wall cabinets generally have both a top and a bottom, but in base cabinets there are different methods of fabricating the top. While it may be tempting to use a solid piece of material for the top, there are several good reasons not to. The solid top will be slightly stronger than one that uses rails or corner blocks for the top, but its use makes the box heavier than it needs to be, makes it difficult to move (cabinets with open tops may be moved by grabbing the rails or corner blocks rather than lifting the entire box from the bottom), and perhaps most importantly makes it quite awkward to fit hardware and drawers in the inside of the box. It is also much harder to finish the inside of a base cabinet with a solid top.

With any sheet material, as the length of a piece increases, so does its tendency to sag, or bend from its own weight. Lengths up to 30 inches do not bend easily, but this changes dramatically beyond that length.

A 48-inch long, 12-inch wide piece of veneer-core birch plywood will bend ⅛ inch with only one-fourth of the weight that would cause a 30-inch long piece to bend, and roughly the same ratio applies to MDF and particleboard. Adding a solid wood edge helps, but as lengths increase over 36 inches, the weight of the material itself, combined

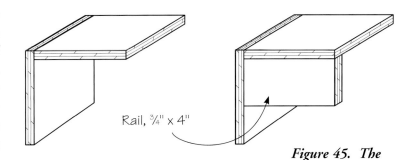

Rail, ¾" x 4"

with adjacent parts, becomes enough to cause the piece to sag significantly. If this piece is a loose shelf, it may sag enough to fall off the shelf pins, and if it is a cabinet component, such as a bottom or a top, it will prevent the front of the cabinet from being square, and doors and drawers will never fit or function properly **(Figure 46).**

Figure 45. The addition of a back rail will keep the other parts square, and will prevent them from racking.

Figure 46. Cabinets wider than 36 inches are liable to sag under their own weight.

How much do shelves sag?
Weight (in pounds) required to create ¼-inch deflection of horizontal piece

Material	Thickness	Span @ 12-inch width			
		30 inch	36 inch	42 inch	48 inch
Poplar lumber	¾"	483	284	175	117
Particleboard (raw or Melamine-covered)	¾"	117	69	43	28
	1"	277	164	102	66
Particleboard (with ¾" x ¾" solid wood edge)	¾"	150	90	63	38
Particleboard (with ¾" x 1½" solid wood edge)	¾"	435	241	152	107
Medium Density Fiberboard (raw or Melamine)	¾"	150	87	54	38
	1"	356	206	128	90

courtesy Architectural Woodwork Institute

Joints

There are many options for connecting the major components, and these options are much the same for both frameless and face-frame cabinets. One important consideration for frameless cabinets, however, is the sequence of applying edge banding to the exposed edges of the box. If the edges are to be covered before the box is assembled, then some variation of a butt joint should be used. It is nearly impossible to put a dado or a rabbet in a pre-edged piece without chipping the edges, since it will be inevitable that in half the cuts, the cutter will exit the sheet material through the edging.

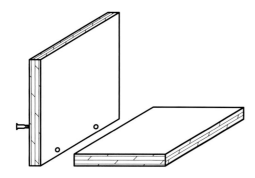

*Figure 47. **Butt-joined cabinets** can be tacked together with staples, then screws can be added to permanently secure the parts.*

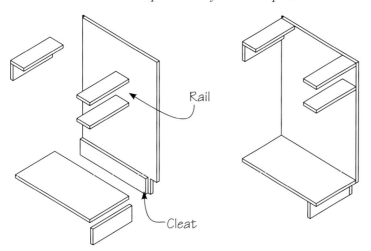

Rail

Cleat

*Figure 48. **A cleat made** of the same material as the rails makes a secure joint for the box bottom, and also a support for the toe kick.*

Butt Joints

Simple butt joints reinforced with glue and screws or staples are strong enough, but are actually more difficult to assemble because the parts do not register against each other. The value of dowels, biscuits, or other joints is largely in the positive alignment of parts during assembly, in addition to strengthening the joint. It takes more time to fasten together simple butt joints because of the difficulty of holding the pieces in perfect alignment while shooting staples and driving screws. Butt joints can be glued and clamped without the use of mechanical fasteners, but staples or screws will reinforce the joint, and prevent the joints from sliding while pressure is applied to the clamps **(Figure 47)**.

Butt joints, if properly glued and reinforced with fasteners, are strong enough to produce a good cabinet, and there are several factors that make the temptation to use butt joints seem appealing. Butt joints greatly simplify the math required to generate cutting lists: the inside width of the cabinet is the finished length of the bottom and rails, there are no additions or subtractions to be made for joints. Butt joints also seems at first glance to be a time saver, since the steps of milling and fitting joints are eliminated. However, this apparent saving of time can rapidly disappear when laying out intermediate parts, and during assembly.

Fasteners can also take the place of clamps. This is an important consideration during assembly, for it will take several clamps for each box. Moving boxes with clamps is more difficult, more room will be taken up by the boxes while the glue dries, and the boxes will need to be moved a second time when the glue has dried, to remove the clamps.

When I assemble butt-joined cabinets **(Figure 49)**, I generally tack them together with 1¼-inch or 1½-inch staples, and then use screws to secure the joints permanently.

Figure 49. Tacking butt joints—If using butt joints to assemble frameless cabinets, apply glue and tack the box together with a few staples.

Figure 50. Clamp while drilling—I always use a corner clamp to keep the assembly square while drilling holes and driving screws.

Figure 51. Clamp pulls warped parts—If any of the components are bowed or warped, use a clamp to pull them into place while driving screws.

Figure 52. Drill from inside—If you are using butt joints and have an interior partition, lay out the joint on the inside, and pre-drill holes for the screws.

Clamps are used to hold the corners square, and pull joints together (**Figure 50 & 51**). The clamps are then removed once all the screws are driven, freeing up the clamps, and saving space in the assembly area. Only finished ends that should not have fasteners showing are clamped until the glue is completely dry. This is one reason for the use of applied finished ends — all of the boxes are held together by the same method, simplifying the assembly process. For interior partitions, lay out the work and pre-drill the screw holes from inside the cabinet, as seen in **Figure 52.**

If toe-kicks are part of the box sides, a cleat may be added below the cabinet bottom, forming a joint where the bottom and side meet, and a surface to nail the toe board to. Although I prefer to use a separate base, this method makes for a stronger cabinet, and the cleat will accurately locate the cabinet bottom, an advantage over the simple butt joint (**Figure 48**).

The Good Box

It fits where it belongs — it connects neatly to its neighbor, or to a wall without any visible gaps.

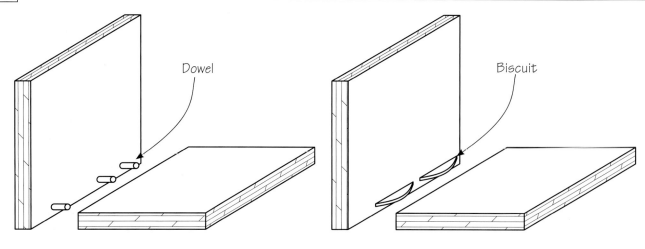

Figure 53. Commercial shops *may prefer dowel joints because they have specialized equipment for making them with precision. In the home shop, dowels are the most time-consuming assembly method.*

Figure 54. Biscuits *are a good alternative to dowels and can be made with a simple slot-cutting machine and some shop-built jigs.*

Dowel Joints

Dowels are widely used in commercial shops, due to the availability of boring machines to drill all of the holes for each joint at one time. In the home shop, or small commercial shop without boring equipment, precisely locating and drilling each hole individually make this method the most time-consuming. Dedicated jigs can be made or purchased to locate the holes and save some time, but this method is still quite tedious. Even when line-boring equipment is used, the gluing and insertion of the dowels can take as long or longer than driving screws, and the gluing and insertion of dowels one at a time is often a bottleneck in commercial shops **(Figure 53)**.

Biscuit Joints

Biscuits are a good alternative to dowels, and have some distinct advantages. Where no adjustment at all is possible during assembly with dowels, biscuits will slide a bit, depending on the depth of the slot, in the same direction as the slot. This allows front edges to be aligned during assembly if there is a slight variation in the size or squareness of

parts. A layout board may be quickly made for each type of cabinet, allowing the slots to be cut in the same locations for every part. In use, a stack of cabinet parts may be marked all at once, with the use of the layout board and a square **(Figure 55 & 56)**.

As shown in the second photo, the layout stick may be used to locate all the slots used for the cabinet. The front and back marks should be located so that the mating slots are centered in the corresponding rails **(Figure 56)**.

The slots may then be cut by working through the stack, milling all the sides, bottoms, and finally the rails. The jig shown in **Figures 57, 58, 59** will locate the slots in the center of the rails, and will allow the end cuts to be made safely. While not as fast as rabbeting a stack of cabinet sides, this method is relatively quick. Assembly of biscuit-joined cabinets will be slower, due to the need to put glue in each biscuit slot. Special glue bottles are made for this purpose that will not only speed this step, but help to regulate the amount of glue used to minimize glue squeeze-out.

The Good Box

Its joints are square (or at the correct angle if other than 90 degrees) and its parts are all straight.

Biscuit Joints

Figure 55. Marking stack of parts—*Using a story board for biscuit layout produces identical joints without measuring each one. These wall cabinet tops and bottoms will have slots cut in the ends.*

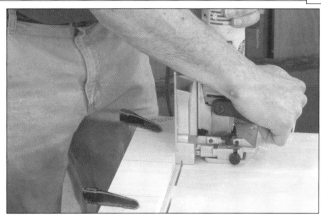

Figure 56. Using story board—*The same story board, clamped to the bench, is used to cut the slots in the mating pieces. The marks on the base of the machine are lined up with the marks on the board.*

Figure 57. Jig for slots in rail ends—*This jig holds the rails while centering the biscuit cutter in the rail's width.*

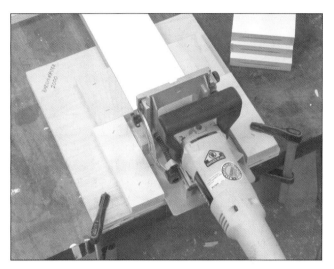

Figure 58. Jig close up with machine—*The guides are set a little wider than the rail, and a little wider than the base of the biscuit cutter.*

Guides for rail

Guides for machine

Figure 59. Jig close up—*In use, the front of the machine stops against the guides for the rail. This centers the slot in the end of the rail.*

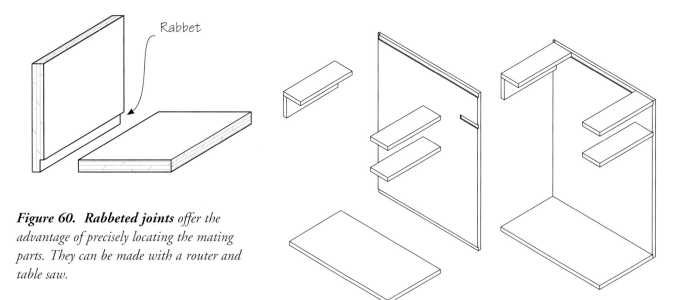

Rabbet

Figure 60. Rabbeted joints offer the advantage of precisely locating the mating parts. They can be made with a router and table saw.

While simple butt-joined boxes can usually be assembled without any clamping (except to hold the corners square) dowel- or biscuit-joined boxes will usually need some force applied to pull the pieces tightly together. Clamps may be used, either left in place until the glue completely dries, or left in place until screws are driven. It is often possible to close the joints with a blow from a rubber mallet or dead-blow hammer, followed by a driven screw, eliminating the need for clamps.

Rabbeted Joints

Rabbeted joints offer some distinct advantages, particularly for backs, the bottoms of base cabinets, and the tops and bottoms of wall cabinets. As mentioned previously, if the front edges of the cabinets are to be finished before assembly, rabbeted joints will not be practical. Rabbets may be cut with a dado head in the table saw, or with a router. The table saw will be the fastest method **(Figure 60).**

A straight cutter may be set up in a router table along with the fence for cutting the rabbets, and provided that the router table is large enough and the router powerful enough, this method will be nearly as fast as using the table saw. A hand-held router, equipped with a rabbeting bit can be used, but this method will be slower as each piece must be secured to the bench in order for the cuts to be made.

In commercial shops, a shaper with a power feeder is commonly used, and this is the quickest, most accurate method, if this equipment is available. The shaper can be set up so that the material being removed is a consistent distance from the machine table. Particularly when using veneer-core plywood, this is a distinct advantage, as variations in the thickness of the material will have less of an effect on the quality of the joints. To accomplish this on a table saw, the parts would need to be run on edge, with the narrow tongue left between the dado head and the saw fence. This practice is not advised, as kickback, or tilting of the part is more likely to occur.

It is also possible to set up a router table similarly to the shaper, but without a power feeder the cutter will need to be covered by an adequate guard, and a featherboard must be used or else kickback is liable to occur.

Face Frame Cabinet Assembly

Figure 61. Staples to start—*Begin assembling the butt joined box by gluing and stapling the bottom of a side to the cabinet bottom.*

Figure 62. Clamp corners—*With the corners assembled, place a clamp in the corner to keep it square, and drill holes for screws.*

Figure 63. Back rail—*Once both sides are attached, put the back rail in place and fasten to the cabinet sides.*

Figure 64. Corner blocks—*Corner blocks cut from scrap plywood hold the back rail and sides square. Screws through the corner blocks will hold down the counter top.*

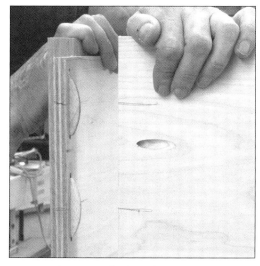

Figure 65. Finished end—*You can use a combination of biscuits and pocket holes to attach a finished plywood end.*

Figure 66. Cabinet base—*A separate cabinet base can be quickly assembled from plywood.*

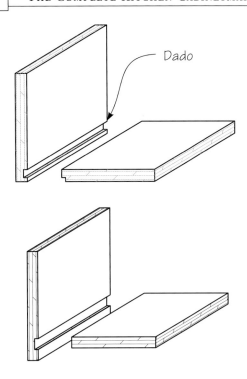

Dado

Figure 67. *A dado joint is stronger than a rabbet, but the difficulty of making a stopped dado limits its use.*

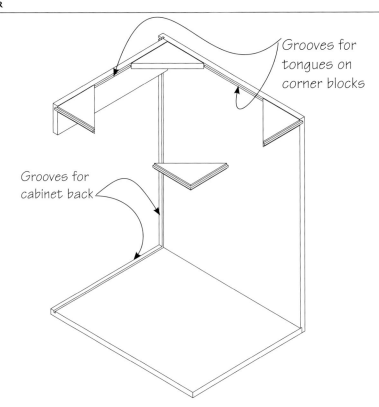

Grooves for tongues on corner blocks

Grooves for cabinet back

Figure 68. *A dado or groove can be run around the inside top perimeter of a face-frame cabinet, for corner blocks with matching tongues, or for rails.*

Dado Joints

Instead of placing a rabbet at the bottom of the end panel, a dado, thinner than the thickness of the bottom piece may be made, with a rabbet run on the edge of the bottom. This will be a good deal stronger than the simple rabbet, and is the first joint shown that would hold itself together mechanically. The parts can be machined as discussed above, and the milling of the rabbet on the bottom piece would be a way to work around the varying thickness of veneer-core plywood. The small piece left below the dado is rather fragile, and if the rabbet is oversized, it can break off during assembly. Where the joint occurs away from the end of the cabinet side, the dado can be made to the thickness of the adjoining part. The difficulty of making a stopped dado at parts that do not run completely across, as rails, makes this joint of limited use. **(Figure 67).**

Another common use of the dado is to run a groove around the inside top perimeter of face-frame base cabinets, for the insertion of corner blocks with matching tongues milled on their edges. These blocks serve two purposes, the first being to hold the sides, back, and face frame securely and squarely together. In addition, the countertop is secured to the cabinet by screws from below, running through the corner blocks **(Figure 68).**

Corner blocks are commonly used in face-frame cabinets, while frameless cabinets incorporate rails, which become part of the finished face of the cabinet. I prefer to use rails in both situations. A top cabinet rail behind the top rail of the face frame will help to keep the face-frame rail flat, and I think it is more efficient to use a consistent method of construction.

The Good Box
It looks good — its parts are in proportion and the finish, whether painted or clear, is nicely done.

Joint Decisions for Cabinet Box Construction

Type of Joint	Advantages	Disadvantages	Notes/comments
Butt joint	Easy to calculate sizes. Minimal machining.	Difficult to line up during assembly. Not as strong as other methods.	Should be reinforced in some manner: fasteners, dowels, or biscuits.
Butt joint with dowels	Easy to calculate sizes. Parts are positively located in relation to each other. Stronger than plain butt joint.	No adjustment of parts locations possible. Time-consuming.	Fast and easy if line-boring and dowel insertion equipment are available — not worth the trouble without equipment.
Butt joint with biscuits	Easy to calculate sizes. Parts are positively located with some adjustment possible. Stronger than plain butt joint.	Time-consuming. Errors in layout can be difficult and time consuming to correct.	Can be used in combination with other methods — rabbets at bottom of cabinet sides and biscuits at rails.
Rabbeted joints	Parts positively located, can be adjusted to align fronts. Very strong compared to butt joints. Machining relatively quick once setup is made. In cabinet side to bottom joints, edge of bottom is covered by side — minimizes glue squeeze-out, and can hide chipped edges in bottoms.	Stopped cuts (as at rails) can be difficult to make. Depth of rabbet must be figured into part size calculations. Inconsistencies in depth of rabbets/thickness of parts can cause problems.	Can be used in combination with other methods — rabbets at bottom of cabinet sides and biscuits at rails.
Dado Joints	If used at top or bottom end of part, both pieces must be machined. Very strong.	Depth of dados must be figured in to parts calculations. Inconsistencies in material thickness (plywood) or in depth of cuts can lead to problems.	Best used for cabinet backs, advantages for other box joints don't outweigh the extra time involved for machining.

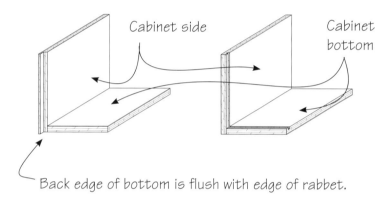

Rails and cabinet bottom are placed flush with edge of rabbet.

If a groove is used, rails are flush with inside edge of groove.

Rabbet in cabinet side is deeper than thickness of back.

Cabinet side

Cabinet bottom

Back edge of bottom is flush with edge of rabbet.

Figure 69. Cabinet backs, *generally of ¼-inch plywood, can sit in a rabbet or slide in a groove.*

Cabinet Backs

Cabinet backs are generally not attached to the cabinets until assembly and finishing are complete. This makes working inside the cabinet — installing hardware, drawers, and accessories — and finishing much easier, and keeps dust and debris from building up in side the cabinet. Backs are usually made from ¼-inch material, and either sit in a rabbet in the cabinet sides and bottom, or slide into a groove in the sides and bottom. In either case, the back should be set in from the back of the cabinet side at least ¼ inch. This allows room for scribing on a finished end, and gives some margin to get the back of the cabinet tight against the wall of the building **(Figure 69).**

Some makers prefer no joint in the cabinet bottom, allowing the bottom edge of the back to run down to the edge, as shown in the drawing at bottom left. This method simplifies some things, but complicates others. There are fewer pieces to be machined, but now the bottoms will be a different width than the sides. For wall cabinets, the cabinet bottom should be treated as a finished surface, so the joint should be included in the wall cabinet bottom, but can be eliminated in the top **(Figure 69).**

If grooves are used for the back joint, the back can be glued in place, either with yellow glue in the groove, or with hot-melt adhesive after the back is in place. I prefer to use hot-melt, as yellow glue will not form a very strong bond if the parts are finished, and it can be messy and time-consuming. If the back is held in a rabbet, a fastener must be used. Because the back is thin, the fasteners do not need to be very long: ⅝-inch screws, ⅞-inch narrow-crown staples, pins from a pneumatic gun, or brads. The rabbets should be made so that there is plenty of surface area for the fastener; it's usual to leave ¼ inch of material in the cabinet side.

If you are using staples, pins, or brads, be careful to drive them straight, as it is easy to angle the fastener and have it come through the face of the cabinet. I prefer to staple backs in rabbets, followed by a bead of hot-melt glue. If the rabbeted back is not securely attached, it is possible for it to be pushed away from the cabinet after the cabinet is installed. If the back is in grooves, it will stay in place, even if the glue joint should fail.

The Good Box

Its moving parts all function well — doors and drawers open and close without binding or being sloppy.

Joints and Materials

The materials used for box construction will also affect the decision on which joint to use. All joints should be glued, as well as fastened with staples and/or screws. If prefinished materials are used, the milled joints will allow wood-to-wood contact for a stronger glue joint. There is a Melamine glue available for holding a Melamine-coated surface to raw particleboard, or to another Melamine surface. It is not at all effective, however, for wood-to-wood joints.

The best joints to use will depend on the available equipment, type of cabinet, materials used, and the builder's preferences. The idea is to develop a system that works for you, and will produce consistent results in an efficient way. Practically speaking, there is very little difference from one type of joint to the other. All of the methods presented here will produce cabinets that are strong and will remain squarely together over time.

In addition to considering the finished strength of various joints, you should also consider the processes involved. In large commercial shops, stacks of parts move from location to location as parts are cut, joints are milled, edges banded, and boxes assembled. If you are working in a small shop, you may not have room to dedicate space for each step of the work, or for very many sub-assemblies. The more work you can do on each piece while it is still a single piece will make the entire process more efficient.

> ### The Good Box
> It is strongly constructed, and resistant to racking out of shape.

As you plan your work, decide what joint you will use at each location...

Box Construction Checklist

Location of Joint	Type of Joint	Personal pluses & minuses
Sides & bottom of base cabinet	1. Butt joint-screwed & glued	
	2. Butt joint with cleat (if toe kick is integral part of cabinet)	
	3. Butt joint with dowels	
	4. Butt joint with biscuits	
	5. Rabbet in sides	
	6. Dado in sides-rabbet on bottom	
Sides & top of base cabinet	1. Butt joint-screwed & glued	
	2. Butt joint with dowels	
	3. Butt joint with biscuits	
	4. Rabbet in sides	
Back of base cabinet	1. Screwed or stapled to back of box	
	2. In rabbet	
	3. In groove	
Finished end of base cabinet	1. Applied	
	2. Integral	
Toe kick on base cabinet	1. Boxes on wood base	
	2. Boxes on adjustable legs	
	3. Integral part of cabinet	

5. BUILDING BOXES: FASTENERS

Figure 70. Staples do the job—Narrow-crown staples hold sheet goods together better than nails, and they can be reinforced with screws. Staplers powered by compressed air are not expensive.

In a lot of woodworking and furniture making, the use of fasteners is considered cheating, and there are places in cabinet construction where you never want fasteners to show. In the majority of cabinetwork, however, it makes sense to speed the work along with the judicious use of screws, nails, staples, and other fasteners.

Fasteners can take the place of clamps, pulling parts together and holding them while the glue dries. They also strengthen a joint, or physically hold parts together without the use of glue. The third function is to fasten hardware, such as hinges or drawer slides, to the cabinet boxes. Different types of fasteners have different qualities, suited to these different purposes.

In commercial cabinet shops the hammer, nail, and screwdriver are nearly forgotten implements of a bygone day. In the modern shop, nails and staples are driven by pneumatic guns, and screws are driven either with pneumatic drivers or cordless electric drills. If you are on a budget, you can certainly hold cabinets together with finish nails, but the price of cordless drills and air-powered guns has reached a point where it makes sense to use them if at all possible.

Staples

A narrow-crown stapler is actually more useful to cabinet construction than a finish nailer or a brad gun (**Figure 70**). Of course, you don't want to use a staple where it will be visible on a finished surface, but it is a good fastener for joints in sheet goods. One staple will hold better than several nails, due in part to its physical nature, but also due to coatings that resist pulling out. During cabinet assembly, I will tack the box together with 1¼-inch staples, and when I am satisfied with the alignment of the parts I will go back and reinforce the work with screws. The 1¼ inch length is also quite useful for fastening two ¾-inch thick pieces face to face. Longer staples — 1½ inch or 1¾ inch — should be used in places where a staple is the only fastener.

Nails

There are three types of pneumatically driven nails, the difference being in gauge and head type. Thin 23- and 18-gauge nails are referred to as pins and brads, and the fasteners can have a slight head or a medium head. The shorter lengths of headless pins leave a nearly invisible hole, and are ideal for fastening thin pieces of trim or edging. While the thin size doesn't leave much evidence behind, it doesn't make a very strong fastener, and if lengths more than 1¼ inch are needed, a heavier-gauge nail is appropriate.

Finish nails are either 15 or 16 gauge, depending on the manufacturer. In use, there isn't a real difference between the two. Finish nailers are really more of a trim carpentry tool than a cabinetmaking tool, but if you are nailing face frames to cabinets, or ¾ inch x ¾ inch edging to plywood, a nail gun will be a great advantage over nailing by hand.

All of the finish nails are flat instead of round, and the head is in the shape of the letter T. Nail heads will be much easier to hide if the length of the T goes in the same direction as the grain of the wood. This can put your hand in an awkward position, but this small detail will make a big difference in the appearance of the finished cabinet.

In addition to being careful about the head direction, you also need to be mindful of where the business end of the nail is headed, and don't hold parts together with your hand close to the end of the nail gun. Squeeze the trigger and release so that if the tip of the gun bounces on the work as the nail is driven, it won't fire a second time. If the gun fires twice, the second nail can hit the head of the first, and bend out through the surface. This can also happen if the nail hits a knot or other hard object hidden inside the wood. If your aim is at an angle, the fastener can also come out the finished surface. The longer the nail, the better the chances are of this happening. Be certain if you are holding parts together while nailing that your hands will be out of the way should a nail or brad go astray. Eye protection is also highly recommended when using power nail guns.

Until a few years ago, all nail guns were driven by compressed air, and were tied to a compressor by a length of hose. This is still the most economical route, and the only available one for narrow-crown staplers and thin-gauge nailers. These devices don't use much air, so unless there is a need for other air-driven tools, a small compressor works well. Lightweight hoses are also preferred over heavier ones.

Cordless finish-nail guns are now available, driven by a flywheel powered by a battery-operated electric motor. At this writing, cordless versions of small-gauge nailers and staplers are not available, but they are in development. The cordless nailers use the same battery packs as cordless drills, and are more convenient to use than pneumatic guns.

A narrow crown stapler is more use in cabinet construction than a finish nailer or a brad gun.

Screws

Screws are the mainstay of cabinet construction, and for a screw to hold parts together properly, it must be fit in the correct hole. Old-style wood screws had an unthreaded shank and the threads tapered to the point. Today the shank has disappeared, and the diameter is constant down to the point of the screw. These differences are a function of how the screws are manufactured; in use, they function the same way. In either case, a good hole has three parts: a countersink that seats the head of the screw flush with the surface, a clearance hole in the part being attached, and a pilot hole for the threads **(Figure 72)**.

The clearance hole should be big enough so that the screw threads do not engage until

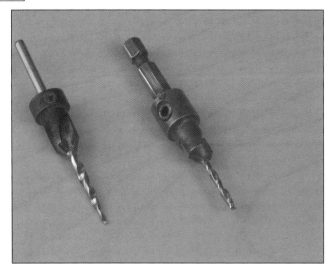

Figure 71. Countersink drill bit—*This type of bit drills a pilot hole, clearance hole, and countersink in one step. The bit on the right is carbide tipped.*

Figure 72. Clearance hole—*The screw threads should only engage in the lower piece, allowing the screw to pull the joint together.*

they reach the part to be fastened. The pilot hole should be the diameter of the unthreaded portion of the screw shank. If the threads do engage in the clearance hole, the screw won't be able to pull the first part down tight to the second part.

While there are people who will drill and countersink in three distinct steps, most makers use a drill with a countersink as shown in **Figure 71**. Tapered bits, such as those manufactured by Fuller, were designed for old-style wood screws, but work just as well for modern screws. In theory, a standard bit will also work, as the unthreaded portion of the shank won't grab in the clearance hole. I think screws in holes drilled with the tapered bits hold better and are less likely to strip the threads.

Some screws claim to be self-drilling or to be self-countersinking, and while they work, they don't work all that well. Get a decent countersink bit, and do it correctly with regular screws.

The old-style countersinks, however, leave much to be desired, particularly when working with modern sheet goods. New-style carbide-tipped countersinks will last several

times longer that the old high-speed steel versions. Hex-shaped shanks will also fit better in the drill chuck, and are quickly interchangeable with hex shank magnetic bit holders.

Magnetic bit holders **(Figure 73)** are preferred over chucking the driver bit in a drill. In addition to being easily changed when a different type of driver is needed, or the bit becomes worn, the magnet will hold the screw in place when reaching to drive it. I like the shortest available bit holder I can find, and use the short interchangeable tips. The longer holders and tips put the hand and wrist too far away from the head of the screw, and make it difficult to apply pressure while driving.

Avoid the tips with the ball-detent as they will be hard to remove from the bit holder. If you get a hand driver that takes the same bits, you can replace an entire drawer full of screwdrivers, and always have a hand driver with a decent tip.

There are some quick-change systems available that let you release the bit holder without loosening the drill chuck itself. These also include drill bits with hex shanks. These

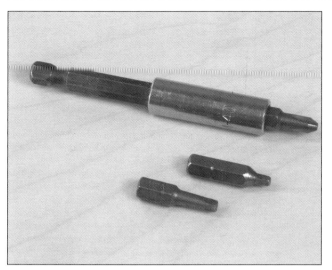

Figure 73. Magnetic bit holder—*Using a magnetic bit holder will speed the work, and make driving screws easier.*

Figure 74. Posidrive/Phillips comparison—*European hardware uses a Posidrive head. At left, the Posidrive bit doesn't quite fit a Phillips-head screw. At right, Phillips bit fits a Phillips head.*

bits will give you 90% of the benefits of the quick-change holders without the expense. Since all of the drill shanks are the same size as the bit holder, all that is needed is to release the chuck, as opposed to making a big change in diameter. If you can afford it, using two drills — one set up with a countersink bit, and one set up to drive screws — will save a tremendous amount of labor.

The most common head type used in cabinetwork is the Phillips head, but square-drive (Robertson) screws hold in the driver better, and are my first choice. A combo, or quadrex head, which combines the Phillips and the square drive, is also available. The combo head drives well with a square drive bit, but not very well with the Phillips. Slotted, or common screws do not drive well with a power driver, and are best avoided. Square-drive screws are available through the mail or online.

The other type of screw head that will be encountered is the Posidrive which is used by most manufacturers of European-style hardware. The Posidrive looks like a Phillips head at first glance, but on close examination the difference can be seen. At the center of the Posidrive screw head, where the familiar lines

of the Phillips head cross, there is a small, square recess. While these can be used with a Phillips-head driver, the proper bit will provide superior performance **(Figure 74)**.

Number 6 drywall screws are often used to join cabinet parts, but they are too thin and too brittle. Screws with similar threads have been engineered specifically to hold sheet goods parts together, and are a better choice. For assembling cabinets, a number 8 screw with a length of 1¾ inches is used the most. 1¼-inch long screws are also used when putting two ¾-inch thick pieces together face to face. For installing cabinets, the same screws used for assembling the cabinets work well for attaching cabinets to each other, but a heavier screw should be used for attaching cabinets to the walls of the building. You need a longer screw to reach through the cabinet nailer and back, as well as the drywall. If you have a ¾-inch thick nailing rail, a ¼-inch back, a ¼-inch space for scribing, and ½ inch of drywall in front of the stud, you need a 3-inch long screw to carry the weight of a wall cabinet. Special screws with a washer-style pan head have been developed for this purpose.

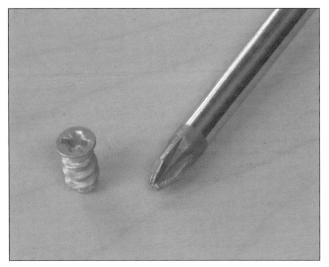

Figure 75. Euro screws—*In factory-made cabinets, Euro screws hold the hardware in the 5mm system holes. These hold best in particleboard.*

Figure 76. Vix bit—*The tip of this bit fits in the countersink of hardware, automatically centering the hole.*

Figure 77. Jig for Euro screws—*A jig like this, which can quickly be located on the cabinet side using a spring clamp, matched with a depth-stop bit, is ideal for Euro screws.*

Special Screws

The washer-style pan head allows for some adjustment in the placement of the cabinet, and these screws are also available in different finishes, to be less obtrusive inside the cabinet. Regular countersink-head screws are also used, and while their appearance is not an issue in base cabinets, some people object to seeing the screw heads in a wall cabinet. Self-adhesive covers, called Fastcaps, are available in nearly every imaginable color and wood species, for quickly disguising any visible screw heads.

There are other specialty screws used that may not be familiar to the average person. European under-mount drawer slides use what appears at first glance to be a standard flat-head screw. The holes in the slides are actually engineered for Euro screws (which we will get to in a minute), and the countersink is not quite the same. This allows a standard flat-head screw to protrude slightly in to the mechanism of the slide, and can catch. These screws have various names — Little Grippers or undercut slide screws — and should be used for this application.

Euro screws have been designed to attach hardware in the 5mm-diameter holes that are line-bored in the 32mm system, and are a superior alternative to the self-tapping screws shown above. The large diameter and thread design holds the hardware more securely, and is far less likely to strip out during use **(Figure 75).**

The disadvantage of the Euro screw is that the depth of the hole must precisely match the length of the screw. This is not an issue if the holes have been bored with a drilling machine or drill press, but it can be a problem when drilling by hand. Vix-style bits are available to drill the 5mm-diameter holes these screws require, and are a good choice for use with jigs to align the holes, and to drill at a constant depth **(Figure 76 & 77).**

Figure 78. Screws for drawer slide—*Full extension drawer slides require a special screws. A regular pan-head screw will jam in the slide mechanism.*

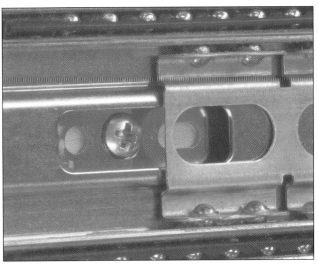

Figure 79. Correct drawer slide screw—*The correct screw won't interfere with the slide mechanism.*

One thing to be careful about with both the Little Gripper and Euro screws is the diameter of the head. Different hardware manufactures vary this dimension on drawer slides, so the screws might go completely through the countersinks in the drawer slides, or they may stick out enough to interfere with the operation of the slide **(Figure 78 & 79).**

Full-extension drawer slides such as the Accuride also require a specific screw, a small (#6 x ½ inch) pan-head screw with a low profile head. These are usually provided with the slides, but if you buy slides in bulk, you need to purchase the screws separately. If you use a regular pan-head screw, the head can catch on the slide mechanism.

Confirmat screws are another European type of screw that was designed for ready to assemble or knockdown cabinets. Some cabinetmakers use these as a standard assembly screw, but I find it hard to justify their use in shop-assembled cabinets. They are considerably more expensive than self-tapping #8 screws, and require a special stepped drill bit. For good results, the drill should also be guided by a jig to keep the hole location in line. The larger diameter does make for a stronger fastener, but the screws they are intended to replace are more than strong enough **(Figure 80).**

If you decide to use pocket screws for assembly, you will need to use yet another special type of screw, #6 pan-head face-frame screws. The 1¼ inch length is used in most applications, particularly with ¾-inch thick stock. Two types of thread are available: fine thread for use with hardwoods, and coarse thread for use with soft woods. In addition to a jig or fixture for the drill press, you will also need a 6 inch long driver bit if you want to drive these with a cordless drill. This bit is included with many of the commercially available jigs. Make sure to do a test fitting to get the depth of the holes and jig placement correct. This system works well,

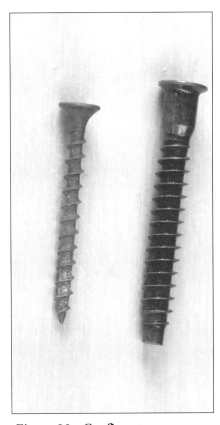

Figure 80. Confirmat screws—*The Confirmat screw (right) was designed for knock-down cabinets, and may be used for assembly, but the regular #8 screws (left) is more than strong enough.*

Figure 81. Drawer front screw— *The washer head on these screws allows some adjustment when placing drawer fronts.*

but must be set up correctly for good results. Square-drive is the most common head type available for these, and is highly recommended. The Phillips heads are likely to strip at the head due to the angle at which they are driven.

Large washer-head screws are an excellent way for securing drawer fronts to drawer boxes **(Figure 81)**. The 1-inch length is used for attaching a ¾-inch thick drawer front to a ½-inch thick drawer box. Drill two ³⁄₁₆ inch to ⅜ inch clearance holes in the front of the drawer box, and you will be able to fine-tune the fit of the drawer front by loosening the screws. After you've done a few, you'll develop the right touch to get the screws tight enough to move the drawer front but still have it stay in place. After you are satisfied with the placement, you can tighten the screws a bit more to hold the fronts in position. You should also run a few countersunk screws to hold the drawer front permanently.

Another odd fastener you may need is the sex bolt which consists of a machine screw (the male) and a coupling (the female). This is used to secure two pieces of hardware to the same system hole, and take the place of a Euro screw, or a Little Gripper.

Handles and pulls generally attach with fine-thread machine screws. These often come with screws, but the manufacturer of the hardware has to guess about whether you are only going through ¾-inch thick material for a door, or through a ½-inch thick drawer box front and a ¾-inch thick drawer box. If you are doing an entire kitchen, you will likely have both conditions present, and need two lengths of screws for the handles.

When you head to the hardware store to get the length you don't have, take a pull with you, or find out from the manufacturer if it is an SAE or metric thread. If SAE, the threads are likely #8-32, and if Metric, M-4. It's hard to distinguish between the two visually, but very easy to tell if you have the wrong size when you try to drive them.

Breakaway machine screws are available, but more expensive than the standard screws. For the money, you can likely get what you need for each of the correct lengths, and avoid the trouble of breaking off the extra length. In an emergency, you can thread a nut on a screw that is too long, and cut it beyond the nut with a pair of side-cutters or linesman's pliers. After you make the cut, unthreading the nut will re-cut the threads.

6. BUILDING BOXES: MATERIALS

Figure 82. Veneer core hardwood plywood—All veneer-core plywood is not made the same way. The sample on top is Baltic Birch, on bottom is a 7-ply domestic product.

Figure 83. MDF vs. particleboard—MDF and particleboard are both man-made sheet materials. MDF (on left) is made from fibers, and is denser, smoother, and more consistent than particleboard (at right).

Solid wood is a wonderful material to work with and to see, but not the best material to use for cabinet box construction. Sheet goods — plywood, particleboard, or medium density fiberboard — are the logical choice for the construction of cabinet boxes. Seasonal wood movement that would cause problems if solid wood were used are not an issue, and it is a responsible environmental use of raw material, as well as a considerable convenience to the cabinetmaker **(Figure 82 & 83)**.

The principle division in materials is often related to finishes; wood on the outside should be on plywood cabinets and plastic laminate should be on particleboard boxes. These are not the only options, however, and there are considerably more choices than the two listed.

Wood veneer and plastic laminate represent the great divide in exterior finishes, with painted wood (or something that looks like painted wood) being a very popular compromise. Cabinet exteriors can also be constructed of solid wood, or can be laminated with other materials ranging from Melamine to metals.

Nearly every exterior treatment can be applied to any of the available core materials, particleboard, medium density fiberboard, or plywood. Cabinet interiors don't necessarily have to match the cabinet exteriors. We tend to assume that veneer on the outside means veneer on the inside, and this is often the case, but a quality cabinet may well have a Melamine finish on the inside and solid wood doors, drawer fronts, and panels on the outside.

There are many myths, misconceptions, and prejudices regarding these materials and their use in cabinetmaking. Plywood is often seen as vastly superior, even though it is usually the least desirable choice for an attractive finished product. Medium density fiberboard (MDF) is seen by some to be inherently inferior, and particleboard is regarded by many as pure evil.

To the practical person with an open mind and a desire to learn the facts, the choice of material should be based on a balanced consideration of cost, suitability for the purpose, and finished appearance.

Technically speaking, any sheet good product with three or more layers (an inner core and two faces of veneer or other material) is called plywood. The differences in core material are spelled out in the product description. What we commonly think of as "plywood" is called "veneer core" in the trade.

If I order red oak MDF core plywood, I will get a sheet of medium density fiberboard with red oak veneer on the faces. If I order red oak VC plywood, it will be a sheet of plywood (VC=veneer core) with the outer two layers red oak veneer. Solid wood, usually thin strips glued together, is sometimes used as a core material, but this is rare.

As with any commodity, there is a great deal of variation in the quality of both the core materials and the face veneers. These differences in quality within a type of sheet material do not necessarily mean that the type is bad. There is good veneer-core plywood and bad veneer-core plywood, quality particleboard and junk particleboard. Knowing the terms and qualities of the numerous choices will avoid disappointments based on the buyer assuming one thing and the supplier assuming another.

"Big Box" home centers and local lumberyards will rarely have much of a selection of sheet goods, but specialists that sell to the cabinetmaking trade will generally have a wide selection of choices, both for core materials and for veneers or other decorative coverings such as Melamine. These sources prefer to sell to the professional cabinetmaker only, and may be hard to find in some locations. If you are going to be building an entire kitchen, however, you will need a considerable amount of material, so it makes sense to track down a supplier, and see if they will make a sale to an individual. Small lumberyards can usually special-order these

materials, but they are not likely to be as knowledgeable as a specialty supplier.

The first myth about plywood (and other sheet goods) is that wood movement is not an issue. The phrase that gets repeated is usually, "Plywood won't warp like solid wood will." This is in fact true; plywood doesn't warp the same way that solid wood does, plywood warps the way plywood warps. Where changes in heat and humidity make solid wood expand and contract mainly in width, these same changes will make plywood, particleboard, and MDF expand and contract in thickness.

There usually isn't enough of a change in thickness to cause problems, unless the edge of a piece is thoroughly soaked with water. With particleboard and MDF this change in thickness can be quite dramatic, and parts once soaked can lose their structural integrity and begin to crumble when the piece later dries out. Any of these sheet goods can and will warp, particularly if they are not stored flat. If you lean a piece of sheet material against a wall for any length of time, it will begin to bend from its own weight, and this bend can become set in the sheet. Sheet goods can also warp as a result of poor manufacturing technique, or from not being stored properly.

Plywood

Plywood used in cabinet construction is made from hardwoods, usually poplar, birch, luaun, or some other imported wood. Softwood plywood, commonly used in construction for floor underlayment or sheathing, has cores and faces unsuitable for quality cabinetwork. It is simply too unstable and too coarse a surface to be usable. Veneer cores are constructed from an odd number of plies, usually rotary-cut veneer. The grain of each ply is at a 90-degree angle to the adjacent ply. These plies are glued together,

> You won't find quality sheet goods at the home center, look for a specialty dealer.

with heat and pressure applied to set the glue and make the sheet flat. This alternating of the grain direction makes plywood more stable than solid wood, and on edge, plywood is quite strong. A measure of this strength comes from the stiffness of the glue itself, and plywood with multiple, thinner plies will be stiffer and stronger than that made from fewer, thicker plies.

Of all the sheet good types, plywood is the most complicated in construction — there are more layers, and each layer of material and each glue joint between layers is an opportunity for manufacturers to cut corners, and for problems to develop. As a result of this, plywood is more likely than particleboard or MDF to have serious problems that make it unsuitable at worst, and difficult to work with at best. In many areas, the quality standards of the Architectural Woodwork Institute do not allow the use of veneer-core material in higher-quality work.

In the manufacturing of plywood, if the moisture content of the plies is inconsistent from ply to ply, then one or more layers will shrink more in width than the others, and the sheet will either warp permanently, or behave much like case-hardened solid wood, bending or warping during or just after being cut. If the thickness of each ply is not consistent, then the sheet will not be flat; it will have an inconsistent thickness throughout the sheet, making joinery difficult and acceptable appearance of the face veneers nearly impossible. These problems are more prominent in cheaper plywood, particularly those that are imported.

In addition to the thickness of veneer-core plywood being inconsistent, it is also always less than the nominal thickness. Taking their cue from processors of framing lumber, plywood manufacturers deliver a product that is smaller than it is supposed to be. The common myth that is applied to this is that undersized plywood is a metric thickness,

and that it has to be that size to meet international standards. The real reason is that if the manufacturer can deliver a product $\frac{1}{32}$ inch to $\frac{1}{16}$ inch thinner than it should be, he has shaved 3% to 6% off his raw material costs. Some cheap imported plywood is now labeled as 18mm, but it is also undersized, often measuring less than $\frac{11}{16}$ of an inch. 18mm is actually close to $\frac{45}{64}$ of an inch, slightly over $\frac{11}{16}$.

So why make a big deal over a little variation in size? One of the reasons is tooling. Standard dado sets, router bits, and shaper-cutters are made to tight tolerances and specific dimensions, based on what should be standard material thicknesses. Undersized bits and cutters are available, but if you sometimes need a $\frac{3}{4}$ inch groove for solid wood or MDF, and sometimes $\frac{23}{32}$ inch for plywood, you now have to duplicate your purchase.

The second — and to me the more important reason — is inconsistency. If you measure a typical piece of veneer-core plywood with calipers, you will find a significant variation in thickness within the sheet. A joint that is the right size for a piece of plywood in the middle of a part can easily be too tight at one end, and too loose at the other. To work with veneer-core material you need to decide on an average size to work to, and then adjust, trim, and live with gaps here and there.

The final problem with veneer-core plywood's inconsistent surface is with finishing the face veneer. It is quite difficult to get a good finish because of its wavy nature. The thin face veneer follows the core below it, and can never be sanded to as flat a surface as can be achieved with other core materials. Often the coarse grain of the core will telegraph through the thin face veneer.

Plywood doesn't move and warp like solid wood — it moves and warps like plywood.

Particleboard

Particleboard is manufactured from wood particles of differing sizes, mixed together with a resin binder, and pressed in to a sheet under heat and pressure. As with any other panel product, there is considerable variation in quality from the cheap stuff to the good stuff. In the better-quality particleboard, the size of the particles at the surface are smaller than those in the center of the panel, yielding a smoother finished surface. Particleboard is not as strong as veneer-core plywood, but it is certainly strong enough for use in cabinet construction, and its flat surface, consistent size, and lower price make it preferable over veneer-core material.

Problems that are inherent to particleboard include sagging over an unsupported horizontal span, moisture absorption, and the tendency to fracture and crumble if it suffers impact damage, such as being dropped on a corner. Screws hold well in particleboard edges, provided they are kept away from the corner of the panel. Screws too close to the edge can split the panel. Cabinet bottoms and shelves less than 32 inches long generally won't sag in ¾ inch thick material. Plastic laminate edging on the front of a particleboard panel will stiffen it to some degree, but a solid hardwood edge is a better solution for spans greater than 36 inches.

Particleboard does expand and contract, mostly in thickness, in response to humidity changes. Real problems will develop if the edge of a piece of particleboard becomes soaked. Three-quarter-inch thick board can become more than an inch thick, and this swelling can force joints to fail and fasteners to let go. If the piece dries out again, the bond between the resin and the particles generally will fail, and the board will start to crumble. This crumbling effect will also happen if the panel is damaged from impact. Once this damage has occurred, there really isn't a good fix for it. You can squirt glue into the damaged area, and try to force things back together with a wooden hand-screw clamp, but the chances of success are slim.

These problems can be avoided by careful handling and a little planning. Design so that raw particleboard edges don't sit directly on the floor, especially in areas likely to get wet, such as a kitchen or bath, or directly on a concrete floor. If you have to put a raw edge on the floor, you can smear a bead of silicone caulk on the edge to seal it, or band it with PVC or other plastic. Sink cutouts in particleboard countertops should also be sealed, but in practice, this is rarely done. Many of the problems associated with particleboard are not flaws in the material itself, but ignorance of the nature of the material on the part of those who use it.

There are special-purpose particleboard products available. Some are manufactured with moisture-resistant resins, and fire-retardant treated particleboard is sometimes used in commercial applications.

Particleboard is by far the most commonly used material for cabinet construction, and is available with a variety of face overlays, either wood veneer, or Melamine. One of the reasons is cost; particleboard adequately performs its job for less money than the other options. In addition to cost, it also provides a flatter, more stable surface than veneer-core material.

Medium Density Fiberboard

Medium density fiberboard is similar to particleboard, in that it is manufactured from tiny bits of wood and resin rather than veneers peeled from a log. The big difference is that the wood that goes in to MDF is precisely sized fibers, rather than little chunks of wood and sawdust. MDF is denser and more stable than particleboard, and the surface is considerably smoother. The smooth flat sur-

Particleboard is cheap enough and strong enough for most cabinet applications.

face is the big appeal of MDF, particularly if it is to be used as the core material beneath hardwood veneer. In high-end furniture, architectural paneling, and cabinetwork, the best-quality veneer finishes will be found on medium density fiberboard cores. The edges of MDF are smoother than veneer-core plywood or particleboard when cut, and can be machined to a profile for painted work.

MDF is incredibly heavy; a 4 foot x 8 foot sheet weighs close to a hundred pounds, and can be difficult for one person to handle alone. There is a lightweight MDF available, but it can only be considered light in comparison to the standard product. Long spans of MDF will sag if not supported, and when machined it produces a lot of very fine dust. MDF does not hold screws in its edges as well as veneer-core plywood or particleboard, and has a tendency to split when screws or other fasteners are driven too close to the corners.

Veneer-core plywood is available in the commonly seen 4 foot x 8 foot sheets, while both particleboard and MDF can be obtained in a wider variety of sizes, up to 5 feet x 12 feet. MDF and particleboard panels are actually an inch wider and longer than their nominal size, so a 4 foot x 8 foot sheet will really be 49 inches wide by 97 inches long.

In quality work, ¾ inch is the standard thickness of most cabinet components except for cabinet backs, which are usually ¼ inch thick. Some makers prefer to use ⅜-inch thick material for cabinet ends and bottoms, but the minimal price difference is offset by the risk of splitting material when fastening parts together. Some factory cabinets are manufactured from ½ inch or even ⅜-inch thick parts, and while this can be and is done, the sacrifice in quality is too great to be justified by the savings in material costs. For finished stile and rail panels, either on cabinet ends or in doors, ¼ inch plywood can be used, but the quality of ¼ inch plywood

and inconsistency in thickness make it nearly unsuitable for quality work. More attractive panels will be obtained by either veneering ¼ inch MDF, or using ½-inch thick material with a rabbet milled to fit the groove in the panel components.

One more sheet good myth that needs to be debunked is that the factory edges are straight, and the sheets are square. Sometimes this is the case, but it is rare enough that the standard procedure in most quality-oriented commercial shops is to straighten edges and square corners as the first step in cutting parts. Allowance for these initial trim cuts is the reason that particleboard and MDF sheets are oversized. In the techniques section of this book I will explain how to deal with this in the small shop.

Other Sheet Goods

Veneer-core plywood, particleboard, and MDF are the three most commonly used materials for most cabinet parts, but there are some other sheet goods that are used in specific situations. Hardboard, commonly called Masonite, can be used for drawer bottoms, cabinet backs, or thin vertical dividers.

There is a combination core which is a veneer-core inner layer sandwiched between two particleboard layers. This sounds like a good idea; the material has the light weight and strength of plywood, and the smooth flat surfaces of particleboard. In reality, however, this attempt to obtain the best of both worlds actually combines the worst features of each material into a product that almost no one ever uses.

For curved work, there are a few varieties of sheet material that are designed and manufactured to be bent. Kerf-core is MDF that has slots cut in one face, allowing the sheet to bend to a radius. A variation of this has a rubber coating on the face that allows it to

Don't expect factory edges to be straight or factory corners to be square, because usually they are not.

be laminated with plastic laminate or veneer before being bent to shape. This works, but necessitates the curved panel being held in place without any fasteners through the face of the material.

The other approach to curved panels is to laminate thin pieces that can be fastened through the face to a curved form below. Most ¼-thick veneer core plywood can be bent to a gentle radius. For a tighter radius, there is a product called bending ply, or wacky wood, which is a 3-ply product consisting of one very thin center ply between two thicker layers of luaun. This is specified at ⅜-inch thick, but is really closer to ⁵⁄₁₆ inch, and the surface is coarse and inconsistent. Two layers glued together will not yield a ¾-inch thick panel.

One-eight-inch thick birch plywood, commonly sold as door skin for hollow-core doors, can be used for making curved panels, either in a stack of six pieces to obtain a ¾-inch thick panel, or as a final layer over two pieces of nominal ⅜-inch thick bending ply. The grain on the face of bending plywood is often oriented at 90 degrees to that normally seen on plywood, but it is also available in its normal orientation. You need to be careful when ordering this material to specify which way the grain should run. An 8 x 4 sheet is not the same as a 4 x 8 sheet — the grain will run in the direction of the second number, not the largest number.

Baltic birch plywood **(Figure 82 page 71)** is imported from Europe, and originated in the Baltic States of the former Soviet Union. Its distinction is the number of thin plies used in its fabrication, and the odd size of the sheets, which are 5 feet x 5 feet instead of the common 4 feet x 8 feet. There are different grades of Baltic birch plywood available, the lower grades allowing a few voids, and a coarser face veneer. This is an excellent material for drawer boxes and for shop jigs and fixtures. It is more dimensionally stable, and stiffer and stronger than regular hardwood plywood. An American version of this material is called apple ply and is made of birch and alder veneers ¹⁄₁₆-inch thick. Apple ply is available in several thicknesses, and in 4 foot x 8 foot sheets.

Most of the time, sheet goods are not seen, but are used as substrates for decorative materials, either wood veneer or plastic laminate or Melamine on the faces and edges. The inside and the outside of cabinets can receive different treatments, and in a practical way, I think this makes sense, both for ease of manufacture and in using the finished product. When the cabinet doors are closed, you really can't tell what the inside of the cabinets are like (unless the cabinets have glass doors) and I think it is preferable to have the interiors finished in a light color, so that you can find what you are looking for inside a cabinet, and with a material that is highly resistant to spills. Finishing the inside of the cabinet the same as the outside greatly increases the amount of work to be done, without any real gain in an aesthetic or practical way.

I prefer a construction method that utilizes applied finished ends. While this will raise material costs slightly, it saves a significant amount of time, and allows efficient techniques to be used in milling and assembling the box parts. Veneer plywood can certainly be used in box construction, and the insides may be finished with either a clear coat, or stained to match the exteriors. If this method is used, it is more efficient to finish-sand all of the interior parts before assembling the boxes.

Many of the sheet materials used for cabinetmaking come already finished. Both the plywood camp and the particleboard camp have an effective, economical product, Melamine board and pre-finished plywood. If you can't stomach the thought of using particleboard, skip ahead a few pages while the rest of us look at Melamine board.

Baltic birch plywood and Apple ply are excellent materials for drawer boxes.

Figure 84. Melamine board and prefinished plywood—Using either Melamine board or prefinished plywood will eliminate finishing the insides of the cabinets.

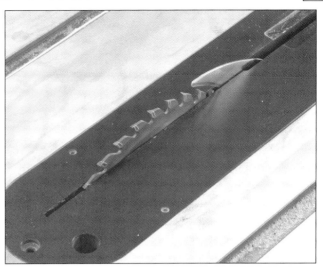

Figure 85. Zero-clearance insert—A zero-clearance insert, combined with an alternate top bevel blade (known as a Hi-ATB blade), will virtually eliminate chipping in Melamine board.

Melamine Board

The surface of Melamine board is basically the top two layers of plastic laminate, permanently fused to particleboard or MDF sheets. The particleboard core is much more common, due to its lower cost. An extremely thin sheet of paper with either a solid color or a printed pattern is impregnated with plastic resins, and covered with a transparent overlay sheet. This is bonded under heat and pressure to a sheet of particleboard on both sides. (One-sided Melamine board is sometimes seen, but it warps almost immediately.) This plastic coating adds about $\frac{1}{64}$ inch to the thickness of the board.

The resulting product has a very durable surface that is resistant to scratching, moisture, and many chemicals. It is easy to clean, and difficult to damage. In kitchen cabinets white and almond are the colors generally used, but other colors are available. Most of the popular patterns used in plastic laminates are also available in Melamine board as the same printed paper is used in both products. The wood-grain patterns don't really look like wood, especially when used in conjunction with real wood veneers or solids. In laminate

cabinets, the appearance is acceptable, and it's difficult to distinguish Melamine from plastic laminate **(Figure 84).**

The main issues in using Melamine board are what to do with the raw edges, and how to cut it without chipping. In large professional cabinet shops, either panel saws or sliding table saws are used to score the bottom of the panel as it is being cut. In the small shop, there are some alternatives that produce consistent, acceptable, but not quite perfect results. Some books have suggested raising the table saw blade slightly and running the panels backwards through the saw to score the bottom face, or cutting every part $\frac{1}{4}$ inch or so oversized and then trimming the edges down with a router. I can't in good conscience recommend working backwards or doing two or three times as much work as is necessary.

In my experience, the proper blade in the table saw, combined with a zero-clearance insert, will eliminate nearly all of the chipping that would otherwise occur. Both Amana and Freud make blades with tooth geometry designed for cutting Melamine, and in combination with the zero-clearance insert they work quite well **(Figure 85).**

Figure 86. Cut comparison—*The sample at right was cut with a zero clearance insert and Hi-ATB blade. The one at left was cut with a standard saw table insert and a combination blade.*

Figure 87. Cutting Melamine—*The key to chip-free cuts in Melamine is a zero clearance insert, and the right saw blade.*

In cabinet construction, one side of the material will never or rarely be seen, and if you get in the habit of keeping the same face up as you cut parts, and using that face in the most visible locations, chipping won't be a problem. Wood-veneered material is also prone to chipping when cut across the direction of the grain. Chipping mainly occurs on the bottom face regardless of material. If you use a zero-clearance insert, a blade with the correct tooth geometry, and keep the good side up, you will only have a minimal amount of chipped material to deal with **(Figure 86 & 87)**.

There is an attachment available for 10-inch cabinet saws that replaces the standard blade with a smaller blade, and a belt-driven scoring blade. I once worked in a shop that used this arrangement, and it worked well when new. Once the blades dulled and needed to be sent out for sharpening, the scoring blade and the main blade were never quite the same width, and we couldn't achieve a clean edge.

Some smaller versions of European cabinet saws are becoming available in the U.S. that are equipped with scoring blades for a little more than the price of an American saw with a sliding table. European saws also usu-

ally come with a sliding table that is more efficient than American after-market sliding tables. Riving knives, a built-in splitter that surrounds the back half of the blade, are generally standard equipment on these machines, and a tremendous improvement on the typical American saw guard and splitter. The biggest drawback to European saws is the short arbor, which prevents the use of a dado set.

Vertical-grade plastic laminate can also be glued to full sheets of raw particleboard or MDF, and then cut to size for use as cabinet parts. One side can be laminated, and if the laminated side is kept face up during cutting to size, chipping will not be a problem. The raw side needs to be laminated shortly after cutting, as the different surfaces absorb moisture at different rates, and parts laminated on one side only will definitely warp. For cabinet interiors, the Melamine surface is adequate. Because the parts are held together structurally, cabinet ends that are Melamine on the inside and laminate on the outside are not likely to warp even though the finish is unbalanced.

Plastic-laminate cabinet doors should have the same material on both faces. In low-end work, a door will often have plastic laminate edges and an exposed face, with a Melamine interior face. Doors made this way will likely warp at some point.

Particleboard and MDF can also be painted, but in most cases they are used with either a Melamine coating or wood veneer. If veneer-core construction is desired for a painted cabinet, birch is the best choice. Poplar and luaun plywood cost less, but are coarser and won't take paint as well.

Pre-finished veneer-core plywood, usually with maple or birch faces, is available with a durable clear coating. Check with your supplier as to exactly what coating is available, and where it is applied. Factory-finished panels can be an epoxy coating that is cured with ultraviolet light. This finish is incredibly durable, and won't scratch while the cabinet parts are being cut and the parts fabricated. Some suppliers will pre-finish panels in-house, and while this can be a fairly durable finish, it is not as tough as the factory finish.

Plastic Laminate

Plastic laminate is a finish material, not a structural one, but it also comes in sheet form. It is made from numerous layers of Kraft paper impregnated with plastic resins, and formed into sheets with heat and pressure. The top layer of paper is printed with a decorative pattern and coated with clear resin. Several thicknesses are available, but the two in common use are standard grade, which is .050-inch thick, and vertical grade which is .030-inch thick.

Standard grade is generally used for countertops and other high-wear situations. It is often referred to as being 1/16-inch thick, but it is actually 1/64 inch less than that. This may be seen as nitpicking, but errors in calculation will accumulate and cause trouble. Vertical-grade laminate is within a thou-

sandth of an inch of 1/32 inch. Postforming grade is in between vertical and standard in thickness, at .040 inch, and is intended for use in countertops that have a rounded front edge.

Plastic laminate without the decorative paper layer is sold as backing material. This should be used whenever a finished surface, such as a countertop, has an unseen and unsupported area of more than 4 square feet opposite the finished side. It is a good idea to use a backer on all countertops, in order to balance the construction to prevent warping. This is rarely done in practice, and is one of the reasons that plastic laminate has a bad reputation. Even if the panel is held in place physically so that it can't warp, moisture entering the unfinished side can attack the glue bond between the board and the laminate on the finished side. This can considerably shorten the life of the countertop.

Wood veneer is also available in sheet form. Normally veneer is sold in leaf form, relatively narrow pieces with irregular edges. When sold in sheet form, the individual leaves are trimmed with parallel edges and applied to a backing sheet, which may be cross-banded veneer, heavy paper, or other thin materials or combinations of materials. Sheets are available with pressure-sensitive adhesive, or without adhesive to be laminated with contact cement or other glue. Numerous species and cuts of veneer are available, as well as sheet size from 4 feet x 8 feet up to 5 feet x 10 feet and sometimes 12 feet. Sheets are also available with the veneer running at 90 degrees to the normal orientation in some species.

Edge Treatments

Visible edges of sheet goods are generally covered for appearance, and also to improve durability. Usually a material similar in appearance is used, but contrasting materi-

While it is a good idea to apply a backer laminate to countertops, in practice almost nobody does it, and this is one reason why plastic laminate has a bad reputation

Figure 88. Sticking edges—A roll of edge-banding with pressure-sensitive adhesive is the easiest way to finish edges.

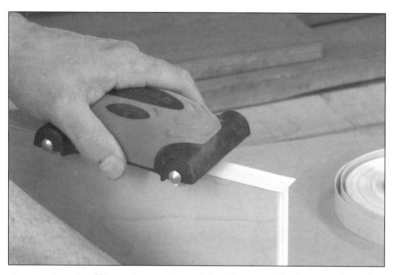

Figure 89. Rolling edges—A special roller, or a block of hardwood, is used to press the edge-band in place.

veyor, applies glue to the edge of the board, and presses on material fed from a continuous roll. After the material is applied, the excess material is trimmed from both ends and from the top and bottom surfaces.

In the home shop, or small shop, this process involves the same steps, but takes considerably longer. The process is simply adhering an oversized material to the edge and trimming it back so that it is flush with the surface. The problem is that in a typical project, you will have lots and lots of edges.

Materials available on rolls save the labor of cutting big sheets into thin strips, and come in both plastics and in wood veneers. Rolls are also available with adhesive applied to the back side, either hot-melt or pressure-sensitive. The plastics that can be applied by hand are generally polyester, and match the standard plastic laminate and Melamine colors. Plastic roll materials used in commercial applications come without any adhesive on the back, as that is usually fed from a reservoir that is part of the edge-banding machine. Some of these may also be applied using contact cement, but if you are attempting this, be sure that the material, substrate, and adhesive are all compatible. Some plastics, notably thicker PVC, won't stick well with contact cement **(Figure 88 & 89).**

Veneers are also available on rolls, with or without hot-melt or pressure-sensitive adhesive. One thing to watch for in veneer edging is the presence of finger joints in the veneer. Obviously, the short lengths of veneer need to be joined every 8 to 10 feet to make a continuous roll. In visible locations, and with light or clear-colored finishes, these joints may be objectionable.

There are a number of devices available for bringing the heat-activated glues up to temperature, but a household iron works as well as or better than most of what is available.

als can be used. In face-frame cabinets, the exposed edges of the plywood parts are covered by the solid wood face frame. In frameless cabinet construction there are many materials that can be used. These materials can be cut from solid wood, veneer, or plastic laminate sheets, or may come pre-cut to a width slightly wider than the thickness of the sheet on a continuous roll.

In commercial shops, the edges of sheet material parts are covered in one step by feeding them into an automatic edge-bander. This machine moves the parts through on a con-

Figure 90. Trimming edges—*A trimmer such as the Virutex can trim laminate against a plywood edge. A sharp block plane would do as well.*

Figure 91. Slitter—*A laminate slitter uses two opposing rollers to trim laminate or veneer for edge-banding.*

After the strip of edging has been heated, it must be firmly pressed in place on the edge. A block of hardwood or a steel laminate roller both work well for this task.

Pressure-sensitive adhesives are a relatively new addition to the edge treatment arsenal, and improvements to the types of adhesives make them a more reasonable choice than they were just a few years ago. This is the least demanding method of application: peel off the back, press in place, and apply pressure with a block of wood or steel roller.

After the edges are glued, the excess material on the edges and ends needs to be trimmed, and there are a number of ways to accomplish this. A router with a flush-trimming bit is too big, noisy, and heavy for trimming this lightweight material, and if used on wood veneer will likely cause the veneer to split and chip. Special trimmers such as the Virutex are commonly used for both plastics and veneers. These gadgets are basically a single-edged razor blade held in a guide. I find it just as effective to use a common trim knife, letting the edge ride on the face surface as a guide (**Figure 90 & 92**).

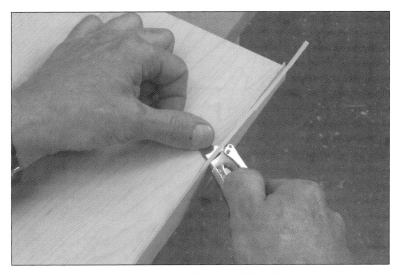

Figure 92. Trimming veneer edges—*While a laminate trimmer can also trim wood veneers, a regular shop knife is just as effective. Guide it by pressing the blade against the face surface.*

While the rolls are convenient, strips can also be cut from sheets or pieces of veneer, or from sheets of plastic laminate. These strips should be cut wider than needed — ⅞ inch for ¾-inch thick material. The table saw, although it can be used, is not a good choice for cutting these strips. Most table saw fences don't come down tight to the table surface, so there is a good chance that the edge of the material being cut will slide under the fence. In addition, it is nearly impossible to keep control of pieces that thin with a push stick.

Figure 93. Trimming solid wood edges—*A router with a mortising bit and a fence on the base plate is the safest way to trim solid wood edges, in this example bonded to Melamine-covered particleboard.*

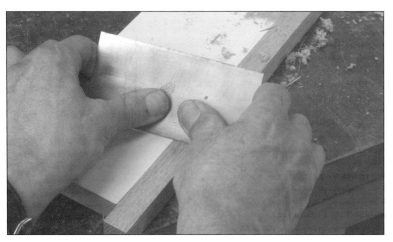

Figure 94. Scraping solid wood edges—*Set the router to leave just a whisker of material, then scrape it down clean and smooth. Scraping works better than sanding because it doesn't leave scratches.*

Figure 95. Sawing solid wood edges—*The last step is to trim the overhanging end of the wood edge. Use a crosscut sled on the table saw, with a stop block clamped to its fence in line with the saw kerf.*

The more sensible choice is to cut the strips with a utility knife and a straightedge, or with a tool called a slitter **(Figure 91).** The slitter will cost about $100, but it is a worthwhile purchase in terms of safety and speed. It consists of two opposing steel wheels and an adjustable fence. The distance between the two wheels is adjusted to suit the thickness of the material being cut, the end of the slitter is placed on the edge of the sheet, and the tool is pulled back along the length of the edge.

The best way to attach laminate edges is with contact cement. Two coats of cement should be applied to the raw board edge, as this edge will absorb the cement more than a smooth face. A disposable 3/4-inch or 1-inch bristle paintbrush is good to use for applying the glue to edges — you can control the flow of glue, and keep if off the faces so you don't have to clean it up later on. The alternative, if there are a lot of similarly sized parts, is to stack them up and apply the contact cement to the side of the stack.

Plastic edges are best trimmed with a router, and the edges then dressed with a file. I find it easiest to keep the pieces flat on the bench, and use a small laminate trimmer held horizontally rather than a large router.

Solid Wood Edges

Solid wood can be prepared for edges, and is commonly used in thicknesses from ⅛ inch up to ¾ inch. The biggest problem with using a solid wood edge is finding an efficient and reliable method of attaching it to the plywood edges. The typical wood glues work well, but thin edges can be difficult to clamp, and the number of pieces involved will require a lot of clamps.

Thicker solid wood edges, ½ inch to ¾ inch, can be nailed on, either with 4d or 6d finish nails driven by hand, or with brads or pins from a pneumatic gun. The nails really only serve in place of clamps, so the smallest nail that will hold is the one to use. Most pneumatically driven nails have a rectangular head, and they are less obvious if the long end of the nail head goes in the same direction as the grain in the edge. Even the smallest nails will likely split solid edge material that is ¼ inch or thinner, so these should be held with glue only.

Thin edges may be held in place with tape until the glue dries, or they may be clamped. The trouble with clamping them is that the thinness of the material doesn't allow the pressure from any one clamp to spread very far, so you need a lot of clamps to get a good joint. Placing a caul made of thicker and wider wood between the edge and the clamp will help distribute the clamp pressure. Another method is to clamp two parts to be edged at once, with the edges in the middle of the assembly. Some people will attach solid wood edges with contact cement, but seasonal wood movement against the relatively weak bond of the contact cement will lead to failure.

Solid wood edges should be slightly oversize, so that getting them perfectly aligned is not required. This means that they must be trimmed back flush to the face after the glue has dried. Edges ¼ inch or less in thickness can be easily trimmed with a block plane or a belt sander. For edges thicker than that I prefer to use a router. A flush-trimming bit with a bearing can be used to trim solid wood edges, but the odds of splitting the edges is pretty high.

Rather than use a standard bit, I use a mortising bit, and the router base plate and fence as shown in **Figure 93**. I set the depth of the bit to cut nearly flush with the surface, and set the fence to leave just a whisker of material where the edge meets the plywood. This can be easily cleaned up with sandpaper or a scraper (**Figure 94 & 95**).

If the finished cabinets are to be painted, the edges can be left raw, but this will involve some extra labor to get a nice clean finish. Wood glue mixed with water at a 1:1 ratio can be brushed on particleboard MDF or plywood. This will raise the grain, and the edge will be rougher after the glue size has dried, but after sanding will be smooth enough to prime and paint. The alternative is to veneer the edges, or apply a solid edge in the same way as if the parts were to receive a clear finish. The solid edge will be more durable than the veneer, but will eventually show a line at the joint as the solid wood expands and contracts due to seasonal movement of the wood.

7. FRAMELESS CABINET DETAILS

Standardization is the key to the European frameless cabinet system. The drawing below shows the standard dimensions that I use for constructing frameless cabinets with full overlay doors. These dimensions are all based on the final finished size of the cabinet box. If for some reason you decide to make the gaps between doors larger or smaller, you can use the same methods to establish your own standard sizes, simply replacing the numbers I use with your own. In the equations that follow, I give the term followed by the measurement that I usually use **(Figure 96).**

I recommend that you get a calculator that lets you work with fractions, rather than trying to convert all the fractions to decimals. I use one that limits the fractions to ½, ¼, ⅛, 1/16, 1/32, and 1/64ths. Scientific calculators will work, but sometimes when you divide, you get a funny denominator that you won't be able to find on your tape measure.

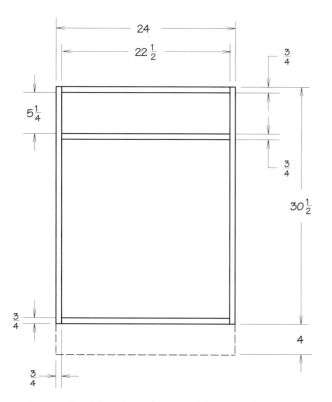

Figure 96. *Elevation of a typical frameless base cabinet box.*

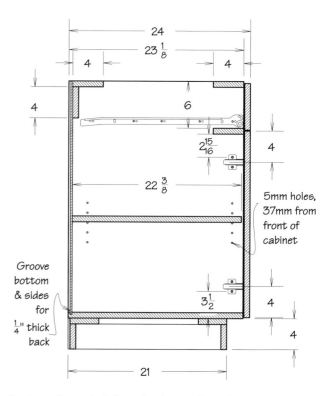

Section of a typical frameless base cabinet box.

One thing about the way dimensions are used in this chapter: I sometimes use inches and fractions, and occasionally will use millimeters. Architects and carpenters will use feet and inches, but a good cabinetmaker never does. The reason for always working in inches is to avoid confusion. 3'-0" is easily mistaken for 30", or vice versa.

I don't think much of the metric system — it's based on a silly premise, and the units don't relate to what people want to measure — but whenever I work with European hardware, I will use millimeters to lay out and size the holes. The reason I do so is that millimeters and fractions don't convert very well. Some metric dimensions, like 19mm for example, are very close to having a fractional equivalent. Others, like ½ inch, fall awkwardly in between 12mm and 13mm. Like working on a car with metric nuts and bolts, it easier to switch systems briefly than it is to try to convert the numbers. I keep a metric tape measure and a 6-inch steel rule that reads millimeters on the backside.

Standard Dimensions

The standard base cabinet finishes at 34½ inches tall and 24 inches deep. These dimensions are with the doors on, and with the cabinet on a separate 4-inch high base. This is also assuming that the countertop is 1½ inches thick. In some areas, and with some materials, 1¼ inches is a standard thickness for kitchen counters. The top of the finished countertop should be 36 inches above the floor in either case. After installation there may be some variation from this around the room, but it is better to plan your work at the standard height. Adding to the height of the cabinet ends and doors is the easiest way to adapt these dimensions and drawings if you are using a countertop that is less than 1½ inches. All of the cabinet components are nominally ¾-inch thick (**Figure 96**).

Remember to measure your material before you begin construction, and be aware of how changes in material thickness will affect the overall dimensions. Melamine board is likely to be ¹⁄₆₄ inch over size in thickness, and veneer-core plywood is likely to be ¹⁄₁₆ inch under. You probably won't need to adjust with Melamine board, but if you are using plywood, the length of all parts that go between the two cabinet ends should be increased by twice the amount the plywood is undersize to maintain the desired cabinet width. If you ignore this, your inside cabinet dimensions won't change, but the outside dimensions will. This will change the gaps between the door edges and the sides of the cabinet box.

The parts that fit between the sides, the cabinet bottom, the front rails above and below the drawer, and the two back rails are all the same length. The bot-

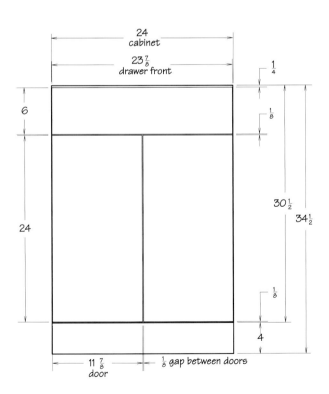

Elevation of a typical frameless base with full overlay doors.

tom is the same width as the cabinet sides. All of the rails are 4 inches wide. The joints for all of these parts are figured as butt joints, which can be reinforced with biscuits and/or screws or other fasteners. Avoid joints that cut into the side panels, such as rabbets or dados, so that the cabinet ends can be edge-banded before assembly.

The doors are ¾-inch thick, but when hung, there will be a slight gap between the face of the cabinet and the back of the door. Also, if you are using plastic laminate on the cabinet edge and door face, the finished dimensions will be in addition to those in the drawings. The cabinet side is noted as 23⅛ inches wide, but you might want to increase that to 23¼ inches, depending on what you use to finish the cabinet edges and face of the door. **(Figure 97).**

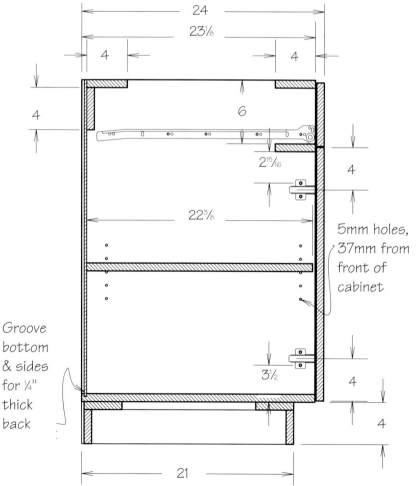

Figure 97. **Section** *of a typical frameless base cabinet box.*

Vertical grade plastic laminate (⅟₃₂-inch thick) on the edge of the cabinet and face of the door will add ⅟₁₆ inch, that, along with a ⅟₁₆-inch gap, will bring the finished cabinet to 24 inches from the back of the cabinet to the face of the door.

The back of the cabinet, at ¼-inch thick, drops in to a ¼-inch deep groove in the cabinet bottom and sides. The width of the back will be ½-inch greater than the inside width of the cabinet, or 1 inch less than the outside width of the cabinet. [24 inches wide cabinet minus two ¾-inch thick sides = 22½ inches.] Since each side of the back fits in the ¼ inch x ¼ inch groove, you add ½ inch (the depth of both grooves) and get 23 inches.

The length of the back is ¼ inch longer than the distance from the top of the cabinet bottom, to the top of the cabinet side. The top of the back runs past the rail, and is fastened in to the back of the rail. [30½-inch long cabinet side, minus ¾-inch thick cabinet bottom, plus ¼-inch deep groove = 30-inch long back.] The groove is set back from the back edge of the cabinet side ¼ inch, which leaves ¼ inch between the wall and the back.

The back can also be placed in a rabbet, ½ inch wide and ½ inch deep, in the bottom and ends of the cabinet. The advantage of the groove is that the back doesn't have to be held in place with fasteners. In an industrial setting, the cabinet is held perfectly square in a case clamp, the back is slid into place and retained with a bead of hot glue down the sides and across the bottom. A few staples in the top of the back rail complete the fastening.

The rabbeted back is a little easier to fit, but must be held in place with fasteners in addition to the glue. The rabbet is made large so that there is some room to shoot a ⅞-inch long narrow-crown staple through the ¼-inch thick back and into the raw edge of the rabbet. Don't depend on staples alone to hold the back in the rabbet. Because the staples are rather short, the back can be pushed out from inside the cabinet. A bead of hot glue works well for this. Some people prefer fastening the back with screws, which is much more time-consuming.

The vertical edges of the doors and drawer front are set 1/16 inch in from the outside edge of the cabinet sides. When two cabinets are set side by side, the two 1/16-inch gaps will form a 1/8-inch gap between the doors. This matches the gap between the doors in the middle of the cabinet, 1/8 inch. Depending on the hinges you are using, you can make this gap a little smaller, but 1/8 inch is as big as it should be. It is small enough to look good, big enough to keep you out of trouble, and it keeps the arithmetic relatively simple **(Figure 98).**

Doors

To figure the width of the cabinet doors, use this equation: width of the cabinet (in this case 24 inches) minus the two 1/16-inch gaps at the sides, minus the 1/8-inch gap between the doors divided by 2 = finished width of each door. [24 inches -1/16 inch - 1/16 inch -1/8 inch = 23 3/4 inches. 23¾ inches divided by 2 = 11⅞ inches.] If there are two drawers directly above the doors, they should all be the same width.

If there is only one door on the cabinet, it should have the 1/16-inch gap on each side, and will be the same width as the drawer front. The width of a single drawer front over two doors is a little easier to calculate; it's the width of the cabinet minus the two 1/16-inch gaps at the edge of the cabinets, in this case: 24 inches - 1/16 inch -1/16 inch = 23⅞ inches. The gap between the top of the drawer front and the bottom of the countertop is ¼ inch. Some types of drawer slides raise the drawer up slightly as it is pulled from the cabinet. This bigger than normal gap makes sure that it clears, and it also helps to make the rest of the math easy. With the ¼-inch gap at the top of the drawer, and the ⅛-inch gap between the drawer and the doors, we now have ⅜ inch worth of gaps in a 30½-inch cabinet face. If we hold the bottom of the door up ⅛ inch from the bottom of the cabinet, our gaps now total ½ inch, and we are left with 30 inches for the drawer and door. The height of the drawer front is nominally 6 inches, and with the gaps at the sizes noted making it actually 6 inches, this makes the height of the doors 24 inches.

Neither the gap below the counter or at the bottom of the door really shows. Raising the bottom of the door also helps to keep it from catching on vacuum cleaners or floor buffers.

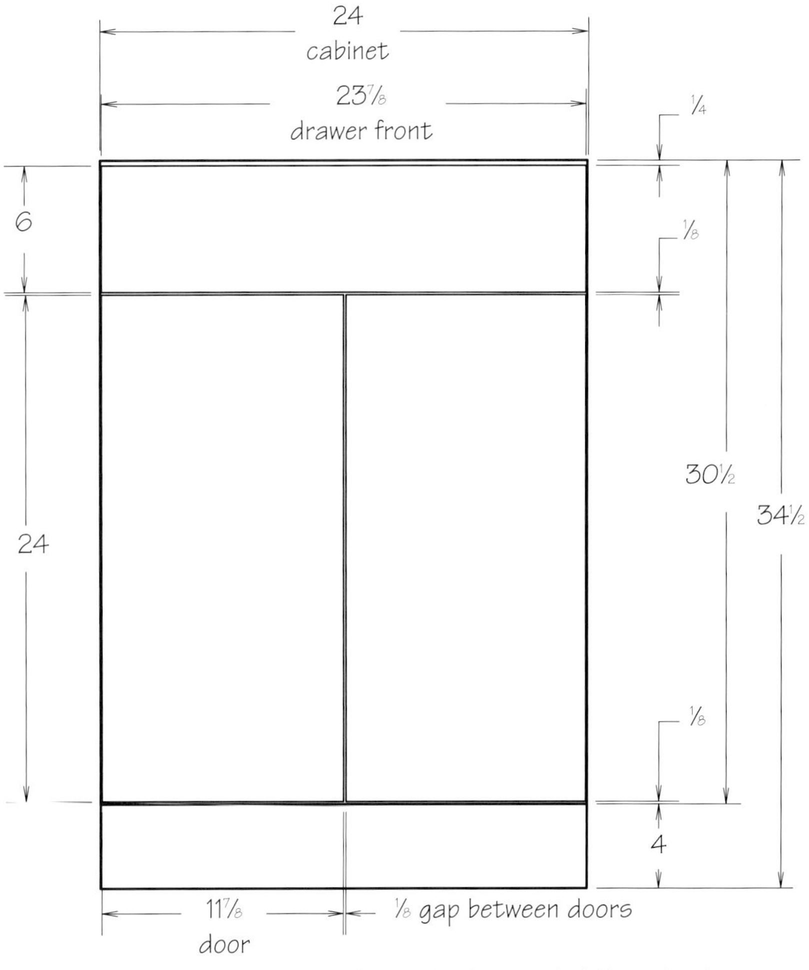

Figure 98. *Elevation of a typical frameless base with full overlay doors.*

> Don't make kitchen drawers deeper than 20 inches, you may need that extra space for wires and waterlines.

Theoretically, the gap between the bottom of the drawer front and the top of the doors should fall in the center of the rail below the drawer. The rail's main purpose is to keep the sides of the cabinet from bowing in or out. This makes the cabinet stronger and keeps the drawer hardware functioning properly. The edge of the rail also keeps the inside of the cabinet from being seen through the gap. Neither of these functions requires the rail to be at a specific distance, so I place it 6 inches down from the top edge of the cabinet.

Holes for Hardware

One of the principles of building frameless cabinets is to take a part as close to completion as we can before assembly. It wouldn't make sense to wait for the cabinet to be put together to put in the groove for the back, yet a lot of people wait to drill the holes for the shelves and the hinge plates. The dimensions on the drawings show the distances to the center of the first hole for the hinge plate. The next hole will be 32mm away, center to center.

Notice that the hinge plates are located on the cabinet so that the center of the hinge cups on the doors is 4 inches from both the top and bottom of the door. I could have set the distances to be consistent in the cabinet opening, but that would make the distances from the top and bottom of the door different, due to the different overlays. It can be hard to tell sometimes which is the top and which is the bottom of a door, and getting the holes in the wrong places will make an expensive raised-panel door useless.

The shelf holes don't have to be the same distance in from the front edge of the hinge plates, or on 32mm centers, and they don't have to be 5mm in diameter. There could also be more of them if you want, but five to seven holes are all that will likely be used. I prefer making the shelf-pin holes ¼ inch in

diameter unless I am using pull-out shelves, and then I will drill them at 5mm.

The shelf itself sits back ¼ inch from the front edge of the cabinet. Sometimes hardware on the back of the doors can bang in to the edge of the shelf if it is out the full distance. The length of the shelf will be a bit less than the inside width of the cabinet. How much less depends on the type of shelf supports used. Some supports are L-shaped and the ends of the shelf must be cut shorter to make room for that. Even if the shelf supports only contact the bottom of the shelf, the shelves should be ¹⁄₁₆ inch to ⅛ inch smaller than the cabinet opening so they will easily go in and out.

Some people make base cabinet shelves half the depth of the cabinet. The reason usually given is that this makes it easier to see and reach what is on the bottom of the cabinet. I think it's just an excuse for using less material.

Drawers

Drawer boxes are usually made from ½ inch thick material, good ones either from a light-colored, smooth-grained hardwood, or Baltic birch plywood. See the chapter on building drawers for construction details. I always make the top drawers on kitchen cabinets 4 inches high, which gives a serviceable drawer without any clearance problems.

I don't like to make kitchen drawers any deeper than 20 inches, although there is room for a few inches more. The extra space at the back of the cabinet may be needed to run a wire or waterline in the future.

The width of the drawers depends on the type of slide mechanism used. European under-mount and Accuride full-extension slides generally need ½ inch of clearance between each side of the drawer box and the inside of the cabinet. The distance can

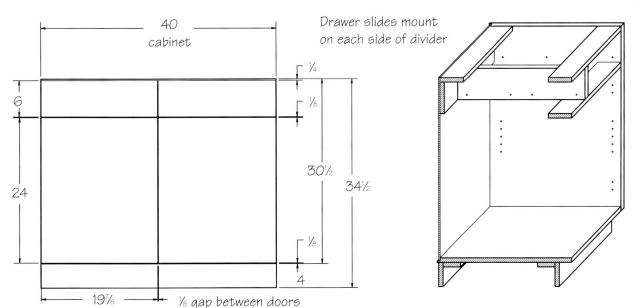

Drawer slides mount
on each side of divider

40
cabinet

¼

⅛

6

30½   34½

24

⅛

4

19⅞
door

⅛ gap between doors

Figure 99. Wide base cabinets need to have a divider so that two drawers can be used. A drawer more than 24" wide will be wobbly.

be a bit bigger (meaning a smaller-width drawer box), but it can't be any smaller. Accuride used to list their tolerances as +$\frac{1}{32}$"/-0" meaning the gap could be ½-inch big, but not any smaller. A lot of cabinetmakers, especially those that couldn't cut a cabinet bottom square, took this to mean a gap bigger than ½ inch was desirable, and routinely made their drawer boxes 1$\frac{1}{16}$ inch smaller than the inside dimension of the cabinet. Accuride decided to dumb-down their specs, and now call for the bigger spacing. The slides work smoother the closer you are to having ½ inch of space on each side of the drawer, and they get sloppy if the drawers are made for a larger gap. If you get the gap too small, however, the drawers will jam and won't work at all.

With the basic parameters established, making different types of cabinets is largely a matter of changes in width. The two ends of the cabinet will rarely change, but the width of the parts between the ends will change, as will the height and spacing of some parts as drawer configurations change.

In some cases, particularly when a cabinet approaches 36 inches in width, you will likely want to replace the single drawer above

the two doors with two drawers (**Figure 99**). Try to keep the cabinet to a reasonable width. Remember that the shelf inside the cabinet will start to sag from its own weight as it increases in length. The only structural difference to the cabinet with two top drawers is the divider that goes from the front edge of the cabinet to the inside of the back rail (**Figure 99**).

This divider can be held in place with screws through the rails. Take care that the rail is square to the front of the cabinet and parallel to the cabinet ends. The drawer slides will fasten to the divider in the same way that they fasten to the ends. Since you will be holding the slides from both sides of the ¾-inch thick rail, you will either need to use alternate holes for the screws, or use sex bolts to use the same hole on both slides.

Figure 100 (next page) shows a standard-height base cabinet with two large drawers in place of the cabinet doors. The top drawer, and its placing in the cabinet, should stay the same throughout the room.

The two drawers take up the same space vertically as a door, so after subtracting the gap from the door height, divide by two for the

Drawer Arrangements

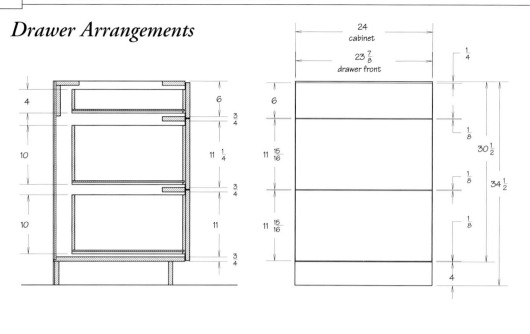

Figure 100. Cabinets with drawers are built the same way as door cabinets, with the addition of a horizontal dividing rail between the lower two drawers.

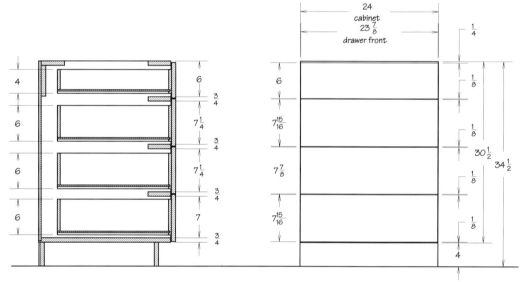

Figure 101. Shallow drawers are more practical than deep ones, which tend to become burial grounds for everything below the top layer of things stored in them. Keep the top drawer the standard height, and make the other three almost equal.

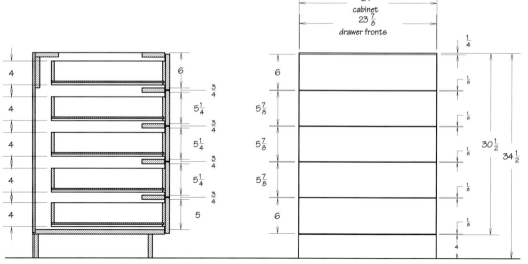

Figure 102. With five drawers in a stack, you can make all of the drawer boxes the same depth, and their fronts close to equal: to maintain consistent gaps, three will be slightly smaller.

drawer front heights. (Height of door minus width of gaps times number of gaps divided by number of drawers = finished height of each drawer front.)

The rails that cross the cabinet horizontally between the drawers are located from the positions of the drawer fronts, and should be centered on the gap, but as with the single-drawer cabinet, a slight change up or down may be made without causing any difficulty. The dimensions on the front side of the section drawing give the locations of the rails within the cabinet, and the dimensions at the back of the section drawing give the heights of the drawer boxes.

Putting three drawers below the top drawer (**Figure 101**) follows the same formula for calculating the sizes of the drawer fronts, but the numbers don't work as neatly because we are dividing the available space into three parts instead of two. If we didn't have to account for the gaps between the drawers, it would be an easy 24 divided by 3 = 8. Taking the gaps into consideration gives us 23¾ divided by 3, which isn't quite as simple. Rather than take all day to make the three drawers exactly equal, make one of them ¹⁄₁₆-inch narrower than the other two, as seen in the drawing. No one but you will ever know that the fronts aren't equally sized.

The section drawing gives the sizes of the drawer boxes, and the locations of the rails.

The last drawer cabinet as seen in **Figure 102** has five drawers. Again, they are close to being equally sized, but the widths have been fudged a little to keep the gaps between the drawers consistent and the numbers more manageable. This fudging is not to be confused with sloppy work. We could make them exactly equal, if we wanted to be measuring to 64ths of an inch. We are changing a size slightly where no one will notice to keep the work moving along.

The section shows the sizes and positions of the drawer boxes and the rails. In all of these cabinets, I have made many choices regarding the actual sizes and positions of these drawers. The goal has been to keep the dimensions in as simple terms as possible, the gaps consistent, and items like drawer boxes the same size and in the same position in relation to the cabinet bottom or rail below them. When it comes time to install all of these drawers, I can build or set a jig to put the drawer slides ½ inch up from the bottom of the rail. I have a lot of variations going on, but each variation mounts the same way. This will save a lot of time when building and assembling.

In situations where the base cabinets are lower than normal, such as in a bathroom or office, take the difference in height out of the doors, and keep the top drawer configuration — that is, the size of the drawer front and drawer box, and the gaps — the same as on the standard-height cabinets.

Office Cabinets

The other variations of drawer cabinets that are likely to be seen are pencil drawers, a small box that fits between two cabinets, leaving an open seating space, and cabinets for file drawers (**Figure 103**).

The pencil drawer consists of two sides and a back, all of ¾-inch thick material, and an upper and lower rail at the front, as well as the drawer box and drawer front. Generally this is mounted so that the top is at 28½ inches above the floor, so that with the counter on, the counter height will be 30 inches, the same height as a table. The gaps from the top and bottom of the drawer front to the box should be the same as in the other cabinets. The drawer can be made taller, but be sure to provide adequate knee space below it.

Figure 103. For a desk, *make standard cabinets shorter. A pencil drawer connects two bases and provides knee space.*

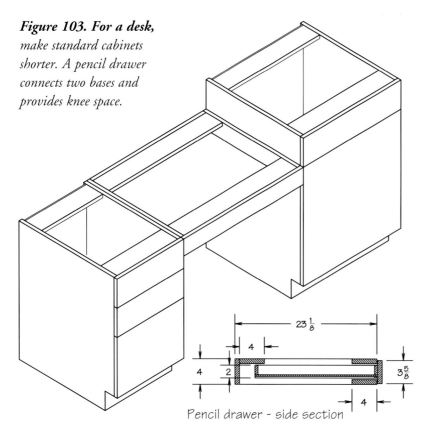

Pencil drawer - side section

Figure 104. It's a tight squeeze *to fit two file drawers into a cabinet with a 4-inch toe kick. It's easier to fit one file drawer with two shallower utility drawers.*

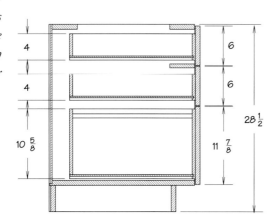

In addition to being used as a writing space in or adjacent to kitchen cabinets, you can combine a pencil drawer with file cabinets to create a built-in desk. Pencil drawers are also popular in a bathroom as a way to provide a place to sit in front of a mirror.

If you are including a desk in the kitchen, or in a home office, you will likely want to include a file cabinet. These are a necessity, but configuring them so that the standard Pendaflex file hangers will work takes some planning, particularly if you want two file drawers in the same cabinet, plus the standard 4-inch high toe space.

If you are in a kitchen, you likely won't have a choice about the toe space; it needs to match the rest of the cabinets in the room. If you are doing an office and these are the only cabinets, it would be wise to make the toe space an inch or two shorter, and add that space to the height of the file drawers. The dimensions given in the section drawings **(Figure 104)** work if the tops of the hanging bars are placed so that the bottom of the file folder is only $\frac{1}{16}$ inch to $\frac{1}{8}$ inch above the top face of the drawer bottom. You also need to consider the tabs that go in the top edge of the folders. If you cut the distances too close in laying this out, you can knock off all the tabs from the folders when you close the drawer. This is why no rail is shown above the lower file drawer in the drawing — you need all the room you can get to do this.

The second section shows two standard-height drawers above the file drawer, and this is less of a squeeze than two file drawers, but you can still run into trouble. If you are in an office and don't have to match other cabinets, making the top drawer shorter, and the file drawer taller will give you some room for the file holders. If you want to make a lateral file cabinet, the construc-

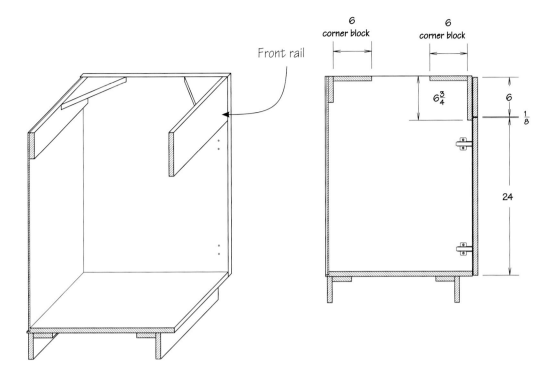

Front rail

6 corner block

6 corner block

$6\frac{3}{4}$

6

$\frac{1}{8}$

24

Figure 105. To install a sink in a standard base cabinet, replace the two top rails with a single vertical rail at the front. This will provide support better support for the counter and the basin.

tion is identical, except that the drawer box should be less than your standard depth, and the rails should mount the other direction. In any file cabinet, use heavy-duty (100 lbs. rating minimum) drawer slides, and attach the cabinet securely to the wall.

Sink Base Cabinet

The sink base cabinet looks like the other base cabinets, with a false drawer front replacing the drawer. Some cabinetmakers will make this as a standard base, with the same rails as the other boxes. This is an easy way out for the cabinetmaker, but introduces two problems. The first will be in making the sink cutout, as at least the top rail will need to be cut to fit the sink in place. With some sinks, the rails between the drawer front and the doors will also need to be cut.

The second problem is structural. In a standard cabinet, the rails and countertop are adequate to support the weight of the sink. In addition to the sink itself, you need to also consider the weight of the water when

the sink is full. When the rail and counter are cut to get the sink in place, very little material remains. A better solution is shown in (**Figure 105**. With the front rail made as a vertical piece, it will not need to be cut to accommodate the sink, and is stronger than the standard arrangement. The false front can also be attached with screws from the back side of this piece. Its width should bring its bottom edge to the same location as the bottom of the standard rail.

The horizontal rails at the top can remain, or they can be replaced with corner blocks as shown in the drawings. The counter can be fastened through these corner blocks, and none of the parts of this cabinet will need to be cut in the field, except for holes in the back for the pipes.

Blind Corner Cabinet

The blind corner cabinet (**Figure 106, next page)** is constructed as a wide-base cabinet, with a vertical divider going from front to back to support the drawer slide. A panel is

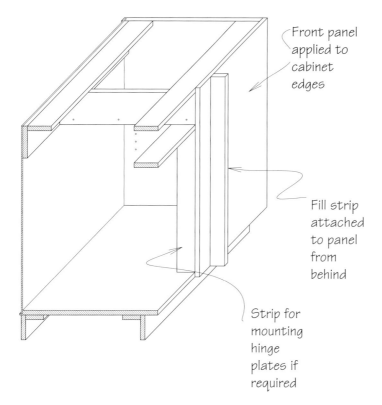

Figure 106. *Turn an inside corner by adding a panel and filler strips to the front of a standard base cabinet.*

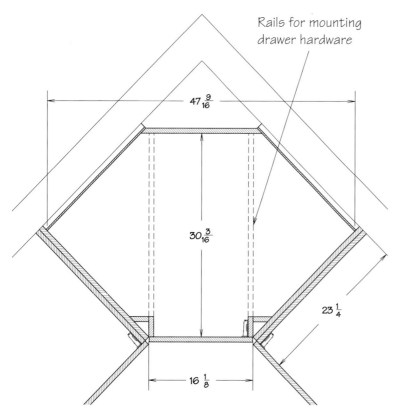

Figure 107. *Make a full-size layout for angled corner cabinets. Clearances with adjacent cabinets are always tight.*

secured over the front of the cabinet to cover the end that goes into the corner. This panel can be inset instead of on the face, as shown. The narrow filler panel that extends out from the face of this panel can be secured with screws from behind. If a regular shelf is used in a blind corner, an additional line of holes for the shelf supports should be bored in the back of the panel.

The simplest way to hinge the door is on the side of the cabinet away from the corner, with the same hinges that are used everywhere else. It is possible to hinge it from the corner side, and there are two ways to do this. Special concealed hinges exist that put the hinge plate in the same plane as the door, instead of at 90 degrees to it. The other option is to run a 3-inch wide strip vertically, at the edge of the front panel. This allows the use of the standard hinge plates, but does intrude into the interior space of the cabinet. If you have a regular shelf, you will need to cut the shelf around it, and it might be in the way of a pullout.

Angled Corner Cabinet

The construction of angled corner cabinets is best explained by looking at the plan view **(Figure 107)**. The depth of the cabinet, from the face of the angled corner cabinet to the corner of the room, needs to be kept small enough so that the completed cabinet will fit through a doorway. The two sides that butt against the adjacent cabinets will be the same depth as standard cabinet sides, and they will be at 135-degree angles to the face of the door.

The width of the exposed face will be the variable that drives the overall size of the bottom, and the ¾-inch thick back that is parallel to the face. The two remaining sides, those that are against the walls of the room can be ¼-inch thick back material, with ¾-inch thick nailers at the top placed on the

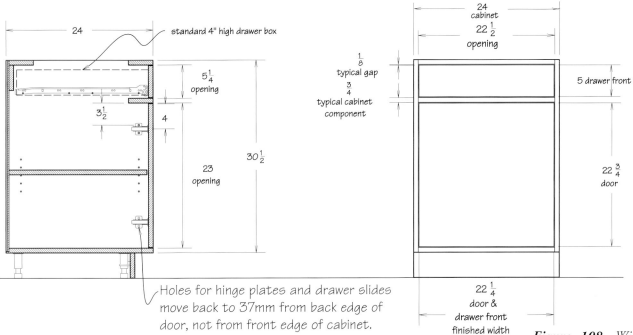

Holes for hinge plates and drawer slides move back to 37mm from back edge of door, not from front edge of cabinet.

Figure 108. With inset door and drawer fronts, the frame becomes visible. Cabinet construction is the same, but the cabinet is deeper, and the hinges move back.

wall side. These rails can be the normal 4-inch rail width, screwed to the cabinet side, and the ¾-inch thick back piece, and serve the usual purpose of attaching the cabinet to the walls of the room.

There are concealed hinges made especially for this type of cabinet, or you can make corner blocks as shown in the drawing and use standard hinges. Make sure of all the sizes and clearances for the door and drawer for this cabinet, and for the doors and drawers of the adjacent cabinets. As the drawing shows, it's a tight fit in the corner. Be especially careful if there is an appliance near the angled corner; it may have some feature that extends farther than the normal cabinets that could get in the way of the door and drawers of the angled cabinet.

The size shown is typical; an important consideration when sizing this type of cabinet is the size required for lazy susan hardware, if it is used. This type of cabinet really isn't very practical without the lazy susan, as the narrow front makes it hard to see and reach what is inside if a standard shelf is used.

Rails to support the drawer-slide hardware should be added between the two front rails, going all the way to the ¾-inch thick back. It helps to make a full-size layout of this cabinet; you can do it directly on the piece that will become the cabinet bottom.

Inset Doors and Drawers

Inset doors and drawer fronts don't impose any major changes to European cabinet construction. The cabinet ends do need to be made deeper, as the finished front will now be at the face of the cabinet edge. Usually in architectural drawings of cabinets, the top drawer front is always drawn at 6 inches high. Some cabinetmakers will build frameless cabinets with inset doors and drawers with the top drawer at this height, but I make it smaller, as shown in the drawing **(Figure 108).**

The same 4-inch high drawer box that was used for the overlay cabinets can still be used with the smaller front. I think these dimensions make the lower part of the cabinet look more in proportion, and make better use of materials, particularly of solid wood.

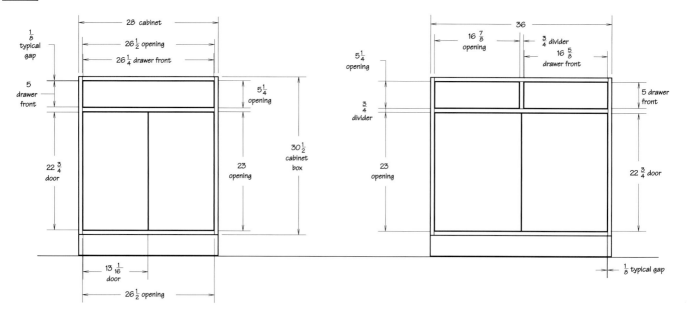

Figure 109. In these two inset-door cabinets, note the difference between the cabinet openings, doors and drawer fronts. The ⅛" gaps shown should be considered a maximum distance.

The door hinge locations remain the same vertically, but the hinge plates must move back by the thickness of the door. Some commercial jigs have an extra set of holes set back from the first so that the same jig can be used with either door style.

One of the difficulties of using inset doors is that the concealed hinges tend to over-close. The springs that make them self-closing, and hold the door tight to the cabinet front with overlay doors, pull an inset door a few degrees past the edge of the cabinet. Door stops should be used to keep the face of the door flush with the edge of the cabinet. Most hinge manufacturers make a small nylon or plastic bumper that is screwed to the cabinet bottom and the bottom edge of the top rail. If possible, the stop on the cabinet bottom should be eliminated, as it tends to get in the way of things in the cabinet.

Figuring the sizes of doors is simpler with inset doors than with overlay doors; for a single door or drawer front, subtract the total width of the gaps from the opening size (**Figure 108**). As the base cabinets increase in width, and two doors or two drawers are used, you need to subtract the total width of the gaps (with two doors there are three gaps, so the equation would be opening minus ⅜ inch)

and then divide by the number of doors. The gaps can be smaller than ⅛ inch; with some hinges it can be as small as 1mm, and ¹⁄₁₆-inch gaps look good in high-end work. Of course, you need to check your hardware and material, and make a mock-up of the door and hinge before you start.

If you are using two drawers (**Figure 109**), you need to add the vertical divider between the drawers to provide a place to mount the drawer slides. It can be exposed, as shown in the drawing, or you can hold it back so that the drawer fronts overlay the divider but fit inside the cabinet opening.

Finished Ends

Finished ends in frameless cabinets can be either the integral end of the cabinet box, or applied. If you are building with veneered plywood, you need to select the end for the best grain pattern, and be careful during construction not to drive any visible fasteners through it, or damage it in handling. With a plastic laminate cabinet, the finished end is often applied after the box has been assembled, so that the construction of all boxes is the same.

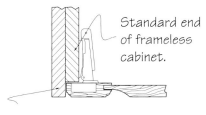

Standard end of frameless cabinet.

Applied end panel makes door appear to be inset.

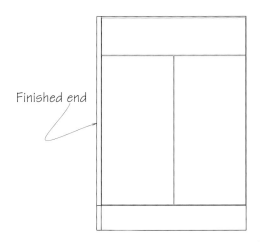

Finished end

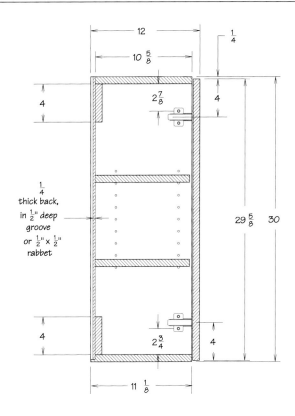

Figure 110. An applied finished end panel *makes the door appear to be inset, even though it is standard overlay construction.*

Figure 111. In typical frameless wall cabinets, *height and depth often vary from the standard dimensions shown here.*

The other option for a finished end in a frameless cabinet is to apply the end panel to the assembled cabinet. The usual way to do this is to make the panel wide enough so that it comes out to the face of the door. This door then appears to be inset.

I fasten finished end panels from inside the cabinet with a few discreetly placed 1¼-inch screws **(Figure 110)**. If you object to seeing the screw heads, you can locate them up in the drawer opening, and behind or beneath the hinge plates.

There is a product available specifically for covering up screw holes in situations like this, called Fast Caps; these are also useful during installation. These are self-adhesive circles of material to match either Melamine material or wood veneer. Once they are placed over a screw head, they are virtually invisible on the inside of the cabinet.

Wall Cabinets

Typical wall cabinets are shown in **Figure 111**, although they can vary in height, and I prefer to make them at least an inch deeper than shown in the drawing. The important thing in deciding the height is the distance from the top of the counter to the bottom of the cabinets, which is typically 18 inches. A 2-inch high light valance is a popular addition, as shown in **Figure 112.** This can be added to the bottom of a standard 30-inch tall cabinet, which will shorten the counter-to-cabinet distance to 16 inches, or the cabinet can be made 2 inches shorter. If the cabinet is shortened, the standard counter-to-cabinet distance is preserved, but it might make it difficult for a short person to reach inside the cabinet.

Parts for wall cabinets are calculated in the following way:

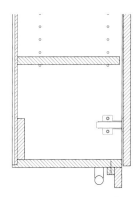

Figure 112. *Light valance must be considered when sizing wall cabinets.*

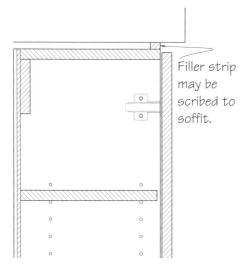

Filler strip may be scribed to soffit.

Figure 113. A small filler piece may be added to the top of the wall cabinet , for scribing to the soffit.

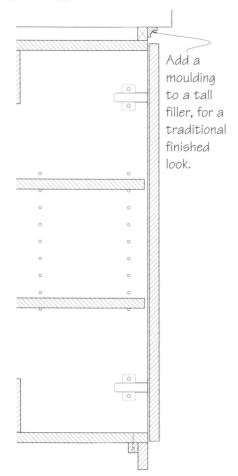

Add a moulding to a tall filler, for a traditional finished look.

Figure 114. If the filler becomes tall, then add a small moulding to cover the join between cabinet and soffit. Be sure to figure these add-ons in the cabinet height.

The sides are the finished height of the cabinet in length, typically 30 inches. The width is determined by subtracting the thickness of the door, and the space between the front of the box and the back of the door from that, from the finished depth of the cabinet, typically 11⅛ inches for a 12-inch deep cabinet.

The bottom is the same depth as the ends in width; its length is the finished width of the cabinet, minus the combined thickness of the two sides.

The top is the same length as the bottom, but is ½ inch narrower, so that the cabinet back may be slid into place after the cabinet is assembled.

The grooves or rabbets in the ends and bottom are milled in the same way as they are in base cabinets. The back extends to the top of the cabinet top, so that there is room to staple or screw it to the cabinet top. The back width will be 1 inch less than the overall width of the cabinet, and ½ inch less in length.

Gaps between the edges of doors and the edges of the cabinet are the same 1/16 inch as in base cabinets. The gap between two doors is ⅛ inch. The width of a single door will be ⅛ inch less than the inside width of the finished cabinet. If there are two doors, subtract ¼ inch (the two end gaps at 1/16 inch each and the ⅛-inch gap between the doors), and divide the result by two.

The length of the doors will be the height of the cabinet, less the gap at the top (typically ¼ inch) minus the gap at the bottom (typically ⅛ inch).

Shelves should be ¼ inch less than the inside depth of the cabinet (10⅜ inches for a 12-inch cabinet) in width, and the length will be the same as the inside width of the cabinet, minus the allowance for the shelf pins and for clearance.

The standard counter-to-cabinet distance puts the top of the cabinet at 84 inches above the floor. Soffits are typically 12 inches down from the ceiling, and the depth of the soffit should be an inch more than the depth of the wall cabinet. Both of these dimensions should be double-checked before the wall cabinets are made. The door on an overlay wall cabinet is ¼ inch down from the top of the cabinet box. This provides a little bit of elbow room if the soffit or ceiling drops in front of the cabinet. As an alternative, a small filler piece can be added to the top of the cabinet **(Figure 113).** If the edge of the soffit is wavy or out of level, this strip may be scribed to keep the cabinets plumb and level.

If the filler is made taller, then a molding **(Figure 114)** may be added to cover the junction between the cabinet and the soffit. If anything is added to the top or bottom of the cabinet, it must be considered when specifying the cabinet height.

Wall cabinets can be made 36 inches or 42 inches high in rooms without a soffit, or in rooms with a higher ceiling. There really isn't a gain in usable space, because it's too high to reach.

Wall cabinets are also often made shorter, particularly when they are above a sink or an appliance. There can be local building code requirements for this distance, so check that when planning the cabinet height in these areas. Remember that the cabinets adjacent to shorter cabinets will have the lower portion of their ends exposed.

The sizes for inset doors in wall cabinets are calculated the same way as for base cabinets. The ends of the cabinets are made deeper, and the holes for the hinge plates are moved back by the thickness of the door. The finished door size will be the size of the opening minus the total width of gaps around the doors. If there are two doors, the width of each door will be the width of the opening, minus the total width of gaps (three total — one at each edge of the cabinet opening and one gap between the doors) divided by two **(Figure 115).**

Cabinets with an open section below the doors, often used to hold microwave ovens, are a standard wall cabinet with a horizontal divider at the top of the open space. The divider will be the same size as the top of the cabinet. The top of the door will be down from the top of the cabinet the same distance as all the other wall cabinets, and the bottom of the door should lie on the divider as if it were the bottom of the cabinet.

Wall cabinets turn the corners as base cabinets do, but if you decide not to extend the cabinets into the corner with a blind corner cabinet, or an angled corner cabinet, you will need to make a filler that extends the cabinet bottoms **(Figure 116).** This should be made larger than necessary and then scribed during installation to fit the

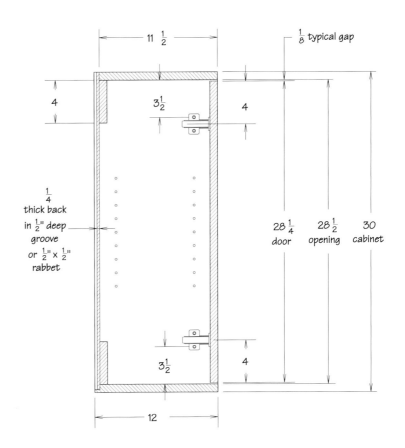

Figure 115. For inset doors, the cabinet ends are wider and the door is sized to fit within the opening.

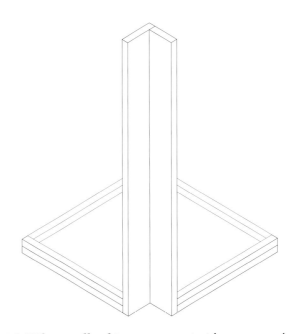

Figure 116. When wall cabinets turn an inside corner, make a filler piece to bridge the bottoms of the adjacent cabinets. Make it oversize then scribe to the actual installation.

corner of the walls nicely. Three-quarter-inch square cleats at the wall will keep the bottom filler in place; it can be secured to the cleats with some construction adhesive and finish nails.

Blind corner wall cabinets are constructed in a similar fashion to blind corner base cabinets: the filler panel is planted on top of the cabinet edges, extending to act as a filler space to ensure that the doors clear each other. A filler for the adjacent cabinet is attached, and it too must include a bottom section. The same methods of hanging the doors used for the base cabinet also apply.

The angled corner wall cabinet also shares much in common with the base cabinet, and it is also best explained by looking at the plan **(Figure 117).** The wall cabinet dif-fers because it extends all the way into the corner, because the bottom of it is visible. Two of the sides are the same as the ends of all the other wall cabinets. The longer sides, or backs, are much wider. One of the backs is of 3/4-inch thick material, and the other is 1/4 inch. The thicker piece adds strength to the box structure, and the thin piece is left off until the cabinet is assembled, and if veneer, finished.

This cabinet is best constructed by making a full-size layout of the bottom, and the actual part can be used for the layout, trimming the piece back to the pencil lines once it is determined that the layout is correct. Like the angled corner base cabinet, a lazy susan is recommended, and the dimensions of this hardware will help determine the size of the cabinet.

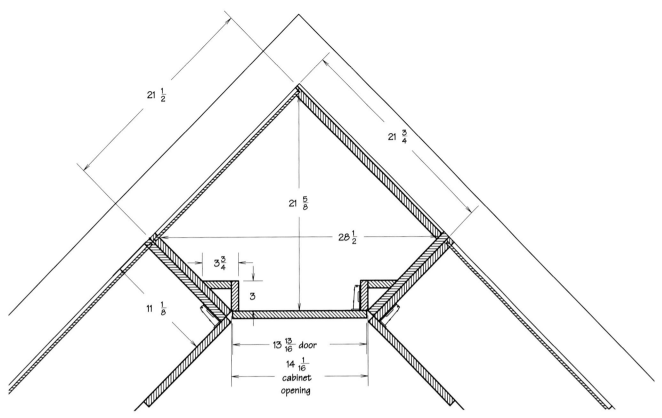

Figure 117. **The angled wall cabinet** *is made with one thick side, as shown in this plan view, so that it can accommodate a lazy susan.*

8. FACE-FRAME CABINET DETAILS

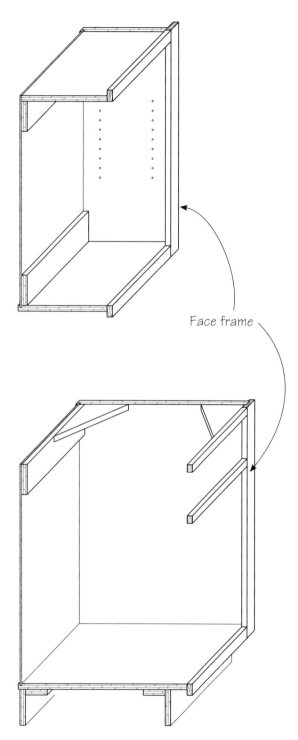

Face frame

Figure 119. The solid wood face frame *stiffens the box and changes its appearance. The cabinet box is assembled using the same techniques as frameless cabinets, but the components differ in size to accommodate the face frame.*

The biggest difference between face-frame cabinets and European cabinets is not in how the basic plywood box is constructed. The big difference is in the presence of the face frame, how that frame is put together, and how it is attached to the cabinet box (**Figure 119**).

There may or may not be a difference in the hardware used. Certainly, with drawer slides, the identical hardware should be employed. With hinges, there are two sensible choices — use butt hinges, or use self-closing concealed European hinges. There are other choices for hinges. Most of the American inventions pre-date the European hinges and were attempts to replace butts with something easier to install, and with some room for adjustment. None of these comes close to the ease of use found in European concealed hinges.

The European alternative, concealed hinges designed for face frame cabinets, are poor cousins to the hinges designed for frameless cabinets. They don't mount as securely, work as well, or look as good in the finished cabinet as the others (**Figure 120 & 121**).

Some of the American alternatives aren't too bad, if you have the dedicated equipment large shops and cabinet factories have to install them, but they are tedious to work with in the typical small shop environment. The rest are a flimsy lot, compared to the alternatives, and really aren't worth consideration for work of any quality.

Butt hinges intimidate almost everyone, which is surprising, since everyone thinks cabinetmakers are so fussy and precise, especially when compared to finish carpenters. Yet, finish carpenters routinely cut mortises in the edge of a door and a jamb to hang a passage door. Most cabinetmakers, requested to hang a cabinet door on butt hinges, will either head for the hills or only attempt the task reluctantly.

I don't think there is a substitute for butt hinges in first-class work, and with a few jigs, a small router, and a sharp chisel, butt hinges can be installed with little trouble.

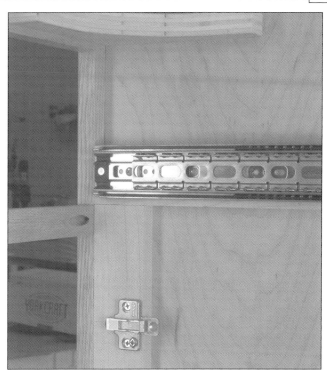

Figure 120. Concealed hinge in face frame—A filler block behind the face frame allows the use of European concealed hinges. The block going horizontally is used to attach the drawer slide.

Figure 121. Hinge and slide in cabinet—With the fillers in place the hardware functions as it would in a frameless cabinet.

Concealed hinges designed for frameless cabinets can be easily adapted to face-frame use, and work as well in that situation as they do in the cabinets they were designed for. In the chapter on doors and hinges, we will go through both methods step by step.

Face Frame 101

The width of the pieces used in face-frame fabrication is fairly well established, but there is a good deal of variation. Generally face-frame stock is ¾ inch thick, and between 1½ inches and 2 inches wide. The vertical parts are called stiles and the horizontal parts are called rails. If you repeat to yourself, "Stiles go up and down," 50 or 60 times, you'll be able to remember this forever.

The simplest face-frame design has all the pieces the same width. **Figure 122** shows a typical base cabinet face-frame with all the stiles and rails 1½ inches wide. This is com-

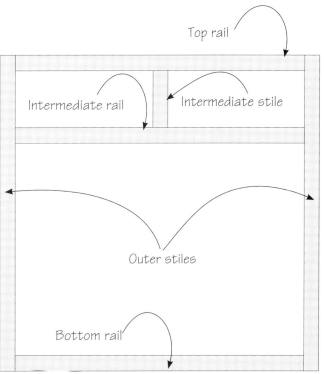

*Figure 122. **The simplest method** of making the face frame is to have all components the same width, usually 1½ inches.*

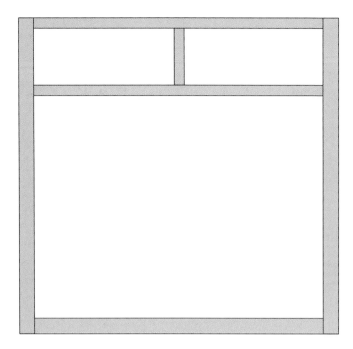

Figure 123. Reducing the width *of the top two rails and the intermediate stile increases the usable space for the drawers and doors, and looks more refined.*

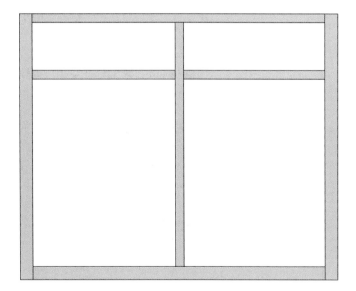

Figure 124. Here is the same face frame *with the addition of an intermediate stile in between the top and bottom rails.*

monly done, but it always seems to me that the top two rails are too wide. The wide frame members at this point take up some valuable space needed for the drawer, and lower the top edge of the cabinet door. **Figure 123** shows the same frame with the top two rails 1 inch wide.

In the step-by-step chapter on building face frames **(page 114)** the various methods of joining the stiles and rails are presented.

Stiles on the outside edge of the frame go the full height of the cabinet; the rails go in between the stiles. Intermediate stiles — that is, a stile that goes between rails, like one that divides a space for two doors or drawers — go in between the rails. If there are intermediate stiles that go all the way from the top rail to the bottom rail, and intermediate rails, the rails will run between the stiles **(Figure 124).** This maximizes the strength of the frame structure, and eliminates exposing end-grain on the edges of the face frame.

Wider stiles and rails are used as design elements in some designs and styles, and while wider elements of the face frame do add strength, the narrower elements shown are strong enough for the application.

Box and Frame Relationships

The large section drawing **(Figure 125)** details the sizes of typical elements of a face-frame base cabinet with inset doors. The overall size of the cabinet, 24 inches deep and 34½ inches high, follows the standard dimensions for base cabinets. The plywood side of this cabinet will be 23¼ inches wide x 30½ inches high when it is exposed, if the cabinet sits on a separate base. If the ends go all the way to the floor, and a separate base is not used, the ends would be 23¼ inches x 34½ inches. Because the bottom of the cabinet is raised to be flush with the top edge of

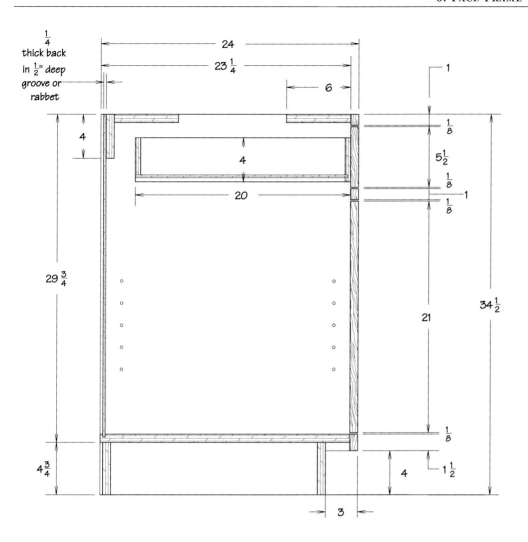

Figure 125. Typical face frame base cabinet dimensions. Note that the bottom of the cabinet is flush with the top edge of the bottom frame rail.

the bottom rail in the face frame, a construction decision needs to be made.

If the exposed height is chosen as the length for all of the side panels, a continuous base for several adjacent cabinets cannot be used, and the cabinet bottom needs to be housed in a dado in the sides. If the shorter length is used, the joinery is simplified, but the exposed end must be longer. In order to simplify things during assembly and installation, I will make all of the box sides the same length, at the shorter dimension, and where a finished end occurs, I will use an applied panel.

How the face frame attaches to the plywood box will also affect the width of the end panels. If the frames are attached with biscuits, or with a simple butt joint and nails

or pocket screws, then the width of the side would equal the finished depth of the cabinet, minus the thickness of the face frame. In this example, that would be 23¼ inches. If the sides are housed in ¼-inch deep dados in the stiles of the face frame (my preferred method), that ¼ inch needs to be added back to the width of the side panels, making them 23½ inches.

Note that many of the elements in the face-frame cabinet are the same, or at least quite similar in size to the elements of the frameless cabinets. If I am building both types of cabinet in the same shop, I want to be as consistent as possible, so if one size of part will work for both frameless and face-frame cabinets, I don't have to reinvent the wheel when switching from one to the other.

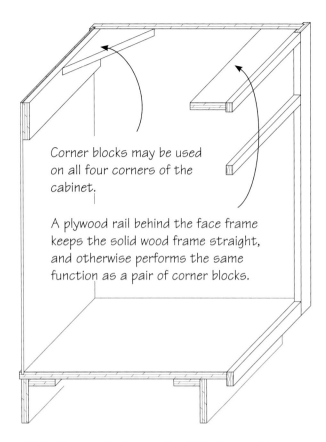

Corner blocks may be used on all four corners of the cabinet.

A plywood rail behind the face frame keeps the solid wood frame straight, and otherwise performs the same function as a pair of corner blocks.

*Figure 126. **Corner blocks** or rails will hold the cabinet square in plan.*

Corner Blocks

One detail that is different in the drawing of the face-frame base cabinet from the frameless cabinet is the absence of horizontal rails across the width of the cabinet at the top. The top rail of the face frame, being solid wood, supports the weight of the countertop above. The corner blocks hold the joints square, and provide a place to attach the countertop with screws from below when the cabinet is installed. The corner blocks shown are cut from plywood scraps, and are about 6 inches long on each leg. If you don't want to make your own, there is a plastic version available that serves the same purpose.

I simply glue and staple the blocks in, but some cabinetmakers like to run a ¼ inch x ¼ inch groove around the inside corners of the cabinet box, and a matching tongue on the

legs of the corner blocks. Corner blocks can also be made from scrap face-frame stock, and an 8½-inch long piece of ¾ inch x 2 inch stock with a 45-degree cut on each end will also make a good corner block.

A 4-inch wide rail, running the entire inside width of the cabinet behind the front rail of the face frame may be used instead, and if the face-frame stock is bowed in or out, this rail will hold the face frame straight (**Figure 126**). In either case, the vertical rail at the back of the cabinet is required to secure the finished cabinet to the wall studs.

End Panels

How the face frame relates to the end panels in plan also affects the sizes the horizontal elements of the cabinet. Traditionally, the inside edge of the panel is not flush with the inside edge of the stile (**Figure 127**). The outside face is either flush with the outside edge of the stile, or it is set in ¼ inch (**Figure 128**). If the end panel is flush with the outside of the stile, when this exposed end is a stile and rail panel, the panel needs to be fabricated before the cabinets can be assembled, and attached to the cabinet box in one of the first steps of the project. It is quite likely that the panel will suffer some damage during the remaining steps. I think the better method, particularly if the stiles are 1 ½ inches wide, is to set the end panels flush with the inside edge of the stile (**Figure 129**).

This allows all of the cabinets to be constructed the same way, whether the end is exposed to view, adjacent to another cabinet, or against a wall. In addition, if European hinges are used, the hinge plates may by mounted directly to the end panel, no blocking or special hinge plates are required (**page 185**).

This way, if the exposed end is a stile and rail panel, it doesn't need to be attached to the

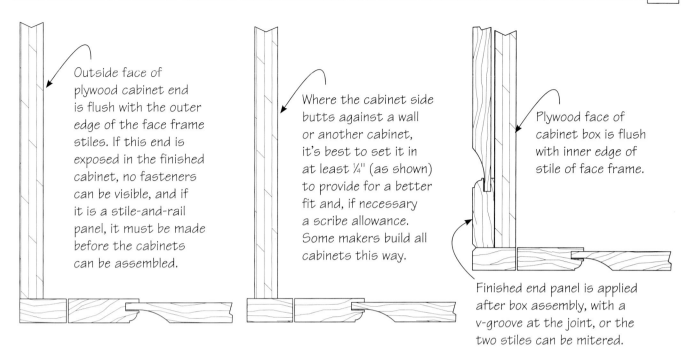

Outside face of plywood cabinet end is flush with the outer edge of the face frame stiles. If this end is exposed in the finished cabinet, no fasteners can be visible, and if it is a stile-and-rail panel, it must be made before the cabinets can be assembled.

Where the cabinet side butts against a wall or another cabinet, it's best to set it in at least ¼" (as shown) to provide for a better fit and, if necessary a scribe allowance. Some makers build all cabinets this way.

Plywood face of cabinet box is flush with inner edge of stile of face frame.

Finished end panel is applied after box assembly, with a v-groove at the joint, or the two stiles can be mitered.

Figure 127. Where the plywood cabinet end *meets the face frame will affect the appearance of the finished cabinet, how and where it is installed, and the sizes of the other cabinet parts.*

Figure 128. Moving *the plywood end flush with the inside of the stile provides a consistent construction method.*

cabinet until the very end of the assembly process. Where the cabinet meets the wall, there is room to run a cleat vertically along the wall to secure the cabinet to the wall. Where the stile meets the wall will likely need to be scribed on installation, and many cabinetmakers like to run a bevel or a rabbet on the long back edge to reduce the amount of material that gets cut away during scribing **(Figure 129).**

If the exposed end is not a stile and rail raised panel, a piece of veneered plywood can be used. This also may be applied to the cabinet, towards the end of the process, rather than being a part of the cabinet throughout the project. This will keep the panel from being damaged during construction. If the exposed end is in a location next to an appliance where not all of it will be seen, a strip of plywood 4 or 5 inches wide can be used behind the stile as a finished end.

If butt hinges are used instead of concealed hinges, one of the advantages of setting the

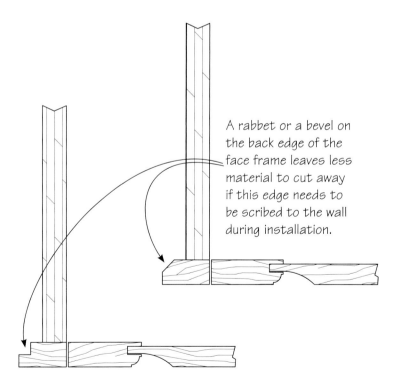

A rabbet or a bevel on the back edge of the face frame leaves less material to cut away if this edge needs to be scribed to the wall during installation.

Figure 129. Making the cabinet end flush *with the inside of the face-frame stile allows using the same method for both finished ends and wall ends, and greatly simplifies the sizing of cabinet parts.*

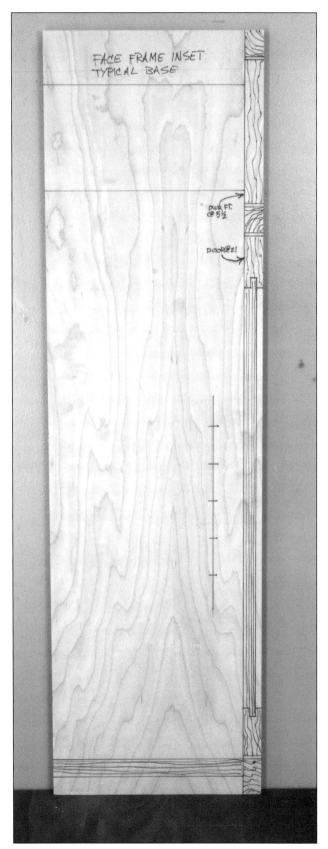

FACE FRAME INSET
TYPICAL BASE

DWR FT.
@5½

DOOR @ 21

Figure 130. Vertical story pole—Draw a full-size section of a typical cabinet to determine the location of common parts and joints.

panel flush to the inside of the stile disappears, and in this case, I prefer to see the face of the panel set back at least ¼ inch from the inside edge of the stile. Regardless of the hinges used, I prefer to leave enough space at the outside edge of the stile for an applied end panel. This may mean making the stiles 1¾ inches or 2 inches wide.

Make a Story Pole

Because of all these variations, determining the sizes for all the parts used in face-frame cabinets will not be as simple as it was with frameless cabinets. But, it isn't quantum mechanics either. If you make a story pole for your typical cabinet, you will be able to establish exactly how the pieces fit with each other and how big each part needs to be.

Using a narrow piece of flat stock, a scrap strip of plywood, or a light-colored piece of solid wood a few inches wide and at least as long as your proposed cabinet, pretend that the front edge is the front of your cabinet. With a square, make pencil marks to indicate the overall width of the cabinet. Now draw a line ¾ inch back from the front edge and parallel to it. This represents the thickness of your face frame. Draw in the locations of the stiles, with perpendicular lines from the front edge to the line. From the line back, draw lines indicating the plywood end-panels, and if there are dados or other joints where the panels meet the stiles, draw them in. I like to scribble in the areas that represent end-grain of solid wood pieces, and draw straight lines inside the lines of plywood pieces (**Figure 130**) to help distinguish parts and visualize the construction. With this full-size layout in front of you, it's simple to measure what the difference between the overall width of the cabinet will be, and how long to make the bottom, shelves, drawer boxes, and rails.

It will also be useful to make a story pole representing the vertical section of both the base cabinets and wall cabinets, and at least the corners where the face of one cabinet meets another. I usually lay out the room plan in AutoCAD, and can zoom in and look at full size details on the computer screen. If I didn't have a CAD program to work with, I would make a full-size story pole for each elevation in the plan. If possible, I would then take the story poles to the actual room, lay them on the floor in the right location, and make sure that my cabinet plan worked with electrical outlets, heating ducts, and plumbing. If the sink drain falls outside your intended sink base cabinet, it's nice to know in advance.

Overlay Doors

Face-frame cabinets don't have to have inset doors. The doors can completely overlay the face of the cabinet, or they may be lipped. **Figure 131** shows a section view of a face-frame base cabinet with overlay doors. All of the face-frame stock is 1½ inches wide, and the doors all overlay their openings by ⅜ inch. Because the front of the cabinet has been moved back by the thickness of the doors, and by the gap between the back of the doors and the face frame, the plywood cabinet parts are not as wide as they are on the inset cabinet. If the doors are lipped, the size of the plywood cabinet parts would be reduced by the amount of door thickness extending past the front edge of the face frame.

Notice also the difference between the two types in elevation (**Figure 132**). In the cabinet with the inset doors, the proportions of the elements of the face frame, and the details of the face frame are more important visually. There is a pleasing regularity in the inset door cabinet, because the lines of the face frame are continuously visible.

In the overlay doors, the lines of the face frame stop and start, and where they appear doesn't relate visually to the elements of the

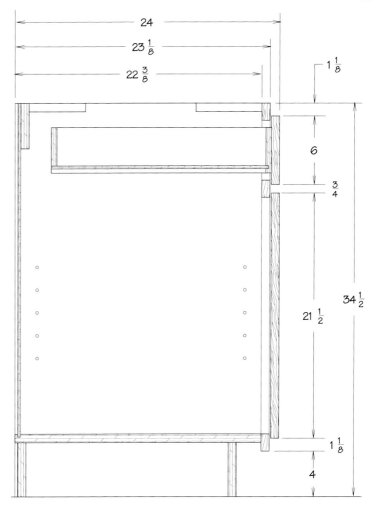

*Figure 131. **Changing to overlay doors** from inset doors will reduce the width of the cabinet ends.*

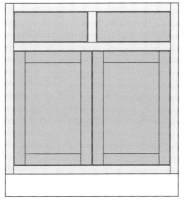

Face frame cabinet with inset doors

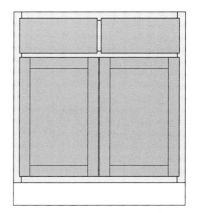

Face frame cabinet with ⅜" overlay or lipped doors.

*Figure 132. **Although they are commonly used**, overlay doors lack the refined appearance of inset doors.*

doors. When viewed at an angle, the inset door cabinet is one unified plane, while the overlay and lipped doors have doors and drawer fronts sticking out here and there.

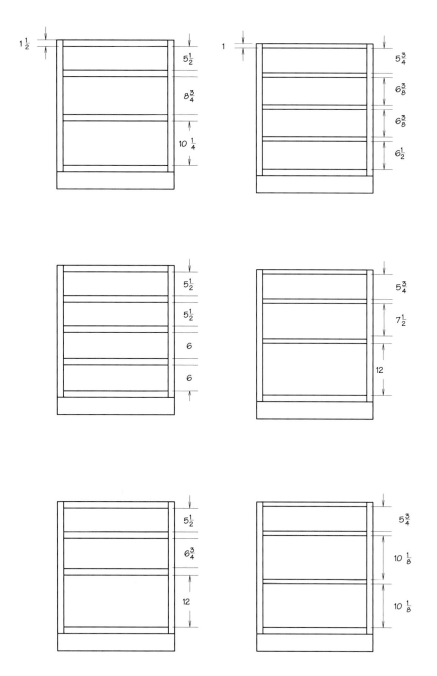

Figure 133. Reducing the width of the rails between the drawers will provide more space for drawer height.

Beads

A bead around the inside perimeter of the face frame adds visual interest, and is often seen in high-end work. Most of the do-it-yourself literature suggests milling the bead stock as separate thin pieces and nailing them in place. While this can be and is done, it introduces some problems that have an impact on the finished appearance of the cabinet, particularly if the cabinets are not painted. The preferred method is to mill the beads on the edges of the face-frame stock. This does make the joint a bit tricky where the face-frame parts join together, but there are several benefits, and the photos on **page 125** demonstrates an efficient method.

If the beads are applied, it is necessary to miter each and every corner, effectively doubling the number of joints to be cut and fit. Gluing of the applied beads must also be carefully done, so that no squeeze-out remains between the frame and the bead. Glue left in this area is hard to see and remove, and will spoil a stained finish. The final problem is the number of nail holes to be set, filled, and sanded. Working the bead in the edges of the face frame requires mastering a new method of joining, but ensures that the color and grain on the face-frame stock match. There is no chance of the joint between the frame and bead cracking over time, little glue squeeze-out to clean up, and no nail holes to fill.

Drawers and Slides

Arranging drawer fronts in face-frame cabinets is not as flexible as doing so in frameless cabinets. Again, the nominal top drawer is 6 inches, but there are good reasons to make it a bit smaller. The drawer box behind the front is 4 inches high, which is accepted as a good height; it fits most silverware and other top-drawer items. If it were any taller, it would be a waste of space. With this drawer box height, a front that is less than 6 inches makes both the doors and the area behind the doors more accessible. If you are using solid-wood stock for the drawer fronts, it will be a lot easier to find material for the fronts without needing to glue-up for width.

The drawings (**Figure 133**) show some workable arrangements for multiple-drawer cabinets. The face-frame rails, of course, occupy some space, and the drawings show possibilities using either 1 inch or 1½-inch wide rails. The dimensions in the drawings are for the openings; the drawer fronts will be smaller.

The best drawer slides to use are the same as for frameless cabinets: either bottom-mount roller slides, or full-extension ball-bearing slides. How the slides attach to the cabinet depends on how the face frame meets the cabinet side. If the inside edges are flush, simply screw the drawer slides to the side.

If the cabinet side is set in from the edge of the face frame, the easy solution is to attach a wooden spacer, the thickness of the offset from the cabinet side to the face frame edge on the cabinet side. This provides a surface

to attach the drawer slides that will be flush with the face-frame edge. There are a variety of brackets available that clip on to the back of the drawer slide, and then screw to the back of the cabinet. These are far more trouble than they are worth, as the exact position of the bracket on the cabinet back is difficult to locate, and the length of the slide must be carefully coordinated with the depth of the cabinet. Even when installed correctly, these only support the slide at the ends, and a heavily loaded drawer can bend the slide, or pull the bracket off its screws.

Inside Corners

Other cabinet configurations, like the blind corner cabinet, are fabricated much like the frameless version. A piece of plywood is attached to one of the face frame stiles where the cabinet extends behind the adjacent cabinet (**Figure 134**). There isn't a significant difference between inset and overlay door face frames, and the most important thing is to remember to provide clearance at the corner, where the next cabinet joins (**Figure 135**). The usual method of making a cabinet with the filler is to make the stile on that side of the

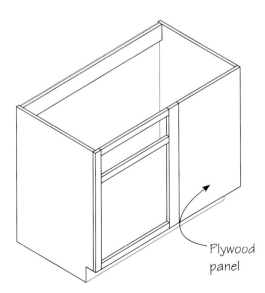

*Figure 134. **Attaching a plywood panel** to the edge of the face frame creates a blind corner cabinet.*

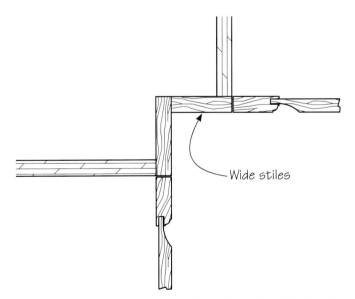

*Figure 135. **In a corner,** extending the width of the face frame stiles is the simplest way to create clearance for the adjacent cabinet.*

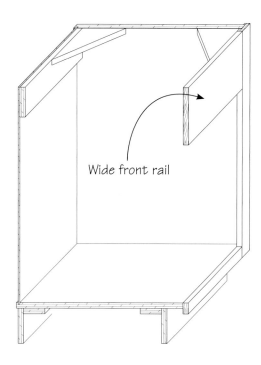

Wide front rail

Figure 136. A single wide top rail provides the best support for the heavy sink in a face-frame sink base.

face frame wider. If there is only one place in the project that you make a full-size layout of how everything fits together, this is the place to do it.

The same cautions apply to angled corner base cabinets. Again, the exact size of everything depends on where the face frame and cabinet meet, and where the doors sit in relation to the frame. Too many variables to cover in this book, but a full-size drawing of the corner, based on requirements of a lazy susan, if used, and the standards set for your cabinet construction in the other cabinets.

Sink Base

In a face-frame sink base, you have the choice of building the frame identically to all the other cabinets or making the top rail one solid piece. If made the same as in the other cabinets, you can hinge the false front from the bottom, and install a tilt-out tray that holds the dish sponge. If the sink is very large or heavy, I would opt for the solid top rail (**Figure 136**).

File Drawers

If you make a file cabinet for use under a 30-inch high countertop, you won't be able to have two functional file drawers and a 4-inch high toe space. Remember that you

need at least 10 inches from the top of the drawer bottom to the top edge of the drawer, plus ½ inch for the file tabs to clear. Start from there, and work up.

Wall Cabinets

For face-frame wall cabinets, the same arguments apply for the ends of the cabinets, as well as some new arguments regarding the top and bottom of the wall cabinet.

As in the base cabinet, the top face of the cabinet bottom is usually flush with the upper edge of the bottom rail. In some factory-made cabinets, the bottom of the box is set down ⅛ inch. This makes finishing easier, especially if the interior of the cabinet has a clear finish, and the face frame is stained. The disadvantage of this is that the inside edge of the face frame can possibly be chipped when removing items from the cabinet.

The bottom stile can also be made wider to provide a valance for under-counter light fixtures. A 2-inch wide rail, set flush with the top of the ¾-inch cabinet bottom, will usually leave enough room.

It is also preferable to have the bottom face of the cabinet top flush, or nearly so, with the bottom edge of the top rail. This allows for a cleat to be mounted to the bottom of the soffit or ceiling to secure the front edge of the cabinet, and allows the frame to be scribed to the drywall if need be.

The section drawing of the typical wall cabinet **Figure 127** shows my preferences for a typical wall cabinet. Usually I build wall cabinets an inch or two deeper than the standard 12 inches. The dashed line at top and bottom indicates the finished 30-inch end panel if it is needed.

Rails for securing the cabinet to the wall are shown at both the top and bottom of the cabinet, although many cabinetmakers omit the bottom one. I like to use both, because these rails also serve to keep the cabinet from racking out of square. Even though the face frame adds some strength to the front of the cabinet, you still need to set a reasonable limit on the overall width of the cabinet. As doors become wider, it is harder to keep them perfectly flat. I don't like to make a door more than 18 inches to 20 inches wide. Even with a solid wood edge, a shelf longer than 36 inches can sag under just a small load.

Inside Corners

Face-frame wall cabinets have the same design challenges as frameless wall cabinets, and the cabinets in or near the corners of the room are the trickiest. You can, of course, leave the corner empty, just widen the stiles on the cabinets next to the corner to serve as fillers, and add a bottom plate. This can be difficult to install if it is attached to one of the cabinets, and it really should be scribed to the walls. Run ¾ inch x ¾ inch cleats on the walls, above where the plate should be, and on the same plane on the sides of the cabinets. Scribe the bottom plate to match the opening, and secure it to the cleats with construction adhesive. Use brads or small finish nails to hold it in place while the adhesive sets **(Figure 138).**

The blind corner cabinet and angled corner wall cabinet are mainly the same configuration as seen previously **(page 94)**. Again, be sure that the bottom of the blind corner cabinet and the adjacent cabinet extend all the way to the corner of the room. Leaving the sides back from the wall will make for an easier installation, but it is easy to forget that the bottoms of the wall cabinets are sometimes visible. The bottoms don't need to be as pristine as an exposed cabinet end, but there needs to be something there so you are not seeing empty space from the breakfast table.

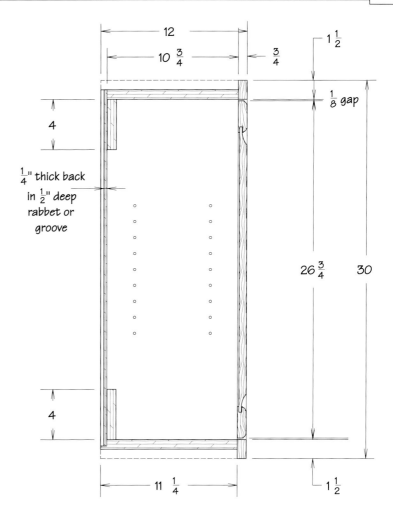

*Figure 137. **Section of a typical face frame** wall cabinet. Note that the ends of the cabinet extend past the top and bottom of the cabinet.*

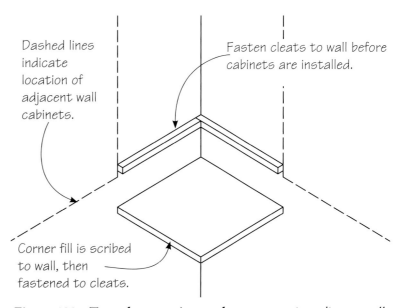

*Figure 138. **To make a continuous bottom** spanning adjacent wall cabinets in a blind corner, use a plywood plate secured by cleats.*

9. FACE FRAME MATERIALS AND ASSEMBLY

Figure 139. Organizing parts—Keep stacks of stiles and rails separate, and orient them at 90 degrees to avoid confusion.

Face frames first or cabinet boxes first? If you can work precisely, and follow your plan, it won't matter which part you start with. If you have the confidence to complete all of your boxes, assemble all of your face frames, and have them fit together, then you are well on your way to a successful project. This is the most efficient way to proceed.

If you don't yet have that confidence, you might want to build a box, see how it turns out, then build your face frame to fit it. Many cabinetmakers, amateur and professional, follow this approach, but I recommend practicing to get beyond it. If you completed your layouts accurately, can use a tape measure and a square, and can cut parts to the sizes you want, there isn't any reason to build one box, one face frame, one cabinet at a time.

If you are fabricating all the solid wood parts for your kitchen, you need to decide not only how you will perform each task, but decide how much wood you need, and how you will purchase it. Don't plan on going down to the local Big Box store or retail lumberyard and asking for a few hundred feet of oak 1 x 2s. While they may have something close in size, you will be paying a lot more than you should.

You do have some choices that will affect your budget and the way you perform the work. It is possible to buy ready-made raised-panel doors, finished end panels, and drawer fronts, so that all the solid wood you need to buy would be the material for the face frames. If that's the case, you should be able to find a supplier to the cabinet industry that sells surfaced face-frame stock, ¾ inch x 1½ inch or ¾ inch x 2 inch in random lengths. Check your yellow pages for "Lumber Wholesale" or "Plywood Wholesale" for a supplier. What you are looking for is a company that supplies the local cabinet shops, and won't mind making a retail sale. If you are buying material for a complete kitchen, it will be a sizable order that the supplier won't want to let go, even though he will likely give you a hard time about making a retail sale, and will pretend to be giving you a break by taking several hundred dollars of your money.

If you have trouble finding someone through the yellow pages, don't be afraid to call a local cabinet shop, briefly explain your situation, and see if you can order the material through them, or if they will tell you who they deal with. If you belong to a local woodworking club, be sure to ask around. You can also check online woodworking forums for a local supplier. There is also an online service at www.woodfinder.com that lets you plug in what type of wood you are looking for and will return all suppliers within a 200-mile radius of your location.

Buying Hardwood Lumber

If you don't buy face-frame stock milled to size, you need to know at least a little about buying hardwoods. Hardwood lumber is sold in random widths and lengths by the board foot, which is a measure of volume of a board one inch thick, one foot wide, and one foot long. If you change the feet to inches, you will see that a board foot is equal to 144 cubic inches. To calculate the board feet in a given board, round up the thickness to the next quarter inch (¾ inch becomes 1 inch) and multiply that by the width (in inches) and the length (in inches). Divide that by 144 and you have the quantity of board feet.

As an example, an 8-inch wide board, 120 inches long, contains:

1 x 8 x 120 = 960 cubic inches

960 divided by 144=6.67 board feet

If all of your face-frame stock is the same thickness and width, you can figure the total amount you need in lineal feet, convert the total number in feet to inches, and multiply by the width and divide by 144.

If, for example, you need 265 feet of material ¾ inch thick by 1½ inches wide, the equation would be:

1 (rounding ¾ inch up to the next inch) x 1½ x (265 x 12) divided by 144 = 33.125 board feet.

Most of what goes in a kitchen is ¾ inch thick, known in the trade as ¾ or four-quarter material. This designation of thickness is simple: the thickness of a rough-sawn board, expressed as an improper fraction, in quarters of an inch. Therefore, ⁵⁄₄ (five-quarter) stock is 1¼ inches thick in the rough, ⁶⁄₄ = 1 ½ inches, etc. When you calculate the board feet of thicker stock, convert the quarters to a decimal number, and use that in the above equations instead of 1.

You can buy it rough, that is, unsurfaced, or you can buy it planed to a relatively smooth surface. In the rough it's as thick as they say it is, but putting it through the planer brings it down in size. Depending on the mill and their practices (or whims), your ¾ surfaced stock may be anywhere from ¾ inch thick to ¹³⁄₁₆ inch thick. When it's sold surfaced, it is referred to as S2S (surfaced 2 sides). Most mills have a great big automatic-feed saw that will put a straight edge on one edge of the board. When that's done the material is referred to as S2SR1E (surfaced two sides and ripped one edge).

Hardwood lumber is sold in random lengths and widths, and where and how you buy it greatly affects the price. If you call up a mill out in the country and say, "Send me 500 board feet of ¾ red oak FAS, S2SR1E," you'll probably get a pretty good price.

If you walk into a retail store in a nice part of town, where it's air conditioned, and someone has looked over every board, tallied the

> Hardwood lumber is sold in random lengths and widths, and where and how you buy it greatly affects the price.

board feet, and figured and marked the price on the board, you're going to pay more for the overhead and handling. If there's a computer barcode on the board, and a Starbucks right around the corner, you're going to pay a whole lot more than if you had "X" quantity pulled at random and delivered.

What you get for your money when you buy retail is the opportunity to pick through the stacks and get the boards you want. If you're buying what the yard sends, you need to figure that a percentage of that lumber may not be usable. Since it's sold in random widths and lengths, you never know until you see it what you will get.

You will have a good idea of what you'll get, because hardwood lumber is graded, that is, there are certain qualities, minimum width length, and number of defects allowed for wood to be sold as a specific grade. The National Hardwood Lumber Association sets standards, and you can download a copy of the grading rules from their web site, www. natlhardwood.org.

Most mills and dealers do the best they can to follow the rules, and although there are a lot of grades in the book, in real life there are only two that you are likely to come across. Selects, or Selects and Better, is usually the best grade available. Most of the boards should be 6 inches wide or wider, and they should be about 85% to 90% clear, that is, without defects like knotholes, splits, etc. This percentage is based on the size of clear-cutting or defect-free pieces that can be sawn from a board. Selects & Better is really a downgrading of what was formerly the highest grade, FAS, or Firsts and Seconds, which required a higher percentage of clear wood.

The other grade you are likely to come across is #1 common. This allows more defects, and the clear pieces that can be obtained from any given board are smaller. #1 common is always less expensive than the higher grade, and if

> If there's a computer barcode on the board, and a Starbucks around the corner, you're going to pay a whole lot more...

the price difference is substantial enough, it can be a great value. Most pieces of solid wood used in a typical kitchen are relatively small, and can be obtained from #1 common with little difficulty. Where the rule of thumb percentage of clear stock in Selects and Better is around 90%, it is about 65% with #1 common. If #1common is less than two-thirds the price of S&B, you will save some money, but you will have to work a little harder to get the clear pieces you need, and you will have a larger scrap pile for the woodstove.

Armed with the information from the elevation sheets and cut lists you have prepared, you should have on hand an organized list, detailing each part you need. It is possible to get too detailed and slow yourself down. I once worked with a man who marked in chalk, on every part, what piece of what cabinet it was. The only problem was that every time he moved the stack of parts for a new operation, most of the chalk would rub off, and he would diligently re-mark them all before proceeding.

From your lists, you will calculate how much wood you are going to need. It's a tedious task but if you don't do it, one of two things will happen: your guess will be too low, and you will have to re-order lumber two-thirds of the way through the job; or, your guess will be too high, and you will have a garage or basement full of hardwood that will be in your way for the rest of your life.

Quick Calculations

There are some tricks to speeding up your calculations.

For items like face-frame stock, figure out how many board feet (actually what fraction of a board foot) is in a lineal foot of the material you need. Then all you need to do is multiply the lineal feet you need by your conversion factor.

Figure each face of a cabinet and each finished end panel as one solid piece of wood. For example, a standard base cabinet 30 inches wide has a face of 7.5 square feet (I'm taking it as 3 feet high and 2½ feet wide) and the side panel will be about 6 square feet (2 feet deep x 3 feet high). This cabinet, since all these parts will be made from ¾ stock, will therefore need about 13½ board feet of material.

Notice that I said about. If I'm ordering material that is 90% clear, I had better keep in mind that I'll be throwing at least 10% of it away. I also need to remember that I'm trying to make specific-sized pieces out of random width and length material. I may need all 3-foot long pieces, and 8-foot long boards may be delivered instead of 10-foot long ones. If tens come in, I'll get three, 3-foot pieces, and only lose one foot out of the ten to waste (10%). If eights come in, I'll only get two pieces out of a board, and 2 feet in 8 will be waste (now it's a 25% waste factor).

I try to come close to calculating the actual amount I use, and if there are any points in the calculating where it is quicker or easier to round off a number, I make sure to always round up instead of down, so that any guesswork won't leave me short. When that is done, I need to figure out a reasonable waste factor, which takes into account the price and grade of wood I am looking at. I usually get at least 15% more, and as much as 25% more if I'm ordering Selects and Better. If I'm ordering #1 common, my waste factor will be between 30% and 40%.

There is often a price break at 100 board feet, at 250 board feet, and at 500 board feet. If the estimate plus the waste percentage is 220 board feet, and there is a price break at 250 feet, I'll go ahead and get that amount.

Having the boards surfaced before they are delivered may or may not be a good idea. It all depends on how the people you are buying from define surfaced and what kind of condition their machinery is in. Most places run both faces of the boards through their planer and call it a day. This will remove the rough saw marks, but it doesn't make the wood flat. The feed rollers in a planer will push a cupped or bowed board flat as it goes through the cutters, but as soon as the pressure is released, the board returns to its bowed or warped condition.

Some mills have a planer that won't do that, or a big jointer with a power feed to flatten the first face of the board before it goes through the planer. Some places take great care of their machinery and keep their knives sharp, and produce a board that is close to perfection. Others haven't sharpened their knives in so long that no one in the place remembers how, and do more damage than good when they surface lumber. Be sure to ask some questions if you're dealing with a seller over the phone, and see some samples if you're there in person.

You can of course have the lumber delivered rough, and if you have a decent jointer and planer available, you can do all of the surfacing yourself. Don't make the mistake of thinking that this will save you lots of money, or even any money. In my area, I expect to pay 30 cents or less a board foot to have both faces surfaced and one edge ripped to a straight line. I can't do a good job fast enough to justify doing this myself for money reasons.

But it is worthwhile for quality reasons. If you can get the raw material you will be working with flat and square to start with, every step of the job will be easier, and the results will be vastly improved over working with run of the mill material.

Cutting Parts

Once you have the material in your shop, the first thing you should do is stack it neat-

> If you can get your raw material flat and square to start with, every step of the job will be easier, and the results will be vastly improved.

When cutting parts, start big and work down to the small ones.

ly, and then ignore it for a few weeks. If the lumber you just purchased was stored outside in a shed, and you bring it inside, it will move as it seeks to reach equilibrium with the new environment. If the environment in your shop is radically different from the environment where your finished cabinets will be, you can expect to have problems due to wood movement. Far too many cabinetmakers ignore these factors and then are surprised when problems develop.

I usually have my cutting lists organized by kinds of parts: face-frame stiles and rails on one list or part of the list, door and panel stiles and rails on a second part, and drawer fronts and panels for the doors and finished panels. If I have room, I like to organize these pieces before I saw, and as I saw. I start to saw the largest pieces first. There are two reasons for starting big and working down. Usually these will be the most visible pieces on the job, and I want to pick the most attractive boards for this. The other reason is that if something goes wrong or I make a mistake, I can usually salvage one or more usable parts from what survives.

I mark the boards I choose for panels and drawer fronts with a piece of chalk or a lumber crayon, sketching roughly where I want to saw, and where the pieces will go. I'm looking for some specific qualities. If I can find a board long enough and wide enough to make all the drawer fronts for an elevation, I mark it and set it aside. If I come across two boards that were next to each other in the tree, and I need to glue up some wide pieces for panels, then I have been fortunate that day. As the pieces I am searching for become shorter and narrower, I begin to look for the straightest-grained stuff in the pile. This will be more stable, and easier to match for grain and color, than material with more flamboyant figure.

My sequence is to do as much ripping as possible before sawing pieces to length, but it is almost always necessary to do a few cross cuts before the ripping can begin. With a sharp rip-blade in the table saw, I cut all the parts wider than they need to be. Boards intended for drawer fronts and panels are sawn to get the widest piece possible from the rough board. This gives me some room to shift parts around to get a better figure match, or to center the figure on a glued-up panel.

Boards that are to become stiles and rails get ripped ⅛ inch wider than needed if the wood is well-seasoned and doesn't move during cutting. If it seems to be a moving target, I'll rip it ¼ inch wider than needed. Ideally, I'll have room to rip these pieces to the rough width, and let them sit in the shop while I cut the plywood parts and assemble the boxes. This gives the solid wood more time to adjust to the atmospheric conditions in the shop.

When I get back to these parts, I still have relatively long lengths of parts. I join one edge of the panel and drawer front pieces. Then I make any rip cuts that are necessary before cutting these parts to a rough length. If I need to glue any boards together to make panels, I go ahead and do that so that the glue has plenty of time to cure before I start to work with it. A glued-up panel may seem like it's dry after a half hour or hour in the clamps, but it takes twenty-four hours or more for it to reach full strength.

One thing I try to avoid is being too specific about parts as long as they are parts. If I'm building eight standard-height base cabinets, I know I will need sixteen end stiles. They will become eight rights and eight lefts, and eventually one will be the left stile of cabinet N-B-2, but when I cut and mill them, they stay a stack of stiles as long as possible.

Once the pieces are acclimated to the environment and have one straight edge, it is time to bring them to their finished size. Pieces for face-frame stiles and rails can be ganged together, and sent through the planer on edge in groups of four to six pieces. This not only brings them all to a consistent finished width, it removes the saw marks from the edges. This greatly reduces the amount of sanding to be done after the face frames are assembled **(Figure 140)**.

Frugality is a virtue, but you will regret trying to save wood by sawing rails and stiles too close to knots and other grain distortions. You want these pieces to be stable and to remain flat, and not to give you a hard time when you get to cutting joints.

If the work is to receive a clear finish, the stiles and rails should be matched as closely as possible for grain and color. The best appearance will be achieved if this stock is as straight-grained as possible, and the work will go better too. After the pieces are cut to size, I keep the stiles in one stack and the rails in another. This will avoid confusion during the process of milling joints that is to follow.

Joints for Frames

There are numerous possibilities for joining stiles and rails in face frames, but really only two that make sense: mortise and tenon joints, or butt joints reinforced with pocket screws. Dowel joints or biscuit joints could be used, but they are more trouble than they are worth.

Dowel joints may offer some strength initially, but over time, as the wood shrinks and swells, they will break loose. Dowels also offer no margin for adjustment during assembly, so any slight misalignment in boring the holes will result in an uneven joint. Standard biscuits are too long to fit within the width of most rails. While it is possible to mill the slots with an offset at the top and bottom, and trim the excess biscuit off, smaller biscuits must be used at intermediate rails. These will not provide the strength

Figure 140. Gang parts through planer—*After ripping the face frame stock ⅛ inch over size, send them through the planer in groups of four or five boards. This will remove saw marks and ensure consistent width.*

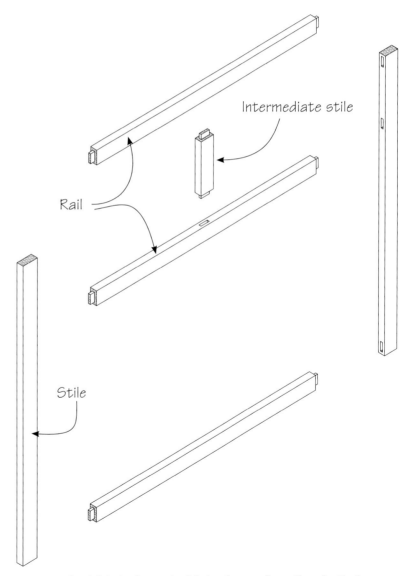

Intermediate stile

Rail

Stile

Figure 141. This is the typical joint layout *for rail-and-stile face frames: all the rails get tenons on both ends, and most of the stiles receive matching mortises. The exceptions are the intermediate stiles.*

Figure 142. Mortise layout —*Use the story board to transfer layout marks to the face frame parts.*

Figure 143. Mortise layout—*Grouping parts together saves time and guarantees that the layout is consistent.*

Figure 144. Mortises—*A hollow-chisel mortiser can be used to make the mortises, or they can be made with a router.*

Figure 145. Tenons—*Stub tenons can be quickly made with a stack dado set on the table saw, or with a straight cutter on the router table.*

of other methods, and cutting the slots in the ends of narrow stock is awkward at best and dangerous at worst.

Mortise and Tenon

For first-class work, there is no joint to equal the mortise and tenon. In typical ¾-inch thick material, the mortises should be ¼ inch wide. The simplest way to cut the tenons is with a stack dado set in the table saw, cutting in ¼ inch from all four sides of the stock

as shown in **Figure 145**. This simplifies the setup for cutting the tenons, and will allow you to cut all the tenons for the face frames at one time. In this situation, I would make all the tenons as stubs ½ inch long.

The simplest way to cut the mortises is with a hollow-chisel mortiser (**Figure 144**), and since these are relatively small, an inexpensive, small-capacity mortiser or a drill-press mortising attachment will do nicely. It is also possible to cut the mortises with a router table, but this will require plunging the

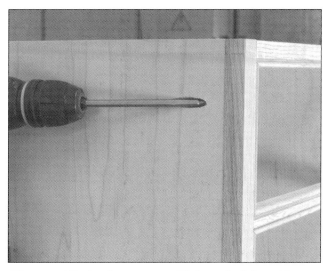

Figure 146. Pocket screws—If the end of the cabinet won't be visible, you can use pocket screws to attach the frame and cabinet.

Figure 147. Pocket screws—A shop-made jig can be used with the drill press to make pocket holes on the ends of all the rails.

Figure 148. Pocket screws—A manufactured jig with a hand-held drill can also be used for drill pockets.

Figure 149. Assembling pocket screws—The vise-grip clamp is essential to hold the parts together. Working with the stile on edge helps you see what is happening.

stock to be mortised onto the router bit, and setting up stops to control the length of the mortises. The mortises could also be cut with a plunge router, but again, this introduces a complicated setup, with a fence set on the router, and some way of setting the length of the mortises, either by eye, or with stops. In addition, the router would be balanced on the narrow edge of the work.

In laying out the mortises, the work will go quickly if the stiles are clamped together, as shown in **Figure 142 & 143** and marked

out all at once. This is also a more accurate way to lay out the joints, because it will result in identical marks on every piece.

Pocket Screws

If pocket screws are used, the layout is simplified, since the stiles will have a rail flush at both the top and the bottom, and only the location of the intermediate rails must be marked. Clamping the stiles together, and making the layout marks at one time will

Joining Face Frames

Figure 150. Mortise & tenon assembly—*With the stile on edge, glue is applied to the tenons and the rails are slipped into place.*

Figure 151. Mortise & tenon assembly—*With the rails in place, apply glue to the tenons and assemble the second rail. Note the clamp holding the rail upright.*

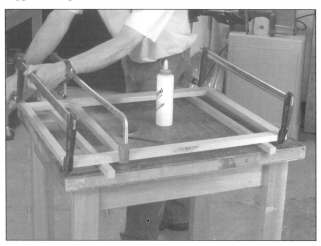

Figure 152. Mortise & tenon assembly—*Mortise-and-tenon face frames will be strong, but they do require clamping during assembly.*

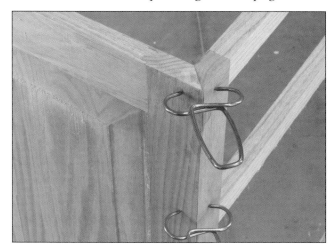

Figure 153. Panel-to-frame joint—*The joint between the finished end panel and the face frame will look better if it is mitered.*

Figure 154. Panel and frame to cabinet—*Assemble the panel and face frame, then attach it to the cabinet box. Putting the cabinet on a pair of low horses lets you work at a comfortable height.*

Figure 155. Clamping—*If you're not using nails, be sure to keep the frame and cabinet aligned as you set the clamps. A few small finishing nails helps guarantee this alignment.*

also speed the work, and make it more consistent.

Commercially made pocket-screw jigs, as shown in **Figure 148** are not cheap, but are the easiest alternative to bore the angled holes quickly and accurately. A shop-made jig used with the drill press **Figure 147** can be fabricated out of common materials found in the typical shop, but you will still need to purchase the stepped drill bit, long driver, and special clamp that come with most jigs, so the savings will not be that great. It can be awkward to set up to mill long pieces avoiding the head of the drill press, so the bench-mounted jig with a hand-held drill is usually more efficient.

If you build your own jig, an angle of 15 degrees works well, and the piece of square stock along the base will keep the bottom of the part to be bored from kicking out during drilling.

Make some test cuts to be certain that the screw exits the rail near the middle of the piece, and that enough of the screw extends to firmly connect the parts without breaking through the face of the part. The two parts to be assembled must be firmly clamped together in the same plane. The vise-grip clamps that come with most jigs are ideal for this purpose. Even though you will be gluing end grain to long grain, this joint should always be glued as well as screwed together.

Pocket-screwed face frames will only need to be clamped together one joint at a time, as the joints are screwed together. Mortise and tenon frames will need to be clamped until the glue has set for the frame. This will likely require a fair number of pipe clamps or bar clamps. When I assemble face frames, I write the time the frame was assembled on the frame, and when I run out of clamps, I remove them from the oldest assembled frame **(Figure 152)**.

Attaching Frames to Boxes

Attaching completed face frames to assembled cabinets will be an important milestone in your project. It is a point where things change from a jumble of parts to an almost completed puzzle. If you have been careful up to this point things will go well.

I rough-sand the front and back faces of the face frames before putting them on the cabinets. All of the joints are brought down flush. If you are using a groove or a rabbet in the back of the frame to fit it to the cabinet, the parts of the frames need to be all in the same plane and flat. The frames can be held to the cabinets with glue only, but you will need a lot of clamps, and a good deal of space to accomplish this. If you don't mind nail holes through the face frames you can save a lot of time by using fasteners in conjunction with clamps.

A dado or rabbet will be stronger than just a glue joint. The main reason I prefer to include a joint, however, is to make assembly easier, not for extra strength. The simple plywood to solid wood glue joint is more than adequate, but a joint will positively locate the frame on the box. What type of joint to use depends on the relationship of the edges of the solid wood parts and the plywood parts of the cabinet box. If the edges are flush, a rabbet will be used, and if they are inset, then a dado will be used. You might have a combination of joints in the project. While you can run a joint on the rails, placing them on the stiles only will save a lot of time, without compromising the structure.

If there is a combination of joints, you should go through all the frames and note which joints are placed on which parts. I run the face frames over a dado set on the table saw, but a router table could also be used. The work should be held down with a feather board to insure a consistent depth. If the face frame isn't perfectly flat on the back,

Attaching face frames to boxes is the moment when a jumble of parts becomes an almost-completed puzzle.

it is likely to snag on some part of the table, so prepare the frames carefully before cutting the joints and be aware of catching corners as you work.

Rather than put the frame on the cabinet on the bench, use a couple of low saw horses (about 20" to 24" off the floor) to support the cabinet. With the cabinet on its back, you can apply glue and place the frame without fighting gravity. If you have dados or rabbets milled in the back of the frame, you won't have to worry about placement of the frame side-to-side. Align the top and bottom and set the clamps **(Figure 154)**.

If you are only gluing the frames on, you will also need to align the sides, or set them at the correct offset. If the edges of the frame align with the plywood, it might be necessary to push or pull the plywood to keep it in line with the frame. If there is an offset, cut a block to the width of the offset to help align the frame and the cabinet box. This is much faster than measuring, and you won't get glue on the end of your tape or rule.

Biscuits can be used to align and strengthen the joint. If the edges of the frame are flush with edges of the box, mark the locations for the biscuits and cut both parts with the same fence setting on the biscuit cutter. If there is an offset, set the fence of the biscuit cutter to the longer dimension, and prepare a small piece of wood to the size of the offset. After cutting the slots in the frame, attach the block to the under side of the machine's fence, then cut the second set of slots.

When the frame is in position, place the clamps. If you are only gluing without a joint or biscuits, be careful that the frame doesn't slide out of position as the clamps are tightened. If you aren't using any fasteners, it is nice to have two sets of horses so that the glue of one cabinet can set while you are assembling the next one. A base cabinet with several clamps on it can be heavy and

awkward to move. If you are nailing the face frame on, set the clamps, then drive the nails. Once the nails are in place, you can remove the clamps and set the cabinet aside **(Figure 155)**.

Another method for attaching the face frames is to use pocket screws, coming through the outside of the cabinet box and in to the back of the face frame. To assemble with this method, the holes should be drilled in the sides of the box, and the frame placed finished side down on the bench or horses. Apply glue in a line on the back of the frame, and set the cabinet box in place. When the box is in the right location, use a few clamps to hold it so that it doesn't shift while the screws are driven.

> Use a pair of low sawhorses to support the cabinet while you attach the face frame.

Beaded Face Frame

Figure 156. Beaded frame parts—An integral bead on the inside of the face frame is better than an applied bead.

Figure 157. Beaded frame end joint—To join the stiles and rails, part of the bead must be cut away at the intersection.

Figure 158. Beaded face frame rail end—The bead on the adjacent piece must be mitered to complete the joint.

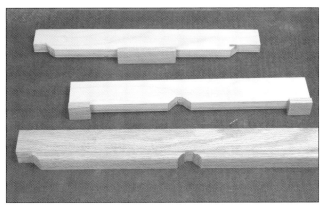

Figure 159. Beaded face frame router jig—These simple jigs allow you to remove the bead and form the mitered joint.

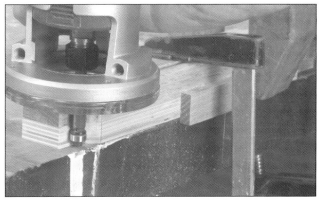

Figure 160. Beaded face frame router jig—The jig is used with a flush trim router bit.

Figure 161. Chisel cut—Complete the miter with a chisel, using the jig as guide.

Figure 162. Clean up—A block plane is a quick and easy way to bring the surfaces flush.

Figure 163. Assembled—The miters can be held together with pocket screws, or a mortise-and-tenon.

10. PREPARING BOX PARTS

Figure 164. Circle saw jig—This shop-made straight edge automatically aligns the blade to the cut line.

Figure 165. Circle saw jig-construction detail—Make the jig from two straight pieces of plywood with the bottom piece a bit wider than needed. Trim the jig by running the saw against the straightedge. The cut edge now indicates the exact location of the sawblade.

One of the most important things to plan is how to get the plywood parts to size, and the sequence of tasks that each part needs before the cabinet boxes can be assembled. This is especially important if you are working in a small shop. You need to provide space for several sheets of plywood, a way to reduce them to a manageable size, and a place to put them while the work proceeds. The goal is to reduce the number of times each part is moved or stacked, and to do as much work as possible to each part before it is assembled.

Of course, much of this depends on the amount of space you have, and the tools at your disposal. The first thing to consider is cutting the sheets of plywood to size. It is possible to do decent cabinetwork without a table saw, but it will require a lot more effort. A circular saw with a straight edge can be used, and if you are tight on space, or uncomfortable pushing full sheets of plywood across a table saw, you might consider this method to make some initial cuts to get the plywood sheets to manageable size.

Jig for Cutting Plywood

A shop-made straightedge (**Figure 164 & 165**) can do most of the cutting. Make the base plate about 12 inches wide so that you have room to clamp it down without the clamps getting in the way of the saw motor. Snap a chalk line along the length to establish a straight line for the fence, setting the fence so that ¼ inch or so of the base plate is beyond the saw blade. Once you have the fence attached, run the saw along the fence, cutting through the base plate. This will serve to locate the guide precisely in line with the blade, and will help to keep the veneer from chipping during crosscuts.

Festool makes a system that includes a plunge-cutting circular saw and a precision straightedge. While this is an expensive option, it works very well. The Festool guide system also works with their router for line-boring applications. If you don't have the space for a large table saw, adopting the Festool system would be a reasonable alternative.

A pair of sawhorses, with four sacrificial 8-foot long 2 x 4s between them, will let you make your rough cuts with the circular saw without worrying about pieces falling as the cuts are completed. Screw the 2 x 4s to the tops of the horses about 10 inches apart, and set the depth of the blade to about ¼ inch below the thickness of the plywood.

While a 3HP cabinet-style table saw is nice to have, it is by no means essential. The materials used in a typical cabinet project are all relatively thin, so a contractor-style saw with less horsepower will do the job. What is important is to have the right saw blade, a reliable fence, and an outfeed table to support pieces at the end of the cuts. If you are working with veneered plywood or Melamine board, you need to be concerned about the material chipping as it is cut. If you have the rest of your life available to build one kitchen, you can cover every cut line with tape, or score each cut with a straightedge and a knife before you cut, as some suggest. If you want to work efficiently, get a zero-clearance insert for your table saw, and get the right blade.

The Right Saw Blade

Most manufacturers have a blade designed for cutting sheet goods without chipping. In an industrial situation, saws are equipped with a scoring blade that cuts partially through the bottom surface of the sheet in addition to the standard blade. With a standard 10-inch saw, a zero-clearance insert reduces much of the chipping. The rest of the chipping can be almost entirely eliminated with the correct tooth geometry. High-angle ATB (alternate tooth bevel) blades with a negative

Figure 166. Giant square—*This jig, combined with a router and a flush-cutting bit, will provide a square corner on a sheet of plywood. Making it a 3-4-5 triangle will ensure its accuracy.*

Figure 167. Giant square—*Clamp the jig securely to the plywood and remove ⅛ inch to ¼ inch with a flush-cutting bit that has the bearing above the cutter.*

hook work very well. If your saw is small or underpowered, a thin-kerf blade will bring improved performance.

There is an attachment available for 10-inch saws that combines a belt-driven scoring blade with a small saw blade. This replaces the standard saw blade and works well until the unit requires sharpening. At that point, unless both blades are ground to the exact width, the cuts will be stepped, and parts won't fit together because of this.

Big Square

Don't depend on sheets of plywood having straight edges or being square. The large square (**Figure 166 & 167**) can be used with a router and a flush-trimming bit with a bearing above the cutter to ensure that parts are square. Put the two legs together with a single screw, and make a mark 36 inches from the intersection down one leg, and 48 inches down the other. Adjust the angle until the diagonal between the two marks is exactly 60 inches. This practical application of the Pythagorean theorem is why you should have paid attention during high school geometry. Once you have proven that your square is at 90 degrees, permanently fasten the two legs.

Planning the Cuts

In all likelihood, you will have numerous parts at the same width. Before you begin cutting your sheet material, use a sheet (or several sheets) of graph paper, along with your cutting list, to plan how you will cut the material. Mark off 4-foot x 8-foot rectangles on the graph paper. If the grid on the paper is four squares to an inch, make the rectangles eight squares wide by sixteen squares long. This gives a scale of ½ inch = 1 foot. Starting with the largest pieces on your plywood cutting list, begin laying out how you will cut each sheet. You don't need to be absolutely in scale. The width of your base cabinet parts should fit two pieces on a 4-foot wide sheet. You can calculate the lengths, and make some rough marks to indicate the parts you need.

For parts like base cabinet sides, you will have several sheets that will be cut identically. I count the number of sides I need, and figure how many I can get from a single sheet. I then make a note beside the sheet layout of how many sheets are cut that way.

> Making the big square relies on the Pythagorean theorem, and is why you should have listened in high-school geometry class.

Cutting the Parts

Once the entire project is planned out, I saw the parts in the following sequence:

• Rip all of the sheets (provided there is room for 8-foot long pieces beyond the saw).

• Square up one end of each ripped piece, and make a pencil mark to indicate the square corner.

• Starting with the longest piece, cross-cut all of the parts to finished length.

• The last cut is a rip cut, bringing the parts to finished width.

If there is a lack of space for handling long pieces, begin by crosscutting the sheets to a rough length, square a corner, then rip and crosscut to finished size. The goal is to make a clean cut on all four edges of each piece, and be certain that the parts are square.

As the parts reach finished dimensions, stack them by where they fit in the finished cabinets. If you have room, make a stack of base cabinet ends, base cabinet bottoms, base cabinet shelves, etc. If you don't have room for a separate stack for each type of part, sort them by the next operation that will take place. If the ends and bottoms are to be rabbeted for the cabinet back, put them in one pile, and put the shelves, which won't receive the rabbet, in another.

Rabbet Joints

With all of the parts cut to size, it's time to consider the joints that may need to be machined to hold the boxes together. If the back sits in a rabbet in the bottom and sides of the boxes, set up the dado set in the table saw, or a straight cutter in the router table and make these cuts (**Figure 168 & 169**). The rabbet in the back establishes a front

Figure 168, 169. Rabbeting—To locate the rabbets on the edge of the plywood panel, set up the table saw with a sacrificial fence. The feather board keeps the workpiece down on the saw table.

and a back for each part, as well as an inside and an outside. The rabbets for the bottom will establish ends that will go on either the left or right side of the completed box. It's easy to get confused at this point, so I like to cut all the back rabbets, separate the bottoms, and make a stack of left ends and a stack of right ends. The bottoms will require no further machining, but the ends will need to be bored for shelf holes, and possibly have joints worked for rails, after the rabbets for the cabinet bottoms are cut.

My preference is to join the cabinets with a rabbet where the side and bottom meet, and a rabbet in both sides and the bottom for the cabinet back. I fasten rails with biscuit joints, cutting the slots in the cabinet ends just before assembly.

Boring the Holes

With the rabbets cut, the next step is to bore holes for the shelf pins, and if it is a frameless cabinet, holes for the hinge plates. In a commercial shop, this work is done on a CNC router, or on a boring machine equipped with enough drill bits to bore the holes for an entire cabinet side in one or two passes. For the small shop, there is a seem-

ingly endless variety of jigs available for line-boring cabinet sides. There are also small line-boring machines that are quicker than drilling by hand, but it is hard to justify the investment in these if you are not building cabinets on a regular basis.

While this might seem like a good place to use a drill press, it is actually much faster to use a jig and a hand-held drill. A drill press is excellent for making your own jig; you can set up a fence to locate a number of holes in a straight line, and the holes will be perpendicular. But it's hard to efficiently get the spacing between holes on the drill press. You don't want to manually lay out every hole in every cabinet side. You want a systematic way to drill the same pattern on each cabinet.

I make my own boring jigs from ½-inch thick plywood. I can tailor them to include only the holes I want to drill, and I save the expense of buying a commercially made jig. A good boring jig needs to be accurate, relatively foolproof, and needs to stay accurate while drilling numerous holes. It needs to be thick enough to keep the bit in a vertical position, and the holes in the jig should not be damaged during drilling. The best way to accomplish this is with a bushing, rather than running the bit through a hole in the

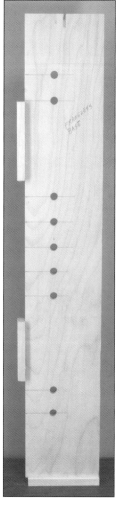

Figure 170. Base cabinet hole jig—*A single boring jig will locate all of the holes needed in a typical cabinet side. The stops on the left side of the jig index it against the front edge of the cabinet side; the stop on the bottom indexes against the bottom edge.*

plywood. Hardened bushings are available from Woodworker's Supply in a number of inside diameters. For ¼-inch shelf pins, T-nuts will make a good bushing, and are readily available. Stops should be provided to locate the jig precisely on the cabinet end and edge (**Figure 170**).

An alternative to using bushings is to use a Vix bit of the appropriate diameter. The holes in the jig must be drilled to match the outside diameter of the collar on the bit. This eliminates the need for purchasing bushings but doesn't work as well to hold the bit straight up and down. Avoid commercially made jigs that require moving the bushing for every hole. This one step can double or triple the amount of time it takes to drill the holes.

An alternative to drilling is to use a plunge router. Festool makes a nice system and there are others available. You can also make your own jig to use a plunge router by boring the holes in the jig to fit the outside diameter of a template guide collar. The depth of the bit is set to the proper dimension, then the router base is placed in each hole and plunged to its limit.

If the holes are not centered top to bottom, you need to somehow indicate the top of each cabinet side. If there is a rabbet for the bottom, this will be clear. If it isn't, a simple slash mark on the top with a magic marker will do.

A battery-operated drill can be used, but a corded drill with higher rpm or a pneumatic drill will be much faster. The holes must be bored to a consistent depth, so some type of stop must be provided to stop the drill against the face of the jig. Metal collars that attach to the drill bit with setscrews are likely to slip. For years, I have used a cheap plastic collar that looks and works much like a drill chuck. It surprised me that it worked in the first place, and continues to surprise me. A

block of hardwood also works, although it can be hard to set the depth precisely.

Clamping the jig to the work is preferred over holding the jig in place. If the jig isn't clamped, it can creep out of place as the drilling takes place, putting the holes out of line. If the holes are put in the wrong places, there really isn't much you can do. You will either have to live with an ugly, patched-up part, or you can start over and make a new one.

I drill a short line of shelf holes in each cabinet side before putting the boxes together. I often wait until the boxes are assembled to drill and install the hinge plates and drawer slides. I do this to avoid putting holes for hardware where it doesn't belong. While the cabinet sides are all the same size, and most of them will have two doors and one drawer, there will always be a few odd cabinets with only one door, or with a stack of drawers.

After the sides are bored for shelves, the next step depends on the material used and the type of cabinet. If they are frameless cabinets, and you have decided to cover the edges before assembly, edge banding will be the next step. If the interiors are pre-finished plywood or Melamine, they will be ready for assembly. If the interiors are veneer, the inside surfaces should be sanded before the cabinets are assembled.

If you are building face-frame cabinets, and don't need to apply any finish to the interiors, the next step is assembly. If you will be finishing them, you want to sand the interior parts before putting the boxes together.

11. Edge Treatments for Frameless Cabinets

One of the advantages of building frameless cabinets is that you save the time you would spend building face frames. The other side of that coin is that you will spend a good deal of time covering or edge-banding the four exposed edges of each cabinet, plus four edges for each door and drawer front.

In a commercial shop, this is a quick and easy process, thanks to a machine called an automatic edge-bander. Parts are fed into this Rube Goldberg contraption, hot glue is applied to the edge, the edge-banding material is stuck on and pressed down, and a series of routers and saws trims the edges and ends. In the small shop, all of these same steps need to take place, but the process is at least ten times slower.

*Figure 171. **Applying edges**—Although it is more expensive than hot melt banding, pressure sensitive adhesive banding is simpler and faster to apply.*

Edging Materials

The edge material should match the face material of the cabinet parts, although sometimes a solid wood edge is used in conjunction with plastic laminate. If you are using veneered plywood, you would use veneer, or solid wood to cover the edges. If you are working with Melamine or plastic laminate, the color of the banding will match, but you have a number of choices for the material itself.

For Melamine or plastic laminate parts, a variety of plastics, vinyl, and PVC are available in rolls that are $\frac{13}{16}$ inch to $\frac{7}{8}$ inch wide, and up to 250 feet long. Most of these are designed to be used with the hot glue of an automatic edge-bander. You can also cut thin strips of plastic laminate. With the exception of the plastic laminate, most of these materials cannot be successfully glued with contact cement. If you want to use plastic, you need to use edging that comes with a heat-activated or pressure-sensitive adhesive already applied.

Keep in mind that this is a thin material, and while it will look nice in the beginning, it is not very durable. Plastic laminate will hold up better, but it is also susceptible to chipping if a hard object hits the edge. With either material there can be no voids in the glue or the material will peel up at the edges.

Edging Before Assembly

The first choice to make is whether to apply the edges before or after you assemble the cabinets. The advantage of doing it before assembly is that you will be working on relatively small, manageable pieces. If you can trim the edges exactly flush to the face of the board, and all of your parts are square and properly sized, the edges will look good when the boxes go together. If the edges aren't trimmed cleanly, and the cabinet parts aren't dead flush at the front edges, it won't look so good.

If any joint other than a butt joint is used, the edging will need to be applied after the boxes are put together. If you are using rabbets on the box sides for example, the edging will be damaged if it is applied before the joints are cut. If you try to apply the edging after the joints are cut, but before the boxes are assembled, you will have to carefully trim the edging at the corners of the joints.

Depending on how you put the boxes together, you should be able to make slight adjustments during assembly to keep the front edges lined up. This is another of the reasons not to use dowels. If your cabinet parts are off a little, you can't move the dowel. If you are using biscuits or butt joints with fasteners, you can.

I put the edging on with the part standing up right or lying flat on the bench. You can put the part on edge in a vise, or in a wood hand-screw clamped to the surface of the bench, if you find it too awkward to work with it sideways. I think this takes too long, and with large parts like base cabinet sides, it puts the part too high. Don't worry, in the

typical project, you will have enough edges to get plenty of practice **(Figure 171).**

Up until a few years ago, I would have used the banding with hot-melt adhesive applied to its back. There is a small heating iron available specifically for the purpose, but I have found that a household iron works just as well. It takes a bit of practice to get the right combination of heat, pressure, and speed to get the edging completely adhered without melting or distorting it. This product is still available, but edging with a pressure-sensitive adhesive will hold more reliably, and be much quicker to apply.

There is a hand-held device that holds a roll of material and heats the adhesive with a hot-air gun. There is also a stationary machine that functions the same way. Either of these will speed the process of sticking the edging down. The edges must still be trimmed, however, so the benefit of using these is slight.

If you are using the hot-melt edging, cut pieces from the roll a few inches longer than you need, and hold one end so that it is ½ inch off the end of the part, and overlaps the sides evenly. Press the iron down on the edging until you feel it slip as the adhesive turns to a liquid. Once this starts, continue down the edge with the iron until the entire piece is attached. A slight amount of glue should bubble out of the edges. Immediately run the shaft of a screwdriver or a block of hardwood with a radiused edge along the surface of the banding. The idea is to press it into place as the adhesive cools.

Using the pressure-sensitive adhesive takes a lot less finesse, and you don't run the risk of melting the material, or burning yourself with a hot iron. Cut the strip of edging a little long, and peel off the backing. Press it in place with your fingers as you move along the part, using one hand to press, and the other to pull the material ahead, keep-

> Pressure-sensitive adhesive needs less finesse than hot-melt, and you don't risk burning yourself.

Figure 172. Trimming edges—*Use a utility knife to trim edge-banding. Hold the knife flat with one hand, pull it with the other.*

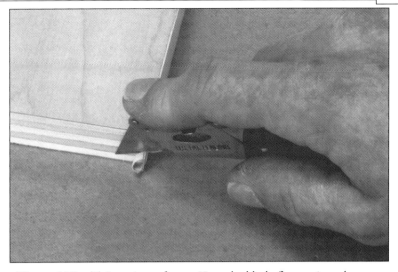

Figure 173. Trimming edges—*Keep the blade flat against the substrate to get a clean cut on the end.*

ing it hanging over both edges. Make sure that it hangs over on both sides. You will be trimming the excess off so it doesn't have to be exactly placed, but be careful that both edges are covered. Once the entire edge is stuck down, run the hardwood block or a hard roller down the edge to press it down permanently.

There are special trimmers on the market for trimming the edging, but I have found that a common utility knife works just as well. With the part flat on the bench, start the cut by laying the point on the flat surface with the rest of the blade back from the edge. Swing the rest of the knife in to the material and along the edge, keeping the blade flat on the part. If you need to, you can use a finger or thumb from your other hand to hold the edge down flat. Trim the ends last, keeping the blade flat to the edge around the corner **(Figure 172, 173).**

The edges hanging over are rather fragile, and you can damage them or pull them off if they aren't handled carefully before trimming. For this reason, I trim each edge immediately after it is applied. If the trimming from the knife is a little ragged, use a laminate file held flat to the face of the part to smooth it. If these are parts of cabinets

that are to be assembled, the edge should be square and sharp so that it doesn't show as a gap in the assembled cabinet. If it is a shelf, or a door, use the file to lightly bevel, or ease, the sharp edge.

Edging After Assembly

You can wait to apply the edges after the cabinet box is put together. The one advantage of this is that you can sand the edges perfectly flush at the joints **(Figure 174)**. The disad-

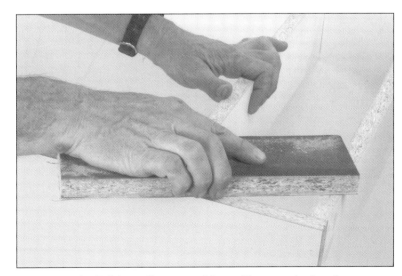

Figure 174. Edging after assembly — *If you apply the edge-banding after assembly, you can sand the box edges perfectly flat at the joints. But you will need to trim the edge ends on intermediate parts.*

Figure 175, 176. Trimming assembled cabinet—*With the edging applied to the long edges, the cross pieces are applied, and allowed to hang over the adjacent edges before being trimmed to fit.*

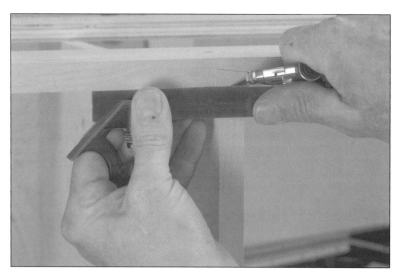

Figure 177. Trimming assembled cabinet—*To get a clean edge, cut through both pieces at the same time. Trim the long edges close to the corner, and then lay a straight edge across the joint.*

Voila *— A perfectly trimmed joint.*

vantage to doing this is that the ends of pieces that run in between other pieces will need to be trimmed. This is done by double-cutting both the edge of one piece and the end of its neighbor at the same time. After trimming the edges up to the joint, place a straightedge along the line to be cut, and with the point of the utility knife make the cut with several light passes (**Figure 175, 176, 177**).

Once you are done cutting, you will need to use the point of the knife to dig the small piece of edge out from under the

end. If you try to cut the pieces exactly to length before applying them, they will stretch under pressure and won't fit. You can cut one edge square and butt it against the edge of the adjoining piece. When you press it in place, work it toward the edge that it butts against.

If you are using PVC edges with plastic laminate, work so that the PVC is applied after the laminate. If you go the other way, the bearing on the trimming bit will likely damage the PVC as you trim the laminate.

Wood veneer is also available in rolls with adhesive applied to the back. The same two types of glue are available, and the methods for applying and trimming are nearly the same. Veneer won't stretch or melt as the PVC will, but be careful when trimming that the knife doesn't follow the grain downhill and split into the face of the veneer. A laminate trimmer with a flush-trimming bit can be used, but it is likely to shatter along the grain and ruin the edge. After the veneer has been trimmed, use a sanding block to bring the edge perfectly flush.

The veneer will also be finger-joined every eight to ten feet in length, and you don't want to see any finger joints on a finished surface. You will waste some material cutting around the finger joints, but you can minimize the waste by saving the cut-offs and using them where you need a short piece of material, as on the edge of a drawer front.

Plastic Laminate

Plastic laminate used for edging is applied with an automatic edge-bander in commercial shops, but it can successfully be applied in the small shop using contact cement. The material must be cut in strips $\frac{1}{16}$ inch to $\frac{1}{8}$ inch wider than the material to be edged. Avoid the temptation to cut these strips with the table saw. They are too thin and too narrow to feed through the saw safely.

A laminate slitter is used to cut the strips to be used for edging. The laminate is guided by an adjustable fence, and cut by the sharp edges of the two tapered wheels. When the slitter is adjusted correctly for the thickness of material, it quickly cuts strips without waste or danger of damaging the material or the cabinetmaker. The slitter also works well for cutting strips of veneer **(Figure 178).**

Gluing Laminate Edging

When applying edges, it is best to apply the contact cement to several parts at once. Stack the cabinet parts so that the edges to be banded are flush, and place a group of strips on a piece of cardboard to keep the

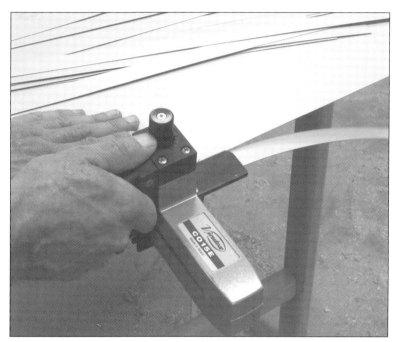

Figure 178. Using the slitter—After adjusting the fence to the appropriate width, the slitter is pushed or pulled to cut the strips.

Figure 179. Gluing strips—With cardboard to protect the bench, roll the adhesive on several pieces of edge-banding at once.

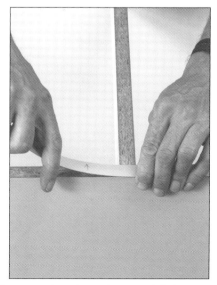

Figure 180, 181. Applying strips—The proper hand grip lets you feel the overhang on both edges as you apply the strip.

Figure 182. Rolling edges—*Laminate held by contact cement needs to be rolled firmly to ensure a permanent bond.*

Figure 183. Trimming edges—*A solid carbide single flute trim bit cuts fast, but can damage an adjacent finished surface.*

Figure 184. Trimming edges—*A trim bit with a bearing guide won't damage a finished surface, but be careful to keep the bearing free of adhesive.*

hold it in your left hand. It should fit at the first knuckle of your thumb on one side, your middle finger on the other side, and your index finger on the end. Gripped like this, you can place the tips of your fingers on the faces of the board. This will keep everything lined up so that the strip of laminate overhangs in every direction. With your other hand, grab the laminate about a foot away in a similar manner, holding it between the first knuckle of your thumb and index finger. Bring the edge in your left hand into contact with the glued surface of the board, and slide both hands along the edge, sticking the laminate down as you go **(Figure 180 & 181)**.

Once the entire edge has made contact, run your thumb along the full length. The laminate should be in position at this point. You now need to apply firm pressure to really stick it down. The preferred tool for this is a steel roller, which will apply more pressure than a rubber "J" roller. If you don't have a steel roller, or are too cheap to go buy one, the rounded edge of a hardwood block will do. Press down as hard as you can. Be careful when you reach the end. If you apply pressure past the end, you can break the laminate **(Figure 182)**.

Trimming Laminate Edging

Don't trim any of the pieces until you have the entire stack of parts edged. With the exposed glue surfaces, you will get chips of plastic stuck to the glue, which will prevent the edge from sticking. Stack the parts on top of a scrap of wood so that the edge of the laminate strip is not in contact with the bench. Place every other piece in the stack with the edges in opposite directions.

Trim the edges and ends with a laminate trimmer and a flush-trimming bit. If the adjacent surface is raw wood, or Melamine, use a solid carbide bit with one cutting edge, and an integral guide. This bullet bit

surface of the bench clean. Using a 3-inch wide disposable roller, coat the raw edges of the cabinet parts, then the back of the laminate strips. Wait a few minutes and give the plywood edges a second coat of contact cement **(Figure 179)**.

Once the contact cement is dry to the touch, take the top piece to be edged off the stack, and let the edge hang over the edge of your bench. Pick up one piece of laminate and

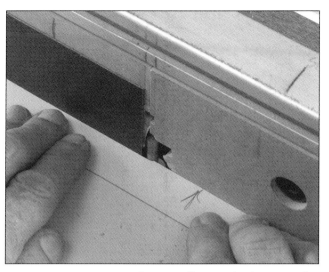

Figure 185. Jointing edges—*Offsetting the fences on the router table makes it function as a jointer, cutting a clean straight edge.*

Figure 186. Fitting edge of cross piece—*A slight bubble in the edge will pull down and leave the joints tight. Too much of a bubble, and the laminate will break.*

will cut much faster than a 2- or 3-flute cutter with a bearing, but can leave burn marks on plastic laminate or finished wood **(Figure 183 & 184)**

Trim with the pieces flat on the bench. This is easier than trying to balance the edge of the laminate trimmer on the edge of the board. Hold the trimmer firmly in, keeping the bearing of the bit lightly in contact with the face of the material. After trimming, use a laminate file held flat to finish the edge. If these are parts to be assembled, you want the edge to be square and sharp. If it is a shelf or a door, you want it to be beveled slightly.

The reason for pre-applying the edges is to save time. It is much faster to apply the glue to a stack of parts than it is to glue and apply one or two edges at a time to a completely assembled box. You also save making a mess with contact cement on the assembled cabinets and filling the cabinet interior with chips from trimming the plastic edges. Any variation from flush in the assembled cabinets, however, will show as a bump in the edges, and if you want the laminate to be perfect, you might want to apply the edges after the box is put together.

Trimming after Assembly

After the box has been assembled, use a sanding block to bring the raw edges flush. Eighty or 100-grit sandpaper attached to a scrap of particleboard works well. I usually take a belt from a portable belt-sander and cut it into two pieces, and attach it to a piece of scrap with contact cement. This will last longer than using a block with sandpaper **(Figure 174, page 133)**.

The strips that run vertically on the cabinet face run from top to bottom, and the strips that are horizontal run in between them. The placement should be the same as if they were stiles and rails on a face frame. The vertical strips should be joined on one edge. Set up the router table with a straight-cutting bit. The outfeed fence should be offset from the infeed fence by $\frac{1}{32}$ inch to $\frac{1}{16}$ inch. If the fences aren't independently adjustable, you can use a piece of laminate to shim the outfeed fence, or apply a strip of laminate to the bottom edge of the outfeed fence. Align the outfeed fence to the cutting edge of the router bit at top dead center **(Figure 185)**.

What you have created with this is essentially a small jointer. Feed the edges of the strips

Figure 187. Underscribe trimmer—This special trim router base cuts the end flush with the adjacent edge.

into the cutter, holding them firmly against the infeed fence until enough material is past the cutter to safely push against the outfeed fence. This will produce a very smooth edge for the ends of the adjacent pieces to butt against. To avoid confusion, draw an arrow in pencil pointing to the jointed edge.

Apply glue to the raw edges on the face of the cabinet, and to the back of the laminate strips. Give the raw edge two coats of adhesive. The jointed edge of the vertical strip should be as close to the edge of the substrate as possible. When the vertical edges are in place, the ends of the horizontal pieces are prepared. I place a piece of scrap on the table of the miter saw, and slowly cut the end of the laminate. After cutting, the sanding block is used to remove any burr that remains.

The first end is easy, it gets pushed against the edge as the laminate is stuck. The second end needs to be cut to exactly the right length, and there are two methods to accomplish this. To trim the length beforehand, butt the squared end against the edge of the adjacent piece, and let the other end overlap the remaining edge. Mark a pencil line, and cut the length on the miter saw, backing up the cut with a scrap of wood as before.

Clean up the freshly cut end with the sanding block and test the fit. If it is too short, throw it away and start over, but if it is too long, you can use a laminate file or a sanding block to bring it down to size. A one or two degree bevel may be filed to help ease the end in place.

When you are happy with the fit, apply the contact cement, and put the laminate strip in place. If it is just a whisker long, you can get a nice fit by placing one end, then about half the length. Stick the remaining end down, which will leave a portion of the material bubbled up from the surface. Carefully stick this down, and if you don't break the laminate, the ends will push tightly against the edges **(Figure 186)**.

The alternative method is to place the first end as outlined above, and use a special base in the laminate trimmer to cut the second end flush with the remaining edge. The under-scribe base uses a ⅛-inch diameter cutter, and a special fence that guides the cutter against the edge. This base is expensive if purchased alone, but it is included in many laminate trimmer kits **(Figure 187)**.

Once it is set up, contact cement is applied to all but the last few inches of the laminate, and the piece is adhered, starting from the already-prepared square end. The under-scribe router is then run along the edge, cutting the end off at the right length. The router bit usually leaves a small burr, which should be removed with the file or sanding block. Once the piece is the correct length, make sure the area to be glued is free of chips, and apply the contact cement with a brush. I prop a drywall screw in between the two pieces to keep them separated while the cement dries. When it's ready, put the end in place first, and roll the entire surface. Once you get the hang of using the under-scribe router, you can prepare and glue all of the horizontal strips for a cabinet at one time.

Figure 188. Solid wood edging— *Mill the edge material to about ⅟₁₆ inch wider than the thickness of the plywood. This makes it easy to apply, and trim later.*

Figure 189. Router edge trimmer— *The jig is made from a ⅜ inch thick piece of Lexan, with a ⅛ inch deep, 1 ⅜ inch wide dado.*

Figure 190. Set the trim— *Set the 1¼ inch diameter mortising bit flush or slightly above the base, then set the fence to the width of the edge.*

Solid Wood Edging

Solid wood edging is best made slightly wider than the thickness of the piece to be banded. For 3/4-inch thick plywood, make it 13/16 inch wide. Neither the substrate nor the edge material will be perfectly straight or flat, and a plywood substrate will vary in thickness. The extra width will make the edge easier to attach, but will need to be trimmed flush to the surface after the glue has dried. I also leave the edge material a few inches longer than needed. It is faster to trim these after they are on than it is to be fussy while attaching them **(Figure 189)**.

The edging can be ¼ inch or ½ inch thick, but these pieces are thin enough that it is difficult to keep them flat. A ¾-inch thick piece will be stiffer, and easier to glue in place. Contact cement will eventually fail if used with solid edging, so regular wood glue should be used. No joint is needed, but you might want to use a tongue-and-groove joint or biscuits to keep things aligned. It doesn't take a lot of clamp pressure to hold the edges in place, but if you are holding them on with glue only, the clamps need to be close together.

1¼ inch or 1½ inch brads can be used to hold the edge to the substrate, but the holes will need to be filled. In frameless cabinets with overlay doors, the nail holes on the cabinet faces will be covered by doors or drawer fronts most of the time. The holes on doors and drawer fronts will also be out of sight most of the time. Normally you wouldn't want to nail in a finished surface, but in this case, you can get away with it.

If you are only clamping and not using any fasteners, place a couple of strips of wood on the bench to support the substrate. I apply glue to the edge of the substrate only, and I try to get just enough glue on the part to hold without the glue squeezing out. There is a glue bottle available with a plastic roller on top that spreads the glue lightly and evenly. After the glue is applied, the edge is clamped on, and the time is marked on the piece. When I run out of clamps, I can then take the oldest piece out of the clamps and continue working. The clamps can be removed in an hour if the shop is warm, but the glue will take twenty-four hours to completely cure.

Figure 191. Router edge trimmer— *Instead of balancing a router on the edge, use this jig to trim the solid edge material.*

Figure 193. Using trimmer—*All but a tiny sliver of edge material is cut away.*

Figure 194. Sanding block for edges—*The rabbet in this sanding block is the exact thickness of the edging, preventing damage to the face material.*

Figure 195. Sanding block—*Make the block by gluing sandpaper to a scrap piece of edge material. Attach a larger piece of scrap to serve as a fence.*

Trimming Wood Edging

After the glue is completely dry, the overhanging ends and edges must be trimmed flush with the face of the substrate. There are several ways to do this, depending on available tools and to some extent the material on the face of the substrate. If the face of the substrate is veneer, you can sand the edges down with a belt sander or random-orbit sander. This is not recommended as it will take a lot of time, create a lot of dust, and the chance of sanding through the veneer is great.

A router with a bearing-guided flush-trimming bit will work, but it too is a risky operation. With the work held on edge in a vise, the router must be balanced on a narrow edge. There is also a good chance that some pieces will split as they are cut with the router bit.

The shop-made jig, shown in **Figure 190 and 191,** allows the edges to be trimmed with the work flat on the bench, and using the bottom edges of a mortising bit rather than the sides of a flush-trimming bit greatly reduces the chances of the edge splitting or breaking. The jig is simply a rectangular sub-base for the router, with a slot in line with the cutter, and a fence attached. The one shown here is made of ⅜-inch thick Lexan, but it could also be made from ½-inch thick Baltic birch plywood.

After cutting the sub-base to size, the holes for attaching the router and the clearance hole for the bit are made using the standard router base as a guide. The ⅛-inch dado along the length lets most of the base lie flat on the face of the work, letting the oversized edge stick up. The slots in the base make the fence adjustable. Use a 1 inch or 1¼-inch diameter mortising bit, and set the depth of cut so that the end of the bit is flush with, or just barely above, the bottom of the base. Set the fence so that the edge of the cutter is even with, or barely inside, the solid wood edge **(Figure 191).**

In use, pressure is applied on the forward part of the fence at the beginning of the cut, and then shifted to the back of the fence at the end. The small amount of material left is cleaned up in different ways, depending on the face material **(Figure 193).**

Figure 196. Finishing with scraper—*A cabinet scraper removes the last bit of edge material without damaging the adjoining plastic.*

Figure 197. Trimming ends—*The stop block on the cross-cut sled is set to the edge of the saw kerf, and is used to trim the end of the edge flush with the shelf or panel.*

Finishing Edging

If the face is veneer, a block plane, a sharp card scraper, or some light sanding will complete the work. If the wood is against Melamine or plastic laminate, you must be very careful not to damage the surface while working on the edge. A block plane is recommended in some texts for this, but I have never been able to successfully plane the wood edge down without shaving the surface of the laminate at some point.

Make a sanding block with a rabbet in the bottom where the width of the rabbet is equal to the thickness of the edge. Glue a piece of sandpaper or a portion of a self-adhesive sanding disk in the rabbet. The edge of the rabbet will limit the sanding to the edge of the solid wood, preventing damage to the surface of the substrate (**Figure 194, 195, 196).**

The ends can be trimmed on the table saw using a cross-cut sled. A stop block added to the base of the sled (**Figure 197**) in line with the edge of the saw blade will locate the part so that the wood edge is trimmed exactly flush with the end of the substrate.

Drawers and Doors

If you are edging doors or drawer fronts instead of panels and shelves, the edging must turn the corner. With veneer, PVC, or plastic laminate edges, two opposing sides are banded and trimmed, and the sanding block is then used to bring the ends of the edging flush with the ends of the substrate. If the entire door is covered with plastic laminate, the vertical edges should be applied first, then the short edges, and finally the face.

If the face of the door is Melamine or plastic laminate, and the edges PVC, the face should be laminated and then the edging applied. With veneer or PVC edges, the sequence is not as important since the edges are not as visible. If the edge is a thicker piece of solid wood, this same method can be used, but mitering the corners will look better.

Pre-cut the miters to the right length, and carefully attach the solid wood edges on two opposing sides. Trim them flush before fitting and attaching the perpendicular pair of edges. To do this successfully, the substrate must be perfectly square, and the miters cut both at a true 45-degree angle and the right length.

12. DRAWERS AND DRAWER SLIDES

Figure 198. Assembling drawer boxes—*Corner clamps will hold butt-joined drawer boxes square during assembly.*

The hardest-working part of any project is the typical drawer. In any kitchen, there is likely to be a drawer that is opened and closed several times for each meal. This can accumulate to thousands of openings over the working life of the cabinets. Even though the drawers and the mechanisms that make them work aren't out in the open, they need to be carefully made and installed properly.

Drawers boxes are typically made with a separate face that is attached to the drawer box at the completion of the cabinets. While this adds some extra material for the drawer front, it simplifies and speeds the entire job. The fronts can be sanded and finished while they are still flat pieces, and the drawer boxes can be finished with a clear finish and installed without fear of damaging the fronts.

Typically, drawers are made from ½-inch thick material, with a ¼-inch thick plywood bottom. A light-colored wood, usually maple or birch, is used, either in solid or plywood form. Drawer boxes are not stained, they are finished with a clear coating. This gives a clean look to the drawers, and there is no good reason to have the drawer boxes match the exterior finish of the cabinets.

The top drawer in a typical kitchen is 4 inches high. Depth can range from 20 inches to 22 inches, depending on the depth of the cabinet. I prefer using 20-inch boxes even when there is space within the cabinet for deeper drawers. This is a good usable depth. Any advantage of having extra space is outweighed by the tendency of things to get lost at the back of the drawer. The height of other drawers depends on the height of the opening, and these heights are given in the cabinet type detail drawings **(Figure 100, page 90, and Figure 133, page 110).**

In lower-end work, Melamine-clad particleboard is used for drawer boxes. If this is acceptable to you, and if the interior of your cabinets is Melamine, you can save money on materials, and with the Melamine surface you don't have to finish the drawer boxes. Some people prefer the sanitary look. You can make a serviceable drawer from this material, but not a first-class drawer.

Figure 199. Typical Drawer Construction

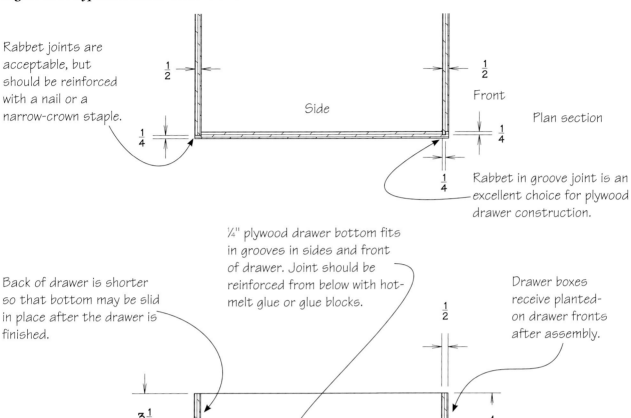

Rabbet joints are acceptable, but should be reinforced with a nail or a narrow-crown staple.

Side

Front

Plan section

Rabbet in groove joint is an excellent choice for plywood drawer construction.

¼" plywood drawer bottom fits in grooves in sides and front of drawer. Joint should be reinforced from below with hot-melt glue or glue blocks.

Back of drawer is shorter so that bottom may be slid in place after the drawer is finished.

Drawer boxes receive planted-on drawer fronts after assembly.

20" in typical 24" deep cabinet

Side section

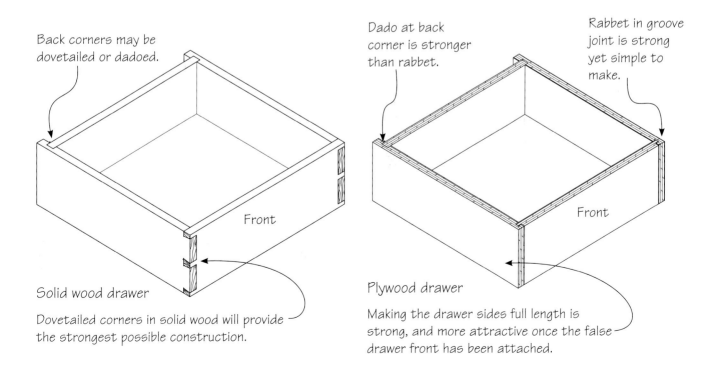

Back corners may be dovetailed or dadoed.

Dado at back corner is stronger than rabbet.

Rabbet in groove joint is strong yet simple to make.

Front

Front

Solid wood drawer

Dovetailed corners in solid wood will provide the strongest possible construction.

Plywood drawer

Making the drawer sides full length is strong, and more attractive once the false drawer front has been attached.

Figure 200. Jig for assembling drawer boxes—*This shop-made jig helps assemble drawer boxes. Be certain that the stops are square when making the jig.*

Building Drawers

I tend to think of drawer quality in terms of the number of years the drawer box may be expected to last. A solid maple dovetailed drawer box could easily last 100 years or more. A plywood box with a decent joint at the corners may last 25 or 30 years. A particleboard or MDF drawer, glued and stapled together, might only last 10 years. Your taste and budget will be the deciding factors.

Most of the force working on a drawer is on the front, and on the joint connecting the front of the box to the sides. The front should be between the sides, with any fasteners or joints connecting the two at a right angle to the pulling and pushing force. This also makes for a better appearance when the drawer is open, all you see is the side, not the ends of the fronts and backs. The drawer box needs to be carefully constructed. The front and back must be square to the sides, the sides must be parallel, and if mechanical slides are used, the finished width of the drawer is critical to success.

With ½-inch thick material joined by simple butt joints, there aren't many fasteners that can be used without splitting the box mate-

rial. Modern glues, along with the right fastener, can hold a butt-joined drawer box together for a reasonable lifespan. Eighteen-gauge brads are the least visible. Narrow-crown staples will hold better, but leave a larger hole to be filled. If using plywood, I staple the box together, and fill with wood putty. If using Melamine, I use brads, and fill the nail holes with acrylic caulking, or with Seam-Fill.

Thicker box material can be used, either ⅝ inch or ¾ inch thick, but it doesn't really give any advantage. Thicker material can be screwed or doweled together, choices that won't work with ½-inch material. If Melamine is used, the top edges should be banded, and it is more efficient to apply the edge banding before the box is assembled. Plywood boxes are sometimes left with raw edges. With Baltic birch or apple ply these edges can be sanded and clear-coated. With other plywood there will be more voids and a rougher end-grain surface, so it is better to edge-band them.

Whatever material and method of joining is used, the drawer bottom should fit in grooves in the front and sides of the box. This method has several advantages, the first of which is that the drawer can be assembled and finished without the bottom in place, making finishing, especially spray finishing, much easier. It is also stronger, and can be reinforced with a bead of hot glue, or a wooden fillet. Typical grooves are ³⁄₁₆ inch to ¼ inch deep, and up ¼ inch to ⅜ inch from the bottom of the drawer.

Drawer Assembly

To assemble butt-joined drawer boxes it helps to use either Bessey corner clamps or a shop-built jig (**Figure 200**).

After the parts have been cut to size, the grooves can be made with either a dado set

Figure 201. Installing bottom—*The back of the drawer is shorter than the sides, so that the bottom can be slid in place.*

Figure 202. Sand parts—*Sand the inside of the drawer parts before assembling the drawer.*

in the table saw, or with a straight bit in the router table. The bottoms should be just slightly narrower than the distance between the grooves in the sides, and should extend to the edge of the back. If you are using Baltic birch plywood for the drawer box, keep in mind that it is likely 12mm thick rather than a full ½ inch. This must be accounted for in determining the length of the front and back pieces, or the drawer slides will not operate properly. The thickness of the drawer

bottom material will also be a factor, but because the bottom of the drawer is out of sight, you can get away with an undersized piece of plywood in a ¼-inch wide groove.

With the corners glued and clamped, brads or staples can be carefully shot into the joints. Because the material is so thin, the shortest possible fastener should be used. I use 1-inch long staples or brads in ½-inch thick drawer boxes. The next step depends

Figure 203. Stapling drawer bottom—*Fasten the back of the drawer bottom in place. Narrow crown staples are fast and hold well, but screws may also be used.*

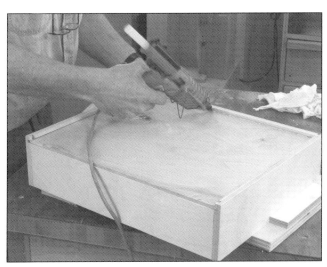

Figure 204. Hot glue on drawer bottom—*After fastening the back edge, a bead of hot glue holds the drawer bottom permanently in place.*

on whether the materials for the drawer are finished before or after assembly. If you are finishing later, set the assembled box aside for the glue to dry, being sure that it doesn't rack out of square while you are moving it. I recommend finishing the drawer parts before assembly, except in dovetailed drawers made of solid wood. In either case, sand the parts on the interior of the drawer completely before assembly **(Figure 202).**

When you're ready to put the bottom in, the drawer box should be upside down on the bench. If you have just fastened it together and the glue isn't dry, keep the corner clamps in place, or set the two front corners in the jigs to keep them square. The bottom should slide into place, if it doesn't slide easily, sand a little off the edges. If the bottom is warped, you may have to push on it to get it seated in the groove in the front of the box **(Figure 201)**. When it is all the way in, fasten the back edge to the bottom of the back. I normally use staples because it is fast, but some people prefer to use screws **(Figure 203).**

The final step is to run a bead of hot-melt glue around the inside perimeter of the drawer bottom **(Figure 204)**. This is admittedly ugly, but it dries quickly and is very strong. If you are making drawers from pre-finished parts, the clamps can be removed in just a few minutes when the hot glue has cooled. If the drawer bottom is thinner than the groove, I push down on the bottom so that some of the hot glue runs into the gap. This keeps the top of the bottom flush with the top of the groove, and looks nice from inside the drawer.

Avoid the temptation to use a thicker drawer bottom, gluing, screwing, or stapling it directly to the bottom of the drawer sides. This puts all of the weight of the contents of the drawer on the fasteners holding the bottom.

Rabbet and Groove Joint

With a simple tongue and groove joint, or rabbet and groove, you can make a drawer that will last several times longer than a butt-joined drawer. The same setup you used to put the groove in the drawer sides and front is used for the drawer bottom. A groove needs to be run across the grain in the ends of the drawer sides. On the table saw this can be made using the miter gauge. Clamp a stop block to the fence ahead of the cutter. This will locate the cut while preventing the piece from becoming trapped between the blade and the fence, which could cause the piece to kick back. On the router table, keep the fence setting the same as it was for making the groove for the bottoms, and use a push block to move the work over the router bit **(Figure 205-210).**

The tongues are made with the same cutter, but the stop block or fence must be placed to form a tongue that is equal in length to the depth of the groove. The height of the router bit or dado set may also need to be adjusted so that the tongue fits in the groove with hand pressure only. The small piece of material that is left beyond the groove is fairly fragile, and can break off if the tongue needs to be force-fit.

Once glue is applied and the tongue inserted in the groove, the joint should be clamped, making sure that the parts are tight, and that the front and the sides are square to each other. If the bottom can be inserted at this time, it will help to hold the other parts square as the glue dries. The procedure for fastening the bottom is identical to that in the first example.

Dovetail Drawer Joint

If you want a premium-quality drawer, then you should use solid wood, and at least the front corners should be dovetailed. I prefer

Rabbet and Groove Drawer Joint

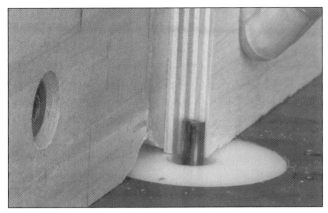

Figure 205. Router table setup—*To set up for the tongue, use a ¼ inch diameter bit and set the outside edge of the bit flush with a piece of the ½ inch plywood drawer-side material.*

Figure 207. Groove the ends—*Use the router table to run a groove across the grain in both ends of the drawer box sides. A push block backs up the cut.*

Figure 209. Milling rabbets—*Make the tongues by running then ends of the sides across the cutter. Use a backing block, and make sure the grooves are facing up.*

Figure 206. Grooves next—*Mill the grooves on all the drawer box sides and fronts. The same set-up makes the grooves for the drawer bottom.*

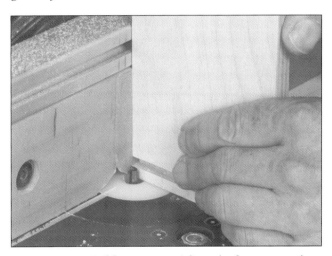

Figure 208. Rabbet setup—*Adjust the fence to cut the matching tongue. Set the height of the bit to the bottom of the groove, and the back edge of the cutter flush with the fence.*

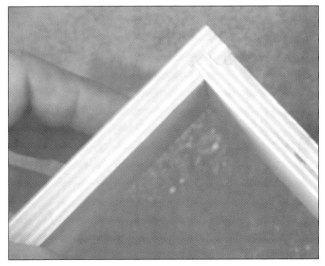

Figure 210. Assembling rabbet and groove—*Check the fit before milling the tongues. Be careful not to force the tongues into the grooves. The narrow strip beyond the groove is easy to break.*

only dovetailing the front, setting the back in a dado across the back end of the drawer sides. The back of the drawer is not subject to the same forces as the front, and the dado makes it easier to accommodate a narrower drawer back. The dovetails should be laid out so that the groove for the drawer bottom is contained within a tail, so that it is not visible from the side of the drawer.

If you want to develop the saw and chisel skills to hand-cut the drawer dovetails, you can, but if you are building a kitchen or other substantial project, you may regret the decision to hand-dovetail the drawers. Once you have gained skill at hand-dovetailing it will take you a half-hour or less per drawer, but while you are acquiring skill it can take several times as long. This can amount to a tremendous amount of time in the midst of the project, and you will have a bunch of nearly completed cabinets gathering dust while you are dovetailing drawers. On the other hand, you will learn how to dovetail.

In a large project, I use a router jig to cut the dovetails for drawers. I prefer the Leigh jig because it is more flexible for arranging the tails on drawers of different widths. Most other jigs have a fixed distance that the tails must be worked to. Other than that, most of the jigs available will produce decent joints in a timely manner. The bottoms of dovetailed drawers are made and fit the same way as any other drawer.

Drawer Slides

Once all of the drawers are assembled and finished, they need to be fit with hardware, and installed in the cabinets. In most cabinetwork, a manufactured slide is used. If you hand-dovetailed all the drawers, and still haven't had enough, you can make all wood slides. This is where I make a distinction between fine furniture and good cabinetry, and use a manufactured slide.

There are three basic types of slides suitable for use: the bottom-mount slide, the full-extension slide, and the hidden slide, which is available in three-quarter and full-extension versions. All are suitable, the choice of which one to use is a matter of balancing budget, function, and the hidden slide's appearance. All have two components, one that fastens to the drawer, and one that fastens to the cabinet. All work well if they are not forced beyond their tolerances by sloppy work on the part of the cabinetmaker. Drawer boxes, and the cabinets that hold them, need to be square, and the sides need to be parallel.

Bottom-Mount Slides

Bottom-mount slides are the least expensive, and function well, but only open to about 80% of their length. A typical 20-inch long slide will extend 16 inches, which provides adequate access to the drawer interior in most circumstances. The slide members move on plastic rollers, and are self-closing. When the drawer is pushed back toward the cabinet, a ramp in the slide is engaged, and the drawer shuts all the way.

The drawer members, which are handed right and left, are placed on an upside down drawer box, and are fastened with screws. A Vix bit will be helpful in locating the screw holes. There are a lot more places to put screws than you need, and in some places, there are slots instead of holes. If the drawers are accurately made, and the slides installed correctly, you shouldn't need to make adjustments. If you're not confident, place screws only in the slotted holes until you have the drawers in the cabinets, then add a few more screws to keep the drawers in place. If you only have screws in the slots, the slides can work loose from the drawer boxes, and slip out of their proper location **(Figure 211, 212).**

Some brands of slides have larger than normal countersinks for the screws, and if you don't use the slide manufacturer's screws, the screws will not catch in the countersinks, and won't hold the slides. The standard size of screw is #6 x ⅝ inch. With some slides, this is too long to screw in from the side of the drawer box. If the screws hit within or below the bottom of the drawer you can use them, but you don't want the tip of a screw poking out into the interior of the drawer. If this happens, use a ½-inch long screw instead.

Generally, the front of the slide is flush with the front of the drawer box, but with some slides, it should be back 1/16 inch to ⅛ inch. If you follow the manufacturer's instructions, and can keep track of which part is the left and which is the right, attaching the slides to the drawer box is quite simple.

Bottom-mount slides are designed for the 32mm system, and if you can locate at least two holes in the side of the cabinet in the right location, you can easily mount the slides in the cabinet. In a dedicated 32mm manufacturing environment the holes are precisely located, and the slides are fastened to the sides of the cabinets before the cabinets are assembled. This is a tremendous savings of labor, and if you can follow this example, you too will save a great deal of time **(Figure 211, 212)**.

You don't need a multiple-spindle boring machine or CNC router to accomplish this. Make a full-size layout of a typical cabinet side, and build a jig like the one shown in **Figure 213.** You can drill the holes for a ⁷/₆₄-inch drill bit through the plywood of the jig, or you can get bushings and drill a 5mm-diameter hole. The larger hole lets you use Euro screws, which will hold much better than the #6 x ⅝-inch drawer slide screws. The smaller holes will begin to wear out as you drill, and you will lose some precision if you drill very many holes.

If you chicken out and wait until the cabinets are assembled to put the slides in, you can still use the jig to locate the screw holes, but instead of working with flat pieces on a bench, you will be working with and moving around completely assembled cabinets. Putting the hardware on while the cabinet side is flat on the bench puts gravity on your side, makes the exact location of the hardware easier to see, and will be faster and more accurate.

Figure 211. Bottom mount slides—*With the drawer box upside-down on the bench, use a Vix bit to drill holes for the mounting screws.*

Figure 212. Bottom mount slides—*Make sure that the screws fit properly in the countersinks in the slides, and that they are short enough to not come through on the inside of the drawer.*

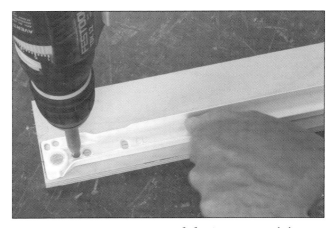

Figure 213. Bottom mount slides jig—*Use a slide to lay out the hole on a jig to locate the holes in the cabinet. Then add a stop to the front of the jig. Reference the location from the bottom of the rail.*

Figure 214. Full extension slides—Once you have determined the location for the cabinet member, a block of scrap, held by the spring clamp, will both position and hold the slide while mounting it.

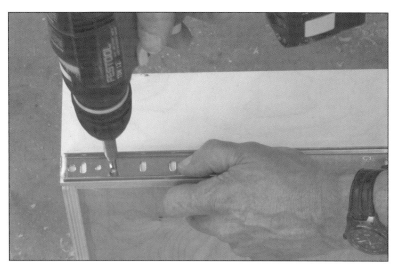

Figure 215. Full extension slides—The drawer member of a full extension slide can mount anywhere within the height of the drawer side. Putting it flush with the bottom is quick and easy.

Most slide manufacturers sell a jig that holds the slide in position the right distance back from the front edge of the cabinet, and parallel to the cabinet bottom. If you use this method, you still need to determine where the slide is vertically on each cabinet side. If you are measuring each one, it's easy to be a little over on all the lefts and a little under on all the rights and end up with crooked drawers. Instead of measuring, cut a piece of scrap material the correct distance from the bottom of the cabinet to the bottom of

the slide, and use that to locate the slides vertically.

If the drawer boxes are too wide for the opening, the drawers will bind when you try to open or close them. If you need to, you can cut a shallow rabbet in one or both sides of the drawer box to give the slide more room. If the boxes are too narrow, the slides usually have one side that captures the roller on the drawer box. This will let the drawer function if you are within $\frac{1}{16}$ inch of your planned width. If you are off by more than that, you can place thin shims behind the slides on the cabinet. Scraps of plastic laminate work will work well, allowing you to move the slides in to the opening in steps of $\frac{1}{32}$ inch or $\frac{1}{16}$ inch.

Full-Extension Slides

Full-extension slides are a step up from bottom-mount slides, but will cost about three times as much. What you gain for your investment are ball bearings instead of plastic rollers, and drawers that extend the full length of the slide. Accuride is the best-known brand, and their model 3832SC is an excellent-quality slide, and pretty much a standard full-extension slide for cabinet applications. Most lower-priced slides are derived from the Accuride design. This is a case where you do get what you pay for, and with a lower price comes lower quality.

Mounting full-extension slides is more flexible than with bottom-mount slides, since they can be located anywhere vertically on the side of the cabinet box (**Figure 214 & 215**). It's easiest to mount them flush with the bottom edge. In any other position, you either need to measure and mark each drawer box, or make a spacer to locate the slides consistently. Both the drawer and the cabinet members should be mounted $\frac{1}{8}$ inch back from the front edge. Accuride full-extension slides use a proprietary screw. It is a #6 x

½-inch with what appears to be a pan head, but a standard pan-head screw extends in to the mechanism of the slide and can interfere with its working.

Locating the cabinet member is equally flexible vertically. As long as you mate with the drawer member in the right place, you can put the slides anywhere vertically. Accuride slides are also engineered to use 32mm system holes. Because the bottoms of the slides are in a straight line, using scrap plywood spacers to locate the slides in the cabinet is more straightforward than with bottom-mount slides. Locate the position of the slides on a full-size layout of the cabinet, and cut a piece of scrap to length. Draw a line ⅛ inch back from the front edge of the cabinet box. Place the scrap inside the cabinet, balance the slide on top, locate the front of the slide with the pencil line, then drill and drive the screws.

With both the bottom-mount and full-extension slides, the outside width of the drawer box should be ½ inch less than the opening in the cabinet. The slides will still work if the gap is ¹⁄₃₂ inch larger, but will not work if the gap is smaller. For this reason, some people, including Accuride, unfortunately, state the width of the drawer box as being 1¹⁄₁₆ inch less than the opening, rather than 1 inch. The problem with this approach is that if you make the drawer box narrower than it should be to begin with, there is no tolerance remaining if it is needed.

Hidden Slides

Hidden drawer slides such as the Blum Tandem offer the easy movement of the ball-bearing slide while remaining completely out of sight when the drawer is open. These are available with many options, full and partial-extension versions, and can be self-closing. These are the most costly slides available, and if you are going to use them, you should

*Figure 216. **Hidden slides** — Hidden drawer slides fit beneath the drawer bottom and are invisible when in place. The drawer back must be notched to accommodate them. Photo courtesy Blum.*

*Figure 217. **Hidden slides**—The manufacturer provides a jig for locating the slide parts on the drawer bottom. Photo courtesy Blum.*

go all the way and use the full-extension, self-closing version (**Figure 216 & 217**).

There are some important technical differences in using hidden slides in the size and location of the drawer sides and bottom. You can't start a project building standard drawer boxes and then decide at the last minute to switch to hidden slides. The hidden slides mount to the bottom of the drawer box, so the bottom needs to be ½ inch up from the bottom of the drawer sides. The slides have a hook at the back that slips into a hole in the back of the drawer. In addition, the manufacturer recommends making the back of the

Figure 218, 219. Slides in face-frame cabinets—*The simplest way to install slides in face-frame cabinets is to place a piece of wood inside the face frame, flush with the inside edge of the face frame.*

drawer box the same height as the sides and front, and cutting two notches at the corners of the back to locate the slides.

Because the slides are mounted inside the bottom of the drawer box, the critical distance is from the inside of the cabinet to the inside of the drawer, not to the outside as with other slides. If the drawer box material is over or under its nominal size, the slides won't operate properly.

The cabinet member of the hidden slides fastens to the inside of the cabinet with screws, in the same manner as other slides. On the bottom of the drawer, at the front, two plastic locking devices are attached with screws. These can be difficult to attach because the screws are tiny, and must be precisely located. Jigs are available from the slide manufacturers to locate the locking devices, and the holes in the back of the drawer boxes.

Once all the hardware is installed, the drawer box is placed on top of the slides and pushed back until the hooks are in their holes. Next the front of the drawer box is pushed down, snapping into the locking devices. To remove the drawers, a lever on each side of the locking device is squeezed, and the drawer box may be lifted up and out.

Slides with Face Frames

To use any of these drawer slide mechanisms in a face-frame cabinet, you need to provide a way to locate the cabinet member of the slide flush with the opening in the face frame. Most slide manufacturers make a bracket that slides in to the back of the slide and screws to the back of the cabinet. The front of the slide is fastened to the inside of the face frame. While this sounds like a reasonable solution, it is quite difficult to get the brackets located in the exact position for the slide to operate properly.

A better method is to add a strip of wood the correct thickness between the slide and the side of the cabinet, so that the slide can be mounted as if it was in a frameless cabinet. This will automatically keep the slide parallel to the drawer box. It will also let you use more screws to attach the slides, keeping it from wobbling as the drawer goes in and out **(Figure 218 & 219)**.

Other Slides

There are other types of slides available, but the three types listed are the best options for

Figure 220. Drawer front adjustment fittings—*These press-in fittings allow some adjustment of the drawer front. After the front is adjusted, use a couple of screws to permanently attach the front to the box.*

Figure 221. Washer head screws—*The large heads on these screws provide nearly the same range of adjustment as the plastic inserts.*

the small-shop cabinetmaker. Other types either require a considerable investment in dedicated machinery to be cost effective, or simply don't function very well.

There are metal slide systems, where the sides of the drawer boxes are actually part of the drawer slides. With this system, the drawer bottom and back are the only parts of the drawer box that need to be fabricated. The drawer front is attached with special brackets that allow it to be adjusted. This limits the heights available to a few standard sizes, and the parts and components are expensive. In a production situation, it might make sense, but for a small shop, it isn't worth it.

Center-mount slides, which use a single slide under the drawer, are difficult to line up, and usually wiggle and wobble in use. Full-extension versions of European-style under-mount slides don't work well, and are troublesome to install properly.

Drawer Fronts

With the drawer boxes in place, the finished drawer fronts need to be attached to the drawer boxes. For the finished fronts to

look right, the fronts of the boxes need to be aligned with the front of the cabinet, and in the same plane. You can lay a straightedge across the front of the cabinet, and adjust the slides if needed. There is often a tendency to place the hardware on one side of the cabinet or drawer boxes a little differently than the other side, and this is when you will notice it. If the drawer boxes or cabinets aren't quite square, it often won't be discovered until this point. With overlay drawers, the alignment of the drawer boxes is not as critical as it is with inset drawers, but it is still important. When you put the fronts on, you will be able to adjust them up and down, and left and right, but in and out adjustments usually must be made with the drawer boxes and slides.

The adjustment of the drawer fronts is similar to the adjustment of the doors with European hinges. It is nice to be able to tweak the fit a little, but don't count on using the adjustments to overcome sloppy work.

Plastic fittings can be pressed in bored holes in the back of the drawer fronts. In the center of the fitting is a threaded metal insert that floats within the fitting. The fronts are

Figure 222. Placing the drawer front—*The points of two screws will mark the location of the drawer box on the back of the drawer front.*

Figure 223. Placing the drawer front—*Using shims the thickness of the desired gaps, the drawer front is placed in position.*

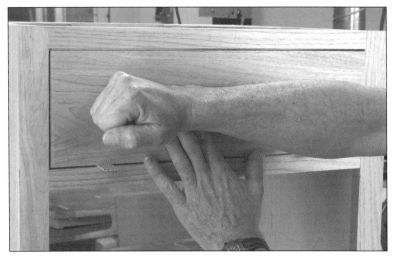

Figure 224. Placing the drawer front—*With the drawer front lined up, tap it so that the protruding screw heads will mark the back.*

attached with a machine screw from inside the drawer box. With the screws snug, but not too tight, the front can be moved in to the right position (**Figure 220**)

These inserts need to be accurately located. You can set up the drill press to locate the holes a consistent distance from the corners of the drawer fronts. If the position of the drawer fronts on the boxes is consistent, you can then make a jig to drill mating holes in the drawer boxes. The inserts are not to be depended upon for permanent attachment of the drawer fronts. Over time, the drawer front can shrink away from the insert, so once the drawer fronts are in position, they should be fastened with at least two more screws.

Washer-head screws (**Figure 221**) will provide nearly the same range of adjustment at considerably less expense. These screws are also faster to use, because you don't need to set up and drill two sets of precisely located holes. If you drill two ¼-inch diameter holes in the front of the drawer box, you can usually run the screws in to the drawer front without further drilling. While these will hold more securely than the inserts, you still should fasten the front to the box with a couple of additional screws.

Positioning the Front

Setting the drawer front on the box initially can cause a lot of frustration. This is the one advantage of setting up the adjusting inserts. If done properly, the holes line up, and the drawer front is close to where it should be. If you are not using the inserts, you need a method to quickly attach the fronts, but still be able to move them around.

I drill two ¼-inch diameter holes in each drawer box, drilling from the inside out, for the washer-head screws. I also drill two smaller-diameter holes, and put in two screws only far enough for the points to protrude through the front of the drawer box (**Figure 222**). With the drawer box in the cabinet, I hold the drawer front in place, and when it is located where I want it, I tap it with my fist (**Figure 223 & 224**). This will leave two dimples on the back of the drawer front, precisely where the screws should be. I then drill pilot holes in the back of the drawer front, and attach it to the drawer box. Once it is attached, I put in two washer-head screws in the large holes.

On an overlay cabinet with a stack of drawers, work from the bottom up. I make a spacer the thickness of the desired gap between drawers, and place it on top of one drawer front to position the next one. If the drawer is above a door, the spacer is used the same way. With the vertical position located by the spacer, I set the side-to-side distance, and tap the drawer front to locate the screw holes.

Most of the time, this method will get the drawer fronts very close to their final positions. You can go ahead and adjust everything until it is perfect, but I prefer to wait until the cabinets are installed. If the cabinet is sitting on a perfectly flat, level surface, and if it is installed in the same condition, these adjustments may be final. More likely than not, something will shift a little during moving or installation, and the conditions of the bench will not quite match those in the field. In this case, the fine-tuning of the drawer fronts and doors will need to be repeated.

Drawer Pulls

Drawer pulls should be located while the cabinets are in the shop, but are often left off until the cabinets are installed. The most common type of pull attaches with two machine screws through the front of the drawer box and the drawer front. Single knobs can also be used. Usually the pull is

centered in both height and width in the top drawer of a typical cabinet. If there is a stack of drawers, the pulls on the lower drawers are located the same distance down from the top of the drawer as in the top drawer. This looks right visually, and makes drilling the holes for the pulls easier.

Because of the number of pulls in a typical project, it makes sense to locate the pulls with the aid of a jig, rather than measuring the location for every one. Commercial jigs are available, in a variety of forms and costs. If you are building cabinets for a living, it might make sense to purchase a self-centering, fully adjustable jig. For a one-time use, a simple jig can be produced that will be just as effective.

The jig should be made to locate the holes vertically, and should reference the centerline between the two holes. In use, the center of the drawer front is marked, the jig held in place, and the holes drilled. A block of scrap wood should be held in place inside the front of the drawer box, to prevent the wood from tearing out when the drill bit exits. The holes should be close to the diameter of the machine screws. They may be a little oversized to provide some adjustment, but if they are too large, it will be difficult to get the handles exactly in position.

If wooden pulls or knobs are used, they can be temporarily attached to a strip of wood so they can be finished as a group.

13. FRAMES AND PANELS

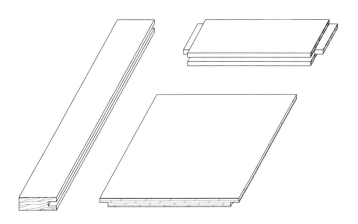

Figure 225. ***Grooves and stub tenons*** *are the simplest way to construct a panel. For a stronger frame joint, make longer tenons with matching mortises in the grooves.*

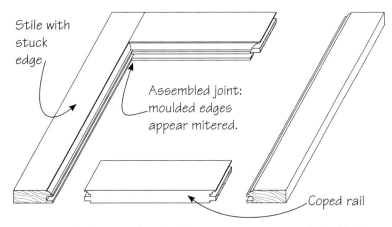

Stile with stuck edge

Assembled joint: moulded edges appear mitered.

Coped rail

Figure 226. ***Cope and stick joints*** *are a common method of holding the frame together. These feature stub tenons that fit in grooves, with shoulders shaped to fit over the moulding on the adjoining stiles.*

Frames and panels, either as doors or as finished ends of cabinets, comprise a large part of many cabinet projects. Developed many years ago as a method of coping with seasonal wood movement, frame and panel construction is an excellent way to showcase the beauty and figure of wood while providing stable construction.

As in other solid wood cabinet components, the key to success is in making good parts from stable material. The stiles, or vertical parts of the frame, and rails, the horizontal parts, are narrow enough that they won't expand and contract enough to cause problems as the seasons and humidity levels change. The panels, however, are large enough to move significantly. Because there is an allowance in the frame for this movement, the panels float, and can expand and contract without causing problems.

If the panels are solid wood, they are trapped within the frame while still being able to move in width. A 12-inch wide panel of oak can lose or gain a quarter of an inch if the environment changes from extremely dry to extremely humid. These swings are common in many areas of the United States, where humid summers can push the moisture content of solid wood to 10% or more. Cold winters, and the methods used to heat houses, can dry wood down to less than 5% moisture content.

The proficient cabinetmaker needs to keep these factors in mind, and accommodate the potential for wood to change its size with changes in humidity. Panels can last for centuries or blow apart in a single year, and it all depends on how they are put together. Seasonal wood movement cannot be stopped, but it can be taken in to account, and cabinets made so that it is never noticed.

Ideally, you should have a moisture meter, so that you know the condition of the wood you are using, and you will do your work in an environment that closely matches that of the interior of the home where the cabinets will be placed.

If you're working in less than ideal conditions, you can still stay out of trouble if you can be patient, and don't expect too much from your materials. Let your raw material acclimate to your shop for a few weeks before you begin construction, and remember that what you make in the middle of a humid summer will shrink, and that you make in the dead of a dry winter will swell.

Frames can be held together with either mortise and tenon joints **(Figure 225)** or with a variation called cope-and-stick **(Figure 226).** Sometimes frames will be mitered, but these are not as strong unless the miters are reinforced with biscuits or splines.

Mortise-and-Tenon

In frames with mortises and tenons, the interior edges of the frame are generally plain, without a decorative profile on those edges. A bevel or other simple detail can be worked around the inner perimeter **(Figure 227)**, but if you do this before assembling the door, you need to be sure to stop before you get to the corner. The door can be assembled without glue, and without the panel, and a router used to run the detail. This will leave a rounded corner. To really look right, these corners need to be squared-up by hand.

A small moulding may be added around the interior as seen in **(Figure 228)**. The corners are mitered, and the moulding can be held in place with a small bead of glue. The best way to hold the moulding while the glue dries is with short, 23-gauge pins. They are small enough to be nearly invisible.

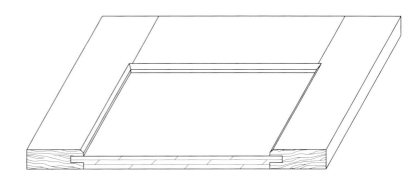

Figure 227. A simple profile can be formed by dry-clamping a mortise and tenon frame without its panel, then running the profile with a handheld router and cleaning up the corners with a chisel.

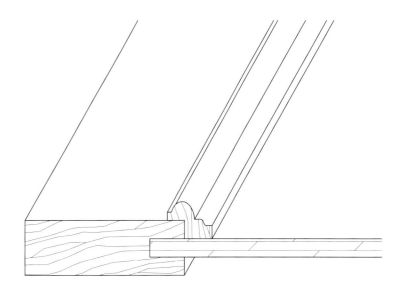

Figure 228. An applied moulding with mitered corners can be used to dress up a plain frame and panel. The moulding can also trap the panel in a rabbet instead of in a groove.

In typical cabinetwork, a ¼-inch wide groove is centered in the rails and stiles for placement of the panels, and the ends of the rails have a tenon worked that also fits in this groove. The width of the groove may be made a little narrower or wider, depending on the material used for the panel. This groove is usually made between ⅜ inch and ½ inch deep. This stub tenon isn't as strong as a longer tenon in a deeper mortise, but it is perfectly adequate for most cabinetwork **(Figure 225).**

Routing Tongue and Groove Joints

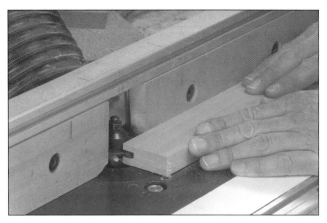

Figure 229.   Groove set up—*A ¼ inch slot cutter in the router table is used to cut the grooves in the stiles and rails.*

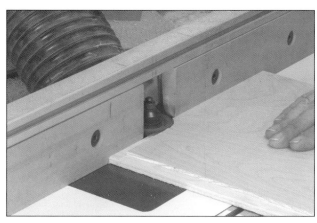

Figure 230.   Rabbet on ½ inch panel—*Without changing the fence setting, a rabbet is formed on the ½ inch thick plywood panel. The bit may need to be raised or lowered slightly for the tongue to fit in the groove.*

Figure 231.   Tongue set-up—*Raise the cutter so its bottom edge is flush with the top of the groove.*

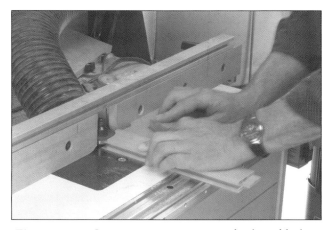

Figure 232.   Cutting tongues —*Use a backing block to cut the tongues on the ends of the rails.*

Figure 233.   Tongue and groove assembly—*The panel is recessed from the front and flush with the back of the stiles and rails.*

Figure 234.   Adjustable groover—*This bit is adjustable to match the actual thickness of nominal ¼ inch plywood.*

You can make a longer tenon, and place a mortise inside the groove, forming the mortise with a hollow-chisel mortiser, or by drilling out the waste with a Forstner bit, and cleaning up the sides and ends with a chisel. I would only do this if I were making an extremely large door, or if I wanted to justify having a mortiser.

The grooves and tenons can be formed in several ways, either on a table saw or with a router **(Figures 229-233)**. With a dado set in the table saw, or with a router table, it is relatively easy to make the groove exactly ¼ inch wide. If nominal ¼-inch thick plywood is used for the panel, however, the groove will be too wide for the panel. In this case, the standard saw blade may be used, set up from one edge of the material, and cutting the groove in two passes. First, set the height of the blade to the desired depth of the groove.

If the plywood were a full ¼ inch thick, then the distance from the fence to the blade would be exactly ¼ inch in ¾-inch thick material. With undersized plywood, the material should be measured with calipers, and its thickness subtracted from ¼ inch. One-half of that difference should be added to the distance between the blade and the fence. The material to be grooved is then run through the saw twice, once with each face against the fence. This centers the groove, and if you do the math and measure right, makes it the right size. If you're not sure of your measurements, start with the fence a little farther away from the blade, and make a test cut. Move the fence closer with each test cut, remembering that if you move the fence in ¹⁄₆₄ inch, and run both faces, the groove will be ¹⁄₃₂ inch wider. If you are going to work by trial and error, work so that your first error doesn't destroy your test piece. Use a procedure that lets you sneak up on a good fit.

Many people will make a big deal about how clever it is to run both faces against the fence to guarantee that the groove is centered. In

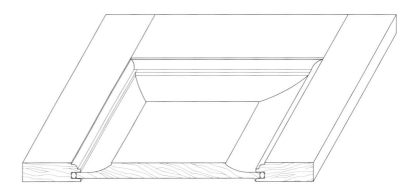

Figure 235. A cope-and-stick frame is straightforward to make and can appear very rich.

reality, whether or not the groove is perfectly centered doesn't make much difference. What you will be guaranteeing with this method is that you will be doing twice as much work, and you'll probably get the groove too wide. It's better to learn how to measure and set up your machinery accurately.

Grooves can also be cut with a router, either with a straight bit, or with a bearing-guided grooving cutter. A router table setup is preferred, although these can be cut with a hand-held router. The big advantage of the router table is ease of setting up, and the gain in speed of not having to clamp each and every piece. Undersized grooves can also be cut with a special adjustable slotting cutter **(Figure 234).**

Cope-and-Stick

With cope-and-stick joints, a decorative profile is cut around the inside of the stiles and rails. The profile is cut in reverse on the ends of the rails, forming the female part of the joint **(Figure 237 & 238)**. This is not as strong as the mortise and tenon, but if it is carefully made, it is more than strong enough for the typical cabinet application.

Figure 236. Stile and rail bits— *In a matched set of stile and rail bits, one cutter mills the profile and the grooves, and the second makes a cope cut and tongue.*

Figure 237. Stile and rail profiles— *The tongue and groove provide strength to the joint.*

Figure 238. Stile and rail profiles together— *When assembled, the coped profiles appear to be mitered.*

Figure 239. Back-up block— *A block of scrap prevents tear-out, and makes the end cuts safely.*

Figure 240. Back-up block— *After the cope cut is made, the rail is removed, and the block pulled back along the fence.*

Cope-and-stick work is done in commercial shops on shapers with power feeders. This provides a considerable advantage in both speed and consistency over the typical small shop use of a router table. Good work can de accomplished with the router table, but it will require more effort to produce quality work.

Router bits are available either as two-cutter matching sets, or as single cutters with a reversible profile cutter. You will save some money buying the single cutter, but will spend a lot more time setting up the cuts so that they match precisely. If you get out of sequence, and have to set them up more than once, you will wish you had the matching set **(Figure 236).**

Which to Cut First?

There are some chicken or the egg arguments regarding which parts to cut first. If it's your first time making coped joints, plan on making some test cuts on scrap before you begin work on the real thing. It can take awhile to be comfortable with the procedure, so plan on spending some time, and wasting some wood. It's also a good thing to have pieces left over from a successful setup to save time the next time, and to calculate the sizes of your panel parts.

I prefer to make the cope cuts (the negative profile cuts on the ends of the rails) first because the pieces tend to chip out as the bit exits the cut. Use a piece of scrap about 6 inches square to push the workpiece past the cutter. The rails are held back to this block, and the block is pushed against the fence on the router table **(Figure 239, 240).** This keeps the part from chipping as the cutters exit. You need to be very careful not to push the rail into the cutters, you only want to hold it to the block. The block must be long enough to always remain in contact with the fence.

A safer method is to add a piece of ¼-inch or ½-inch plywood to the bottom of the block, and a hold-down clamp to secure the rail as the end is moved over the cutter **(Figure 242, 243).** Remember when setting the height of the cutter to account for the thickness of the bottom of the sled. In either of these methods, the backing block won't work if the edge of the rail has a profile in it. If you do run the profiles first, you can make a backing block with the coped profile in one edge, but that will only work for one end of each rail. You will still need a flat back-up block for the opposite ends, and switching back and forth, trying to remember which end gets which backer isn't worth the trouble.

The Cope Cut

I set the cope cutter up so that the smallest diameter edges of the cutter are flush with the face of the fence. The bearing on the cutter should then be flush with the face of the fence **(Figure 244, 245).** No material should be removed from the end of the rails as the cut is made. The height is usually set to leave ¹⁄₁₆ inch before the pattern

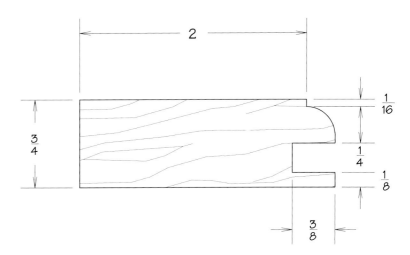

Figure 241. *Typical stile and rail profile dimensions.*

Figure 242. Coping sled—*Adding a baseplate and hold down clamp to the push block is a secure way to make the cope cuts, but remember to account for the thickness of the baseplate.*

Figure 243. Coping sled—*The sled securely holds short rails.*

Figure 244. Cope bit set-up—Set the height by measuring, or by matching a marked workpiece.

Figure 245. Cope bit set-up—Save a successful sample to use for setting up the next time.

Figure 246. Cope bit set-up—Use a straightedge to align the fences with the bearing on the bit.

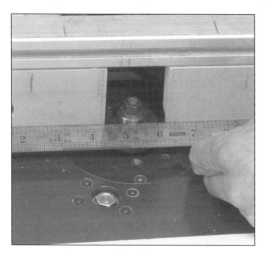

Figure 247. Stick bit fence—Align the bearing with the fences using a straightedge.

Figure 248. Stick bit set-up—After all the cope cuts are made, change cutters, and use a coped piece to match the height of the stick cutter to the coped profile.

begins from the face, leaving ⅛ inch from the bottom to the groove **(Figure 241)**. This can vary from cutter to cutter so be sure to check the one you have. You can hold the cutter up to the end of a piece of scrap the proper thickness to get an idea of where the height should be.

The Stick Cut

I set up the stick cutter (the profile on the inside perimeter of the frame) so that the flat edges above and below the groove are flush with the fence. The bearing on the cutter should be flush with the face of the fence **(Figure 247)**. I'm careful to have straight stock prepared, and I don't want to remove any material from this edge. Some people will set this up so that the fences are offset, with the outfeed side of the fence flush with these edges, and the infeed side ¹⁄₁₆ inch away. This serves to join the entire edge, but doesn't work consistently with hand

feeding the work in a router table, and leaves the parts at odd widths.

The height of the sticking cutter is best set from a piece that has already been coped, rather than trying to hit a specific measurement. If you get your eye in position so that you're looking directly at the cutter, rather than from above, you can hold the previously cut piece flat on the table, and line up the intersecting points **(Figure 248)**.

You will likely need to make a few test cuts to get the height exactly where you want it. Obviously, if your parts aren't straight, or at a consistent thickness, you can't expect them to fit together nicely and make a flat door or panel. Some test cuts may also be needed to determine the exact length of the rails.

Mill all of your stock at the same time to ensure consistency. After ripping the pieces ⅛ inch oversize, run one edge over the joiner, and send the pieces on edge through the planer in a group to obtain clean edges and consistent width **(Figure 249)**. You might want to make the stiles and rails ¹⁄₁₆ inch to ⅛ inch wider than your finished width, so that you can plane the edges to fit after the panels are put together. Some people will leave the stiles long, and trim the entire end of the panel once it is assembled.

The Right Size

While it can be argued that leaving parts a little big so that they can be made to fit is good practice, this is often an excuse for sloppy work. I find it easier to make everything the right size to begin with, and put the parts together carefully. If you make everything too big, you will end up doing a lot more work in the end, and the width of your stiles and rails will probably not be consistent. If you can't cut four pieces of wood to the right length, and put them together square, or can't make a cabinet with the right sized opening, you should get some practice before you tackle a large project.

When you run the profile on the edges, you should use featherboards to hold the pieces against the fence and down to the table **(Figure 250)**. This is for consistency as much as it is for safety. Hand feeding without these aids will result in edges that vary if the wood is not perfectly straight, or if it is not fed evenly. Because the profile will become part of the finished joint, in a visible location, you need to do a good job of milling.

Short rails should be avoided if at all possible, as it is risky to cope the ends of pieces shorter than six inches. If you must, make sure you have a means of holding the work safely. Short rails will also result in narrow panels, which are even more dangerous to machine.

Figure 249. Gang stock through planer—After jointing one edge, send the stile and rail stock through the planer as a group to guarantee consistent width.

Figure 250. Featherboards for sticking—Featherboards hold the stock down on the table and in to the fence. This makes for consistent and safer cuts.

Coping Arched Rails

The top rail may also be arched, along with the top of the panel. To lay these arches out, pick a consistent distance down from the top of the panel for the curve to start and stop, and a consistent distance for the peak of the curve at the middle of the panel. You can then draw the curves by bending a thin strip of wood across these three points **(Figure**

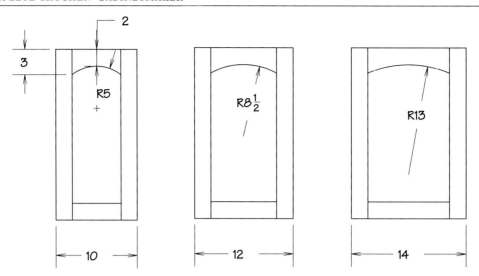

Figure 251. For arch-top panels, the radius will vary as the widths change, but the center of the arches, and the intersections with the stiles, are constant.

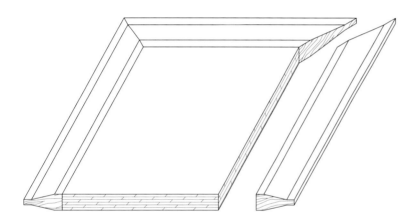

Figure 252. A solid wood edge surrounding a veneered panel is stable and attractive, but labor intensive to make.

251). You really don't need to know the exact radius of any of the curves. If you do your layout work in a CAD program, you can draw the radii as described above, and let the computer calculate the arcs. If laying out manually, draw them with a large compass or trammel points.

Once the curves are drawn, run the cope cuts in the ends before cutting the curves. You can cut them just outside the line with a jigsaw or band saw. Remove the saw marks with a drum sander, a spokeshave, or a sanding block. If you have several rails the same length, with the same arch, you can clean up

one, and use it as a pattern for the others. Use double-sided carpet tape to hold the pattern to the part to be routed. Don't make the entire cut with the router, instead trim the rail with a band saw or jigsaw, staying 1/16 inch to 1/8 inch outside the line. You can then use a bearing-guided flush-trimming bit to make an exact duplicate. To route the stick pattern, you will need to remove the fence on the router table, and run the material against the bearing.

Panels

Panels can be either a veneered panel product or solid wood. Veneered panels are usually flat, although if you like to do a lot of extra work, a solid wood moulding may be glued around the perimeter **(Figure 252).** The grain direction at the top and bottom will be at 90 degrees to the panel, and the corners of the moulding must be mitered. The resulting panel will, however, be more stable than one made entirely from solid wood.

A variety of patterns is available for the cope-and-stick pattern, as well as for solid wood raised panels, as seen in **(Figure 253 to 258).** Flat veneered panels can also be used, instead of solid wood raised panels.

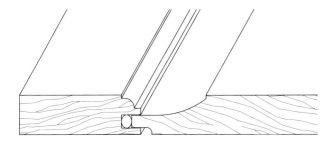

Figure 253. *The tongue* on the panel may be formed by shaping on both sides.

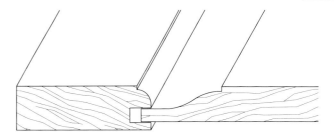

Figure 254. *This panel is moulded* on one side and flat on the other.

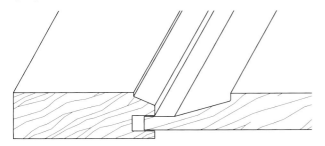

Figure 255. *This panel has a flat bevel* and a straight tongue, with a matching bevel moulded on the frame.

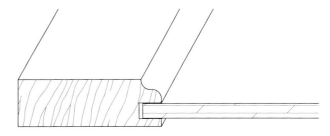

Figure 256. *A panel made of thin plywood* fits the frame grooves without further shaping.

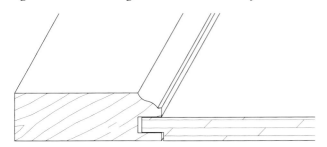

Figure 257. *A thick plywood panel* will need a rabbet to fit the grooves in the frame.

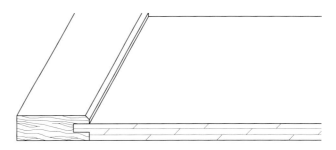

Figure 258. *This rabbeted plywood* panel fits the groove in a thin and minimally shaped frame.

Veneered panels can be made from nominal ¼-inch thick hardwood-veneered plywood, or from thicker plywood with a rabbet cut to fit in the groove **(Figure 256, 257)**. The problem with ¼-inch plywood is that it is thinner than its stated size, and if used in a groove made with cope-and-stick cutters will leave a visible gap. If you are making panels with a simple groove instead of a pattern, you can make a smaller groove, which will almost solve this problem.

One-quarter-inch veneer-core plywood also tends to vary in thickness, so it is difficult to get a good fit. Better results will be obtained if you veneer your own panels on ¼-inch or ⅜-inch thick MDF. The edges of the panels will need to be rabbeted to fit the groove in either case, but the finished panel will have a better appearance.

Solid wood panels should be prepared before milling the stiles and rails. If you need to glue up parts for width, you want to allow at least twenty-four hours for the glue to set before doing any milling. Because these will be one of the most visible parts of your cabinets, you want to use your best material,

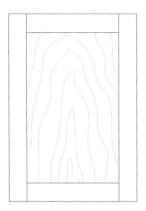 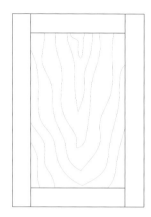

Figure 259. *The arches* *of cathedral figure should point upward, as at left.*

Figure 260. *Panels*—*The triangle marked on the parts for the panels keeps them oriented.*

Figure 261. *Panels*—*Leave the panel in clamps for several hours, and wait 24 hours before machining. Don't use too much glue.*

Figure 262. *Panels*—*If the panel isn't flat across the joint, adjust the clamps and add cauls clamped across the joint to hold it in place.*

and pay attention to the grain and figure of the wood.

If your stock has been dried properly and acclimated to your shop environment, you can use a single, wide piece of wood for the panel. Don't listen to anyone who tells you to rip a wide board into several pieces and glue it back together, especially if they tell you to flip every other piece over. All this will do is create extra work, introduce an opportunity for failure at every glue joint, and make an ugly panel.

More often than not, you will need to glue up for width to make panels. The goal is to make an attractive panel that looks like a single piece of wood. There are a lot of myths about gluing up panels, and most of them are nonsense. Again, if the wood is properly dried, and at equilibrium to the shop environment, how the growth rings are oriented or how wide the pieces are makes no practical difference.

No joint is necessary for gluing boards edge to edge. A well-prepared butt joint will be strong enough. In addition to making extra work, methods used to join boards edge to edge can create more problems than they solve. Dowels and biscuits should be considered as aids to alignment, but must be carefully placed so that they are not exposed when the panels are raised. Tongue-and-groove joints are also sometimes used, again mainly as an aid to keeping the faces of the individual boards flush. These too may look odd when the panel is raised.

I lay out the boards to be glued up on my bench, and when I'm satisfied with the arrangement, I mark a triangle on the face **(Figure 260, 261, 262).** This quickly and positively keeps the boards in order. As I prepare more panel material, I simply add legs to the triangle on either side of the point. If the boards get mixed up, it's easy to tell which one goes where.

I like to joint the boards just before gluing them, and I will run one marked side facing out from the jointer fence, and the next side facing in. If the joiner fence isn't perfectly square to the table, the edges will form complementary angles, and still line up.

Because the panels are so visible, you want to pay attention to the figure of the wood, and the direction of the grain. Arched patterns or cathedrals in the figure will look better if they point up, as in **Figure 259**. If they point down, they don't look right, and you want a consistent, elegant look in the finished elevation. Spend some time laying out the work so that panels next to each other have a similar appearance. This is one of the advantages of veneered panels. You can use veneer sheets that are sequence matched, that is, kept in the order in which they were cut from the log, and have virtually identical panels across the room.

Gluing Up Panels

There are several strategies for gluing-up solid wood panels for appearance. One is to re-saw

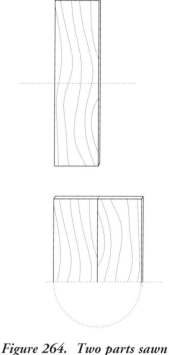

Figure 264. Two parts sawn from the same board and flipped on end make an attractive panel.

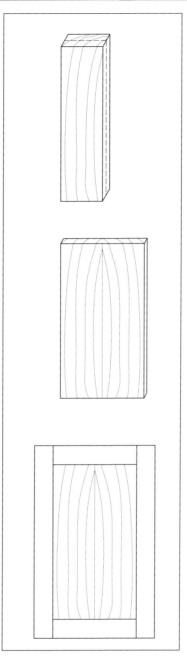

Figure 263. Resawing a thick piece of wood and turning the edges together will yield an attractive book-matched panel.

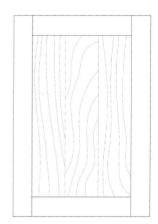

Figure 265. Gluing up panels without matching figure usually results in an ugly composition, typical for manufactured panels.

the panels from a thicker piece as in **Figure 263**. If you slice the board in half, and flip one piece before gluing them together, you will have a book-matched panel, with a nice cathedral pattern down the middle. This is an expensive and time-consuming approach, but worth the effort.

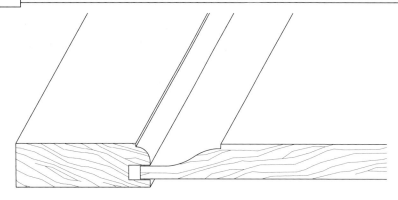

Figure 266. The solid panel *for a ¾ inch thick door should be ⅝ inch thick, so its face ends up in the same plane as the face of the frame.*

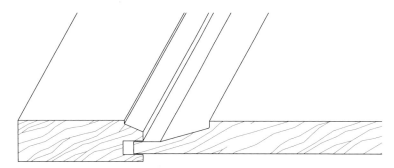

Figure 267. Making the panel thinner *than the door allows you to glue it up from 3/4-inch material, then level it in the thickness planer.*

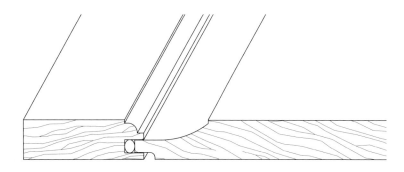

Figure 268. Some panel-raising cutters *form the tongue with a back cut, so full-thickness material may be used.*

If you can take both parts of your panel from the same board, your chances of getting a panel that looks like a single piece of wood are much better. Cut two pieces from a length of material, and flip and slide them around until the grain matches (**Figure 264**). If you just glue panels from random narrow material, the panels will look like **Figure 265.**

Traditionally, the solid panel for a ¾-inch thick door would be ⅝ inch thick, as seen in **Figure 266 & 267**. The face of the panel should be in the same plane as the face of the stiles and rails. The advantage of the thinner panel is that you can usually glue up two pieces of ¾-inch thick wood, and run the panel through a thickness planer to clean up the glue joint. The disadvantage is that the thickness of the tongue on the panel must be achieved on the last pass over the panel-raising cutter. The panel can also receive a back cut (**Figure 268**) so that material a full ¾ inch in thickness may be used. Some panel-raising cutters have a built in relief cutter that makes this cut, and sizes the tongue to the correct thickness.

Raising the panel

While it is possible to make beveled raised panels on the table saw, I don't recommend it. If you do this, you need to install a higher fence to support the board as you pass it on edge with the blade angled to about 15 degrees. If the panels are perfectly flat, and you feed consistently, you can make a decent panel, but any variation will result in saw marks or burns that are difficult to sand out. In either case, it will take a great deal of sanding to make the saw cuts smooth.

A router mounted in a table can mimic what is done in a commercial shop with a shaper. You should be able to achieve cuts that require little or no sanding. Where the panel is raised at the top and bottom will be mostly end grain, and it's difficult to get a good surface if a poor router cut makes it necessary to do a lot of sanding.

To allow the panels to expand and contract as the seasons change, the tongue should not extend all of the way in to the groove. Generally speaking, you want to go about halfway. If you are building in the humid summertime, your panel will likely be as wide

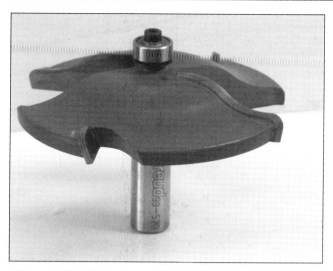

Figure 269. Raised panel bit—*This large router bit will cut the profile for the panel. Use the slowest possible speed on a table-mounted router.*

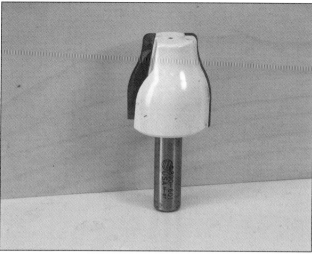

Figure 270. Vertical raised panel bit—*This bit raises panels by running them on edge. There is less strain on the router, but a tall fence extension should be used.*

as it ever will be, so the panels should be cut a bit wider. In dry areas, or at dry times of year, you would make them a bit narrower.

In theory, the tops and bottoms of the panels can extend further into the grooves, as the panel won't change in length, only in width. In practice, make them the same all the way around the panel so that you have a consistent reveal.

I wouldn't attempt to raise panels on a router table without a variable-speed router with a ½-inch diameter shank. Panel-raising cutters with ¼-inch shanks are made, but the mass of the cutter requires a large shank, and a slow speed. A 2HP router will work, but a 3HP machine will perform without straining. Set the router at its slowest available speed, which is usually around 12,000 RPM.

Plan on making at least three passes on the router table, with the last pass removing only about ¹⁄₁₆ inch of material or less. How you set up the router table will depend on whether or not your cutter has a built-in back-cutter or not. If it does, you need to set it up so that the height of the tongue is in the right place, and move the fence in toward the cutter with each pass. For the final pass, the fence should

Figure 271. Cross panel cut—*Cut the end grain profile first, and use a backing block. This prevents tear-out at the end of the cut and makes it easier to mill the end of a narrow panel.*

be flush with the bearing on the panel-cutting bit. **(Figure 269, 270).**

With a cutter that only mills the face, I set up the fence where I need it for the final cut, lower the cutter, and then raise it with each successive pass.

Set up the table as if you were going to make the cut in one pass. The bearing should be flush with the fence. If you are not making a relief

*Figure 272. **Raised panel bit with back cutter**—This router bit makes a relief cut in the back of the panel. The multiple cutters for the profile leave a very clean surface.*

cut on the back, your cut should leave a tongue that is ¼-inch thick. If your panel-raising cutter has a second cutter for making the relief cut, the tongue size should be set. You want to set the height so that the relief cut is about ⅛ inch. If the thickness of your stile and rail stock is more than ¾ inch, set up the cut so that the face of the panel is flush with the face of the frame parts.

If you are moving the fence with each pass, draw a pencil line on the top of the table to indicate where it must be for the final pass. This lets you repeat your setup exactly without needing to measure. If you are raising the cutter with each pass, and you have a plunge router in the router table, set the depth stop on the router for the final location.

With the panels cut to size, and the router table set up, you are almost ready to rout the faces. Take a few moments to go over your setup to be absolutely certain that everything is secure, and double-check the fence and the router settings. This is likely the largest cutter you will ever run on the router table, and you need to be careful.

Begin by making a cut on the end of a panel, going across the grain **(Figure 271)**. This cross-grain cut is the most likely to tear out at the end of the cut. By making it first, the long-grain cut to follow will clean up any torn areas. Be aware of where your hands are at all times, and keep them out of the area near the cutter.

When you start the cut, apply pressure on the infeed fence until the leading part of the panel is past the cutter. As soon as possible, apply pressure to the outfeed fence, while maintaining a steady feed rate across the cutter. The two fences and the bearing on the bit must be in a perfectly straight line. If not, you run the risk of a corner of the work catching on the corner of the outfeed fence.

It helps to have a push block when making the cross-grain cuts. It requires a bit more coordination, but it greatly reduces the risk, especially if the panels are narrow. Push the panel back against the push block, and move the push block against the fence. Once the leading edge of the panel is beyond the cutter, push it against the fence while continuing to push with the block.

Because the edges going with the grain are longer, these cuts are easier to make. There is also less resistance to the cut when going with the grain. Each direction will behave a little differently due to the physical properties of the cutting. Feed the work at a steady pace, without putting a strain on the router.

The quality of the cutter used will make a big difference in the amount of work that remains to be done after raising the panels. The goal is to reduce the amount of sanding required to an absolute minimum. A few dollars invested in a superior router bit may make the difference of many hours in sanding.

Freud makes panel-raising cutters with two sets of carbide edges to make the panel cuts **(Figure 269 & 272)**. In use, one cutter removes most of the waste, and the following cutter shears off a small amount of material, leaving an excellent surface.

The end grain is the most difficult area to sand, and it is here that a good cut will be most appreciated. With some profiles, you can sand with a quarter-sheet pad sander, or with a profile sander. If you are sanding with

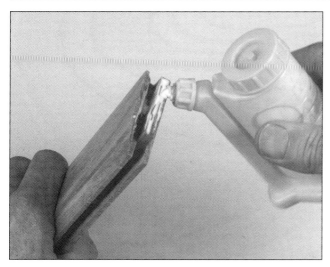

Figure 273. Cope glued—*Be frugal in applying glue to the cope cut. You don't want any to squeeze into the groove for the panel.*

Figure 274. Panel in clamp—*There should be little or no glue squeeze out when the rail and stile are clamped.*

Figure 275. Panel assembly—*With the stile on edge, the rails are put in place.*

Figure 276. Panel assembly—*The panel is slid in between the rails, and glue applied to the ends of the rails.*

a machine, you run the risk of knocking off sharp edges of the profile, changing the profile, or reducing the size of the tongue. In quality work, the machined edges should be crisp, and there should be a nice line coming out of the corners of the panel. Sanding sponges or a soft, flexible pad work well to sand these areas by hand.

If the profiled edges of the rails and stiles were well-machined, you shouldn't need to do any sanding on them before assembling the panels. In any case, you do not want to sand the edges at the ends of the stiles where

the ends of the rails join, this will ruin the fit of the cope and stick joints.

If there is any chance at all of the panels shrinking and you are planning a stained or painted finish, then the panels should be partially finished before assembly. This is taking the work out of sequence, but if the panels shrink in width, raw wood can become visible as the panels dry out. Do a sample to see if your finish can be blended in once part of it is dry. It is better to just stain or paint around the edges if you can and finish the rest of the panel along with everything else.

Figure 277. Panel clamping—*Strips of wood on the bench provide a level surface for the assembled panel to be clamped.*

Figure 278. Pinning joint—*Short pins are used to hold the joint together.*

Figure 279. Spacers—*Foam tape cut in short pieces and placed in the groove will center the panel.*

Figure 280. Panel clamping—*Make sure the assembly is square as it is clamped tight.*

Assembly

To assemble the frames and panels you should have a flat area to work on, and enough clamps to keep you busy for an hour. If the parts are machined well, you should only need one clamp per joint, and you don't need much clamping pressure. It's more important to apply pressure directly in line with the joints than it is to apply great force. In fact, over-tightening the clamps can cause the joints to buckle.

Start by gluing one end of both rails into place in one of the stiles **(Figure 273).** Avoid using too much glue. I usually put glue on the

coped parts of the rail only. Vary the amount of glue until you get just a few tiny beads of glue squeezing out **(Figure 274).** Using a glue bot will help you control the amount of glue applied. You can also use a brush, but that will take longer.

If you are using yellow glue, you have about fifteen minutes to assemble a panel before the glue starts to set up. It shouldn't take any longer than that, but if it's your first time, and you run in to trouble getting things lined up and square, the glue might start to set before you want it to. You can use a glue with a longer open time, but if you have a lot of panels to put together, you won't be able to take the clamps off already-glued panels to keep the work flowing.

I set the stile on edge, and push the rails down in to the groove until they bottom out **(Figure 275)**. Next I drop the panel in place, put glue on the exposed ends of the rails, and put the remaining stile on from above **(Figure 276)**. Hand pressure, or just a light tap from a dead-blow hammer, is enough to put the panel together. Sometimes a stile or panel may have a slight bow that needs to be pulled straight while assembling the panel. If you do this, be aware that your chances of having a straight door are greatly reduced, but you might get lucky.

Once all the pieces are together, I lay the assembled panel on two strips of wood on the surface of the bench. These strips will keep glue from getting on the bench, and give you room to place and line up clamps. I check that the panel is square with a speed square or a drafting triangle on the inside of the joint before tightening the clamps, and again after the clamps are tight **(Figure 277, 280)**. If I have a lot of doors to put together, I shoot a ½-inch long 23-gauge pin through the back of the joint, so that I can remove the clamps if I need them for another piece **(Figure 278)**.

It is important that the panel itself be centered within the frame. If there is a hard edge on the panel profile, place a block of soft wood on it and tap the block with a hammer to move it to the proper position. Once the panel is centered, shoot a pin from behind at the midpoint of the panel at the top and bottom.

Good alternatives that will center the panel are ¼ inch diameter surgical tubing, foam weatherstripping, or a product specifically designed for this purpose, called Spaceballs **(Figure 279)**. The Spaceballs, or foam tubing cut into short lengths, are inserted into the grooves before the panel is put in place. They will push the panel evenly to the center, and will contract if the panel expands.

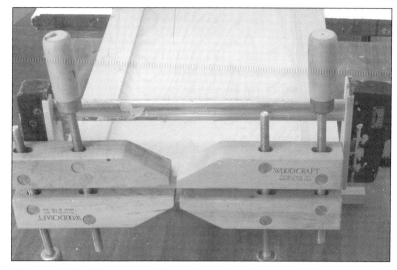

Figure 281. Keep panel flat—A wood caul, or wood clamps across the joints, will prevent the stile and rail joint from pulling up under pressure from the clamps.

Plywood panels should be sized to just fit within the grooves. You don't need an allowance for the panel to shrink or swell. Unlike solid wood panels, you can, and should, glue plywood panels in place. Don't use much glue, a line 3 inches or 4 inches long in the middle of each stile and rail will be enough to add considerable strength. Sanding the veneered panels before assembly will enable you to sand them with a random-orbit sander rather than by hand.

Before setting the assembled panel aside for the glue to dry, check to see that the stiles and rails are in the same plane. If they aren't, you can either adjust the placement of the clamps, or clamp a caul above and below the joint to hold the assembly in line. A small wood hand-screw can also be used for this purpose **(Figure 281)**.

I mark the time in pencil on the panel once I have the clamps in place. This helps to keep track of which panel has been in the clamps longest. I set the panels aside for the glue to dry. I leave each panel in the clamps for at least one hour. As the work proceeds and I run out of clamps, I remove the clamps from the oldest panel. Although the glue is dry enough after an hour to remove the clamps,

Figure 282. Sanding joints—*A random orbit sander is effective at evening out the joints. Keep the sanding pad perfectly flat at all times or it will score the work.*

Figure 283. Planing joints—*A block plane is effective at leveling the joints.*

the panel needs to set for 24 hours for the glue to truly cure and achieve its maximum strength.

After removing the clamps, the panels should be stacked flat to insure that they dry straight and flat. After waiting for the glue to dry, the panels are ready to sand. If the preceding stages have gone well, only minimal sanding will be required. Often in cabinetwork, you need to work through a following step to understand how careful you need to be. To look good as doors or end panels, the assembled panels need to be perfectly flat. If the joints were prepared accurately and assembled carefully, they will be in this condition.

Sanding and Finishing

Some sanding is usually needed, and in a large commercial shop, the assembled panels are fed through a large wide-belt thicknessing sander. Smaller drum sanders are available, and work fairly well, but at a much slower pace than their industrial cousins. With either machine, the stiles and rails can be sanded flush, but the rails will be sanded across the grain, and these scratches must be removed.

If the stiles and rails are close to being flush, a random-orbit sander with 80-grit or 100-grit paper will put the faces in line **(Figure 282)**. Be careful to work the high points down, and keep the disc flat on the surface being sanded. If the sander is tilted at all, it is much less effective, and you are likely to introduce dips instead of achieving a flat surface. After the joints are flush, the entire panel should be sanded with progressively finer grits until no scratch marks are visible on the surface. The final sanding should be done by hand, backing up the paper with a firm block on the flat surfaces and with a sponge on the profiles.

A belt sander can be used to flush the joints, but it is quite difficult to control, and cross-grain scratches will need to be removed with a random-orbit sander. A smooth plane or a block plane is quite effective at reducing the high spots, and a card scraper can be used to complete the smoothing **(Figure 283).**

Finally, sand or plane to ease all sharp edges and make them hand-friendly. Some makers cut a tiny chamfer, perhaps only ¹⁄₁₆ inch wide, for this reason. Easing the sharp corners also helps finish stick there.

14. HINGES

Butt Hinges

Few things are more terrifying to many woodworkers than setting butt hinges. Even professional cabinetmakers and furniture makers will avoid using them. It seems that with the advent of European hinges and no-mortise hinges everyone has forgotten how to do what is actually a basic task. There isn't a better way to hang a door than with quality butt hinges, set in mortises. Properly done, the butt hinge will be stronger, operate better than other types of hinges, and will last virtually forever **(Figure 284).**

No-mortise hinges put the entire load on the screws, and European hinges are just plain ugly. Both of these alternatives are sloppy to begin with, and will become more so as the years go by. A good door in a well-made cabinet deserves to be hung on quality hardware. The keys to success are making parts the size you want them, in the location you want them, and square to each other.

You need to work carefully and precisely, both in constructing the door and its opening, and in locating and cutting the hinge mortises. It's possible to fit a door to a crooked opening, but that is a lot more work than doing it right the first time. Often the advice is given to make the door bigger than the opening, so that it can be trimmed when hanging it. Stiles are frequently left a few inches longer than needed. This is only necessary if you are chopping mortises for the rails with a mallet and a chisel. If you make the door oversized, you need to be extremely careful when trimming it to keep the width of the stiles and rails a consistent size. If you can accomplish that, you have the skills to make the door the right size to begin with.

I recommend making the door to the exact size of the opening, this still allows some margin to fit a less than perfect opening, but minimizes the waste of material and time. With an inset door, the gaps between the door and the frame should be the same all the way around the perimeter of the door. I usually determine the size of the

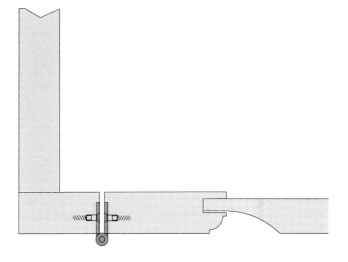

Figure 284. Mortised butt hinges *are the best way to hang an inset cabinet door. There is no equal in terms of function or longevity, and installing them is easier than most people imagine.*

Figure 285. Positioning—*With the door shimmed up from the bottom, mark the hinge location on the door and cabinet stiles.*

Figure 286. Layout—Use a hinge to mark the exact size of the mortise.

Figure 287. Layout—Set an adjustable square to mark the back edge of the hinge mortise.

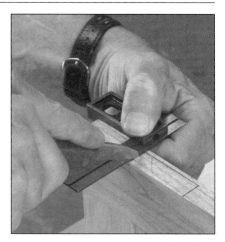

Figure 288. Layout—Use the other end of the square to mark the ends of the mortises.

gap based on the gap between the two leaves of the hinge when the hinge is in the closed position. The easiest way to do this is to close the hinge, and measure the thickness of the leaves next to the barrel of the hinge with a caliper. Then measure the thickness of one of the leaves. This thickness (times 2) subtracted from the overall thickness will give you the desired gap.

Measure the width and height of the opening at several places, and check each of the corners with a good square. If the door is the same size as the opening, you should be able to fit it to the opening with minimal trimming. A plane works well for trimming the width, but I trim the length on a crosscut sled on the table saw. If you made the door oversized so you could trim it later, you now have several hoops to jump through. If either the door or the opening is out of square, you need to determine where it is out, and by how much, before you can hope to make any corrections. When the door will just fit in the opening, you can fine tune the gaps, and lay out the mortises for the hinges.

Start work with the hinge stile. Make it straight to use as a reference, and trim the bottom edge of the door to fit the opening. If the opening is slightly out of square, place a thin shim at one end of the hinge stile, between the stile and the fence on the

crosscut sled, to make the angled cut. With one corner established, place the door in the opening, tight against the hinge stile and the bottom. Measure the gap at both sides of the top of the door. Trim enough off the top so that the gap is twice the desired finished gap. I prefer to set the hinges before trimming the long edge of the other stile.

Place the door in the opening, and insert some shims at the top and bottom to hold the door in place with uniform gaps. When you're happy with that, you can set the locations of the hinges. There really isn't a set distance for the hinges to be placed. For appearance sake, I line up the ends of the hinges with the inside edges of the rails. If the rails are wide, then I'll center the hinges on the edge of the rail **(Figure 285).**

Make a mark across both the cabinet and door stile to indicate the end of the hinges, and remove the door. Place a square on the mark, and put the hinge against the edge of the square. Wrap the hinge around the corner as shown in **Figure 286**, this will locate the back edge of the hinge. With a knife, mark the edges of the hinge on the edge of the stiles **(Figure 287 & 288)**. You now have the exact size of the mortise you need to make, and because you marked the cabinet stile and door stile together, you have the exact location.

Figure 289. Setting up router— *Use the hinge to set the depth of the router bit, then carefully rout close to the layout lines.*

Figure 290. Chisel ends—*With the flat back of the chisel in the knife mark, press down to define the end of the mortise. Be careful not to split the wood at the back.*

Figure 291. Paring—*carefully pare the bottom of the mortise by resting the flat back on the area cut by the router.*

There are several ways to cut out the recess. You can do it entirely by hand, using a chisel to remove most of the waste, and a router plane to get the depth right. I prefer to remove the waste with a straight bit in a laminate trimmer or other small router, and use the chisel only to clean up the edges. If there are a lot of doors to do, as in a kitchen, it's worthwhile to make a template to guide the router, but if there's only a door or two I just guide the router by eye, coming to within ⅟₁₆ inch to ⅛ inch of the lines. It is helpful to clamp a piece of scrap wood to the edge of the stile to support the router base and keep it from tipping. The advantage of using the router is that the bottom of the mortise will be flat and at a consistent depth.

Set the depth of the cutter directly from one of the hinge leaves **(Figure 289).** With the router upside down, place one hinge leaf on the base of the router, next to the cutter. Adjust the depth of the cutter until it is even with the top surface of the hinge. Make a test cut in scrap to confirm the proper cutting depth. The face of the hinge should be flush, or barely proud, with the surface of the wood.

Use a chisel that's a little wider than the hinge and you can make the end cuts in one shot, ensuring a straight line. Set the edge of the chisel in the corner of the knife mark, with the bevel of the chisel facing into the mortise. Push down and rock the chisel back toward the edge, stopping when the edge of the chisel meets the depth mark **(Figure 290).** The long edge is cut the same way, working from each corner in to the middle of the mortise. Once the edges have been cut to the right depth, paring cuts will remove the small amount of remaining waste. Be careful paring to the back edge, as it is easy to split the wood there **(Figure 291).**

The hinge should fit snugly in the mortise. If it doesn't, take a close look at the edges. If those cuts are angled slightly the hinge won't fit. With the hinge in place, drill one hole and set one screw. A Vix bit will help locate the screw hole **(Figure 292),** but you still need to be careful the drill bit is at 90 degrees to the edge. If you have brass screws, set them aside and use a steel screw temporarily until you are happy with the way the door hangs. I go ahead and tighten a steel screw and then remove it in each location so that it will be easier to tighten the brass screws when fitting the door.

Figure 292. First hole—The hinge should fit snugly in the mortise. Use a Vix bit to drill the middle screw hole in the door, and do the same on the cabinet stile.

Figure 293. Cabinet—Use one screw in each of the door and stile leaves to hold the hinge in place, and check how the door swings.

Figure 294. Steel screw first—With brass hinges, use a steel screw of the same size to cut the threads for the fragile brass screws.

Fasten the hinges to the door, and carefully put the remaining leaves in the mortises on the cabinet, having screws and screwdriver handy to fasten the door in place (**Figure 293 & 294**). The door should fit well, but in case it doesn't, there are a few ways to make some minor corrections (**Figure 295 & 296**). If the hinges are too deep in the mortises, or if the gap on the opposite side of the door is too big, place a piece of cardstock or veneer under the hinge to adjust the gap. If the door needs to move vertically, or farther in or out in relation to the cabinet, you will need to move the screw holes, and enlarge the mortise. Before

you can re-drill, the old screw hole needs to be filled by whittling a piece of scrap to fit and gluing it in place.

If the mortise only needs a slight increase in length, re-cutting the end and paring out the waste will leave only a small gap . A gap larger than ⅛ inch should be repaired by cutting and fitting a small piece to entirely fill the mortise. Match the grain on the patch to the face of the door, and bevel the ends so that the repair isn't so obvious. Once the glue holding this in place has dried, the mortise can be cut again.

Figure 295. Check fit—Check the fit of the door and adjust if necessary.

Figure 296. Brass screws—When you are satisfied with the fit, replace the steel screws with the brass ones.

European Hinges

European hinges have made the once intimidating task of hanging doors a quick and reliable operation. Hidden from view, different types of Euro hinges exist for nearly any imaginable situation, and with a few simple tools, and an understanding of how these hinges work, any fool can hang doors.

The concept behind the design of European hinges is to set up a repeatable process that accurately places the components of the hinges, both on the door and on the cabinet. These hinges are also adjustable after being installed, so that minor errors in the sizing or squareness of the doors or cabinet openings can be corrected.

While Euro hinges are an excellent solution in many cases, they are far from perfect, and aren't always the best solution. Hidden from view when the door is closed, Euro hinges can be very ugly when the door is opened, and can get in the way of other cabinet components, or the contents.

The variety of options available can be bewildering, but most of the confusion can be resolved by answering two questions: do you want the door to sit in the opening or to overlay the opening, and how far do you want the door to open?

The big decision to make is whether to have the doors sit inside their openings (inset doors) **(Figure 298)** or on the face of the box (overlay doors) **(Figure 297)**. If the doors overlay the opening, they look better if they come nearly to the edge of the box, this is called full overlay. Half, or partial, overlay hinges exist, primarily for the purpose of fitting two doors to a common cabinet partition. Leaving a big reveal around an overlay door doesn't look as good as a full overlay **(Figure 299).**

When using conventional butt hinges, how far the door opens is rarely a consideration. The door swings until it hits some other part of the box, and this is generally farther than needed to get at whatever is behind the door. With Euro hinges, there are built-in limits to opening, due to the engineering of the hinges.

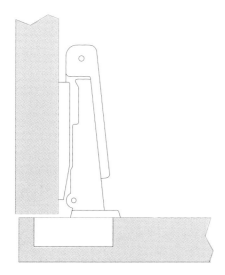

*Figure 297. **With overlay doors, t**he door almost completely covers the cabinet elements, there is a reveal of about ⅟₁₆ inch. The overlay hinge takes comparatively little space within the cabinet. While it always helps to work to exact size and squareness, with overlay doors there is some room for minor adjustments.*

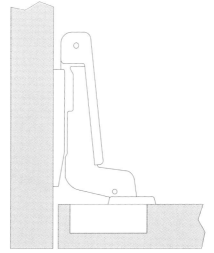

*Figure 298. **With inset doors,** the hinges take up more space inside the cabinet, and a stop must be provided to keep the hinges from over-closing. With inset doors, it's critical to accurately size both door and opening, and to make sure both are perfectly square.*

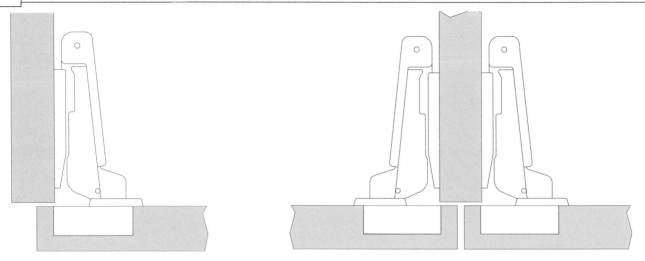

Figure 299. The half-cranked hinge *leaves the edge of the door approximately at the mid-point of the edge of the cabinet. It was designed for use where two doors are both hinged from one panel, as shown at right. In other situations, it leaves a large reveal between the edge of the door and the edge of the cabinet, and intrudes even farther into the cabinet interior. The same effect can be achieved using the standard hinge, and a taller mounting plate.*

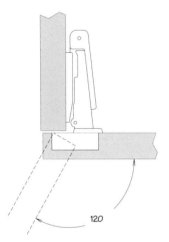

Figure 300. With a full overlay *120-degree hinge, the door does not clear the opening.*

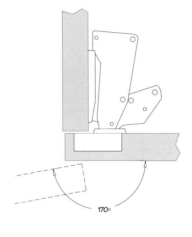

Figure 301. A 170-degree full *overlay hinge does throw the door clear.*

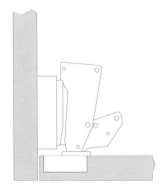

Figure 302. A 170-degree inset *hinge also clears the door but is large and eats interior space.*

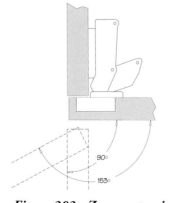

Figure 303. Zero-protrusion *hinges throw the door clear, and take up less interior space.*

The most common hinge is full overlay 120-degree opening. When the door is completely open, its inside corner will interfere with pullout trays. People also expect the door to open farther than 120 degrees, so they force it, which stresses the mounting plates. With two cabinets side by side, the ⅟₁₆ inch reveal will leave a gap of ⅛ inch between the doors, so duplicate this ⅛ inch gap between two doors on a single cabinet **(Figure 300)**.

Wider opening hinges, to 165 degrees to 180 degrees, are expensive, and take up a lot of space inside the cabinet. The amount of overlay and the reveal can be controlled by the placement of the hinge cup holes, and the thickness of the mounting plate. Wide-opening hinges do throw the door clear of pullout trays; however, the vertical location of the hinge may need to be changed so the hinge itself doesn't interfere. A compromise is the 153-degree zero-protrusion hinge available from some manufacturers. It opens nearly as far as the 170-degree hinge, but does not take up as much interior space. When open to 90 degrees, the back edge of the door will clear the inside edge of the cabinet, so pullout trays don't hang up **(Figure 301, 302, 303)**.

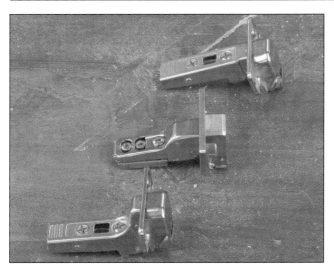

Figure 304. Hinge cranks—*The three types of cranks in Euro hinges provide different door overlays.*

Figure 305. Base plates—*Base plates of different heights can also be used to obtain a different overlay.*

Euro hinges have two distinct parts, the hinge (which goes on the door, **Figure 304**) and the base plate (which goes inside the box, **Figure 305**). Different combinations of hinges and base plates can be used to vary the degree of opening, the amount of overlay, or the size of gaps on inset doors.

There isn't a lot of quality difference among the various European manufacturers. Blum is the most commonly available from mail order sources and better hardware stores, so I will use their terminology in these examples. Concealed hinges manufactured in Asia have recently become available and are available from Internet based hardware suppliers such as Grizzly and Custom Service Hardware.

To successfully use Euro hinges, you need to do two operations: drill the right size hole in the right place on the door for the hinge cup, and locate the base plate in a precise location on the cabinet (**Figure 306**).

The hinge cup sits in a large (35mm) hole, and is usually attached to the door with two #6 x ⅝ inch screws. The locations of the two small screw holes vary from manufacturer to manufacturer, and in commercial applications the screws are in plastic ribbed dowels that are pressed in place. The location of the large hole determines how the

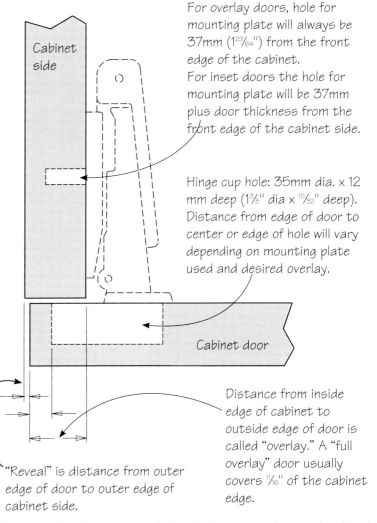

Cabinet side

For overlay doors, hole for mounting plate will always be 37mm (1²⁹⁄₆₄") from the front edge of the cabinet.
For inset doors the hole for mounting plate will be 37mm plus door thickness from the front edge of the cabinet side.

Hinge cup hole: 35mm dia. x 12 mm deep (1⅜" dia x ¹⁵⁄₃₂" deep). Distance from edge of door to center or edge of hole will vary depending on mounting plate used and desired overlay.

Cabinet door

Distance from inside edge of cabinet to outside edge of door is called "overlay." A "full overlay" door usually covers ⅟₁₆" of the cabinet edge.

"Reveal" is distance from outer edge of door to outer edge of cabinet side.

Figure 306. Placing the hole for the hinge cup *closer to the edge of the door moves the door in the direction of the outside of the cabinet, giving you a smaller reveal with overlay doors, or a smaller gap with inset doors.*

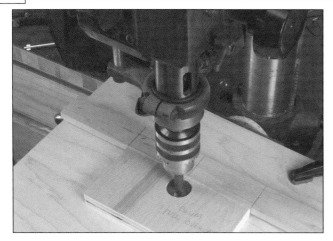

Figure 307. Hinge cup holes—*The sample from the test fitting is used to set both the depth stop on the drill press, and the fence position.*

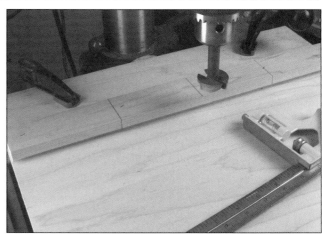

Figure 308. Fence—*The fence is just a piece of plywood with a rabbet in the bottom to keep chips from building up. Mark the centerlines directly from the bit.*

Figure 309. Marks on fence—*The measurements to each end of the door are made from the centerline, and marked on the fence.*

Figure 310. Door being drilled—*Lining up the corner of the door with the mark on the fence locates the door for drilling the cup holes.*

door looks and functions when it is in place. There are a number of jigs and fixtures available to locate and drill these holes, ranging from inexpensive jigs for drilling by hand to dedicated machines. For the first time user, I would recommend using a drill press, and the shop made jigs shown (**Figure 307, 308, 309, 310**).

One of the issues to deal with is which measurement system to use, metric or imperial. I'm no fan of the metric system, but I find it much easier to use it when laying out Euro hinges since all of the specifications from the manufacturers are in metric dimensions. Converting back and forth can be a chore,

and small errors due to conversions can lead to big problems.

One of the givens with Euro hinges is that the holes for mounting the base plates are 37mm (1²⁹⁄₆₄ inch) back from the front of the cabinet for overlay doors. For inset doors, add 37mm to the thickness of the door to locate the plates. The distance from the top or bottom of the door to the center of the base plate can vary, and for most cabinet applications the distance should be between 3½ inches and 4 inches (96mm to 100mm) (**Figure 311**).

The hole in the door is 35mm (3 thousandths over 1⅜ inch) and for Blum hinges 11.5mm deep (²⁹⁄₆₄ inch). If you are using overlay doors, and want a profile on the edges, make sure that the hole for the hinge cup and the moulding profile don't intersect **(Figure 312).** The distance from the edge of the cup hole to the edge of the door is usually 3mm to 5mm, so there isn't much room for a profile on the door edges. Add half the cup diameter (17.5mm or ¹¹⁄₁₆ inch) to the desired distance between the cup and the door edge to locate the centerline for the cup holes. **Figure 307** shows a drill press set up for drilling doors, with a mark on the fence to indicate the location of the hole from the edge of the door. If you get the hole locations reasonably close, you will be able to use the height adjustment on the hinge to compensate for any small errors.

Once you have established where the holes should be in the cabinet, you can make a jig (as shown in **Figure 313**), or use a manufacturer's jig **(Figure 314)** so you can consistently drill the base plate holes without lay-

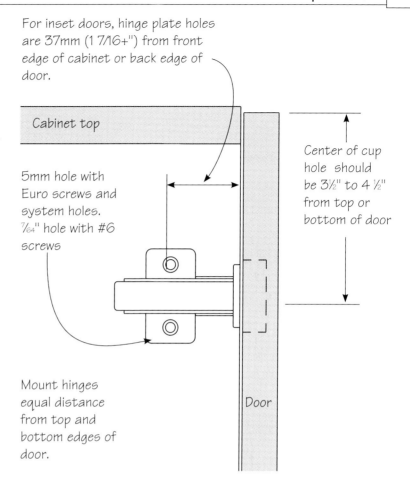

For inset doors, hinge plate holes are 37mm (1 7/16+") from front edge of cabinet or back edge of door.

Cabinet top

5mm hole with Euro screws and system holes. ⁷⁄₆₄" hole with #6 screws

Center of cup hole should be 3½" to 4 ½" from top or bottom of door

Mount hinges equal distance from top and bottom edges of door.

Door

Figure 311. Location *of hinge elements in sectional elevation.*

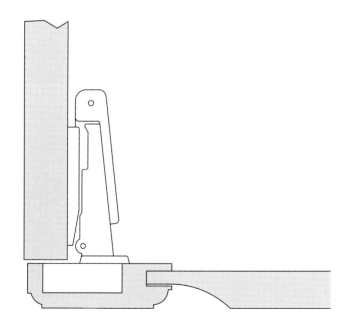

Figure 312. With frame and panel doors, *the stiles need to be wide enough for the cup hole to be drilled without interfering with the groove for the panel. Any profile must be small enough to not intersect with the hole for the hinge cup.*

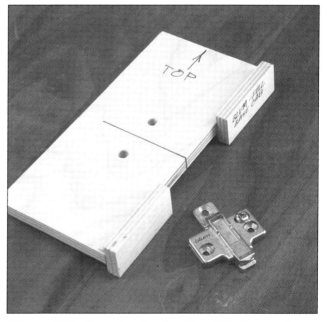

Figure 313. Baseplate boring jig—*This shop-made jig locates the holes from the top and bottom of the door opening. This allows the holes in the doors to be drilled at a consistent distance in from the corners, while providing differing overlays at the top and bottom.*

Figure 314. Metal jig—*This simple jig locates the hinge plates from a centerline marked on the cabinet.*

Figure 315. Lining up the hinge—*With the hinge inserted in the cup, the lipped alignment block ensures that the edge of the hinge is parallel to the edge of the door.*

Figure 316. Baseplate—*If the jig is set correctly, the hinge plates can be mounted in seconds.*

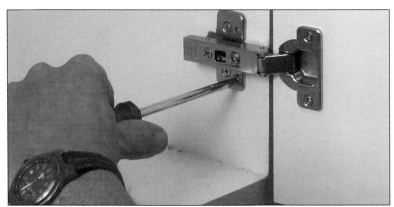

Figure 317. Hinge mounting—*Slide the hinge onto the plate from the front until you hear it click into place. If it doesn't quite fit, loosen the height adjustment screws.*

ing out each and every location. These holes are 32mm (1¹⁷⁄₆₄ inches) center to center, and can be drilled at 5mm (¹³⁄₆₄ inch) diameter for Euro screws, or ³⁄₃₂ inch if you are using #6 screws. The Euro screws will hold better, particularly in particleboard. The #6 screws are sturdy enough for holding in plywood.

In the 32mm cabinetmaking system, a line of holes is bored for installing base plates and other hardware **(Figure 316).** In the small shop, it's a lot easier to drill only the holes you need, and the cabinet won't look like it has been shot by a machine gun.

Most European hinges attach to the base plates by a mechanical clip. Thus you mount the base plates to the cabinets and the hinges to the doors **Figure 315,** and hang the doors by simply snapping the hinges on to the base plates. If things don't quite line up, you can still clip the doors on if you loosen the height adjustment **(Figure 317).**

When the doors are in place, you can fine-tune the fit with the adjustment screws. There are three adjustments that can be made. There are two different ways to adjust the height of the door. With some hinges you do it manually: loosen the screws on both hinges just enough to let the door move. You can then

Figure 318. Adjusting—Check which way each adjustment screw moves the hinge. This screw adjusts the hinge vertically.

Figure 319. Adjusting hinges—This screw adjusts the hinge in and out from the front of the cabinet.

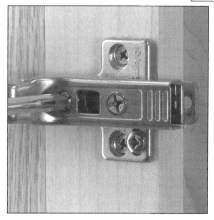

Figure 320. Adjusting hinges—The third screw moves the hinge right and left.

slide the door up and down with one hand, and when you have it where you want it, hold it in place and tighten the screws. Some hinges now have the height adjustment on a cam. Turning the screw one way raises the door, and turning it in the opposite direction lowers it (**Figure 318**).

The position of the door in relation to the face of the box can be adjusted with one of the screws located on the hinge arm (**Figure 319**). The third adjustment screw moves the hinge arm in relation to the base plate, changing the overlay, or the gap at the side of the door (**Figure 320**).

The adjustments can be a great help, but they can't magically fix doors or openings that are out of square, or not the right size.

To use Euro hinges with a face frame, you can either add blocking behind the frame and use standard base plates, or use special face frame plates that attach directly to the face frame. Some manufacturers offer hinges designed for face frame applications, but they don't function as well or provide as many options as frameless style hinges.

Figure 321. Here are four ways to use concealed Euro hinges with face-frame cabinets.

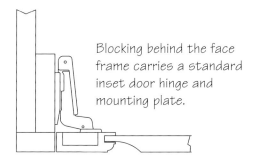

Blocking behind the face frame carries a standard inset door hinge and mounting plate.

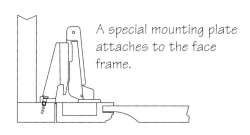

A special mounting plate attaches to the face frame.

The cabinet side can be flush with the inside of the frame instead of the outside being flush. This is the simplest choice.

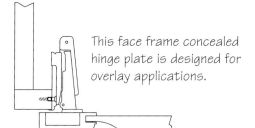

This face frame concealed hinge plate is designed for overlay applications.

15. WORKING WITH PLASTIC LAMINATE

Figure 322. Perfect corner—Plastic laminate is very workable in the small shop, and with a little care can be finished as neatly as this corner.

High-pressure decorative laminate, commonly referred to as plastic laminate, can seem like a foreign substance to many woodworkers, yet it is one of the most common materials used in cabinetmaking. It isn't appropriate for every situation, but when you need a colorful, durable, easy to maintain surface, it works very well. In this chapter, we will look at the general properties of the material, and how to apply it to frameless cabinets. In the chapter to follow, we will look at countertop applications.

Plastic laminate is formed from several layers of Kraft paper, saturated with Melamine plastic resin, and formed into flat sheets under heat and pressure. Near the top of the stack of paper layers is a layer with the decorative pattern printed on it. The top layers are clear resin to protect the printed pattern. The clear layer may have a matte finish, or it may be glossy. The matte finish is far more durable than the glossy, which can scratch if you walk by thinking about something sharp.

It was originally developed for use as an electric insulator, decorative uses for plastic laminate were an afterthought. The major American manufacturers are Formica, Wilsonart, Nevamar, and Pionite. There isn't a significant difference in quality from one manufacturer to another. In recent years, generic laminate, known as commodity laminate, has appeared, and there is a significant difference in quality between it and the brand names. The commodity laminate has a much thinner clear top layer that wears away quickly. Once the top layer has worn, the other papers layers are exposed and are susceptible to staining. The money saved by buying commodity laminate will be money wasted.

There are several grades or thicknesses available, two of which are applicable for general cabinetwork. Horizontal grade is the thickest, measuring .050 inch in thickness. This is usually reserved for use in countertops. It is often referred to as being $\frac{1}{16}$ inch in thickness, but it is 12.5 thousandths of an inch under that. Vertical grade is .030

inch in thickness and is usually used for surfaces that don't receive much wear and tear, like cabinet sides and doors. Vertical grade is often referred to as ½ inch thick, and it is just a little over one thousandth of an inch over that. In most cabinetwork, all exposed laminate surfaces will be vertical grade. In between is post-forming grade, at .040 inch thick.

Post-forming grade is thin enough to be bent to a tight radius when heated, but still thick enough to make a durable countertop. Plastic laminate tops that have a built-in backsplash with a tight cove between it and the countertop, or a lipped, radiused edge at the front of the counter are post-formed. Post-forming requires special equipment to heat the entire edge of a long top to a specific temperature. There is a narrow window of temperature where the material will bend readily without melting or burning the plastic. This type of work just isn't possible without the equipment, so if you want this type of counter you will have to buy it.

For flat work in cabinets and countertops, and radii within a reasonable range, plastic laminate is fairly easy to work with, once you know how to handle and work with it. It can be cut with a table saw and router, and it doesn't require a vast collection of specialized tools for fabrication and finishing. A special roller and a file are likely the only tools you will need to obtain if you already have standard woodworking tools.

Horizontal-grade laminate comes in a wide range of sheet sizes, from 30 inches x 6 feet to 5 feet x 12 feet. Vertical grade is only available in 4 foot x 8-foot sheets. The actual sizes of sheets are 1 inch larger than the nominal dimension, that is a 4 foot x 8-foot sheet of laminate is actually 49 inches x 97 inches. Plastic laminate will shrink and expand slightly in reaction to changes in humidity, but not as much as solid wood or sheet goods like particleboard or MDF. It's

Figure 323. Fence mask—*A piece of Masonite with a rectangular hole keeps the edge of the laminate from slipping under the table saw fence.*

a good idea in extremely hot or extremely cold weather to let the sheets acclimate to the shop environment for a few days before using them.

Sawing Laminate

Plastic laminate is brittle, and the thinner vertical grade is fragile until it is adhered to a substrate. When carrying a sheet, hold it vertically by one long edge, and be careful not to let the sheet buckle when laying it flat. The easiest way to cut laminate is with a table saw, but you need to prevent the edge of the sheet from slipping under the edge of the saw fence. The Delta Unifence can be turned 90 degrees to provide a low ledge for the laminate to ride over while being cut. In most shops, a piece of ¼-inch thick Masonite or plywood is used, as in **Figure 323**. Cut the piece a few inches longer and wider than the table saw fence, and make a rectangular cutout so it can be dropped over the fence. With this bridge, a carbide-tipped ATB saw blade, and a zero-clearance insert, you are equipped to saw laminate.

Because the sheets are so flexible, they can be awkward to cut down to size. Having

Figure 324. Sawing laminate—*Holding the back edge of the sheet up in the air allows you to control the front of the sheet. Make sure the leading edge doesn't catch on the outfeed table as it comes off the saw.*

Figure 325. Sawing laminate—*Complete the cut by pushing the laminate sheet past the saw blade.*

flat support on both the infeed and outfeed ends of the saw will help to keep control of the material. You can also bend the end of the sheet up toward you so that you can locate yourself close to the blade to keep the sheet pressed against the fence while cutting **(Figure 324 & 325).**

An alternative method to cutting sheets to size, or at least to sizes that are manageable to get through the saw, is to clamp a straightedge to the bottom of the sheet along the line to be cut, and use a router with a flush-trimming bit to make the cut.

Except in rare circumstances, the laminate is cut ¼ inch to ½ inch larger in each dimension than the piece it is to be applied to, and trimmed flush after being adhered to the substrate. How much larger depends on several factors. Because contact cement adheres immediately when the laminate touches the substrate, there is no second chance of adjusting the placement of the sheet. If it is oversized, you have a better chance of getting it where you want it without leaving part of the substrate exposed. If it is too large, however, it's harder to see what you're doing, and you make more mess when you trim.

Substrate

Particleboard is the most commonly used substrate, either in its raw state or coated with Melamine resin. Usually the interiors of cabinets and the inside of cabinet doors will have a Melamine surface, and the exposed parts will be vertical-grade plastic laminate. Ideally, you want to follow the rule of balanced construction as you would in veneering. If you have different materials on opposite sides of a board, they will give off or absorb moisture at different rates, causing the substrate to warp. Nearly all of the Melamine board available is coated on both sides, and for a good reason. If it were coated on one side only, it would begin to warp almost immediately after being made. Most cabinet parts don't have a finished side, so you want to use two-sided Melamine in these locations. Finished cabinet ends are usually supported well enough by the structure of the cabinet that warping of cabinet ends is not a problem when they are covered with plastic laminate.

With cabinet doors, however, the odds are about 50/50 that a door with laminate on one side and Melamine on the other will even-

Figure 326. Applying adhesive— Use a disposable roller to apply contact cement to large flat surfaces.

Figure 327. Applying adhesive—A disposable brush is used to apply cement to raw edges. Wait for the first coat to completely dry and then recoat.

tually warp. Usually this is not severe, but for first-class work, both the back and front of the door should have plastic laminate. If you're making several doors, it makes sense to apply an entire sheet of laminate to a sheet of particleboard, and cut the door parts from this. If this is done, the second side needs to be covered within a day, or the material will begin to warp due to its unbalanced state. Saw it with the laminated side up.

If you are laminating over a Melamine-coated material, you need to scuff-sand the surface or the laminate will not bond to the substrate. Eighty-grit sandpaper in a belt sander or random-orbit sander works well. Wear a good respirator for the dust cloud that this will create. Clean the dust off the surface before applying the adhesive. If you can vacuum it up you will maintain a cleaner environment than if you blow it off with compressed air, or a brush.

Contact Cement

Contact cement is used to bond the laminate to the substrate. There are two types of contact cement, water-based and solvent-based.

There are also two types of solvent-based cements, flammable and non-flammable. The solvents in the flammable type are quite volatile, and should not be used anywhere near a flame or where there is a chance of a spark. The solvents in the non-flammable type won't ignite, but they are quite dangerous to breathe. Given the dangers of both types of solvent-based material I won't use either of them. I use the water-based cement instead.

Water-based contact cement will take longer to cure in cool or humid conditions, but if it is not spread too thick, it is ready to use in the same amount of time as the solvent types. For large surfaces, use a disposable paint roller to apply the adhesive (**Figure 326**). For thin surfaces, like the edges of cabinet or door parts, use a cheap, disposable bristle brush (**Figure 327**). Lay a thin coat down quickly and evenly, but don't roll over the applied adhesive more than you need to. On raw particleboard, apply two coats, as the first coat will soak into the board. On the back of the laminate, and on Melamine-coated board, one coat is sufficient.

Commercial shops spray on the contact cement, but until you reach the point where

Figure 328. Sticks—A smooth wood like birch or maple makes excellent sticks for keeping the glued laminate elevated from the substrate. Place the sticks on the dry glue surface every 6 inches to 12 inches.

Figure 329. Laminate on sticks—Put one edge of the laminate on the sticks, then lower it into place.

you are laminating all day every day, stick to rolling and brushing it on. The material is thick enough that regular spray guns don't work very well. Commercial shops use dedicated guns and pressure pots to spray the glue. If you have the equipment to spray lacquer, don't gunk it up by trying to spray glue.

Before applying the adhesive, clean off the surfaces to be coated to be sure they are free of dust or little chips of laminate. Don't sand or trim any laminate near where you have glue curing. The contact cement will be ready when you can touch it without any of it sticking to your finger. This takes about ten or fifteen minutes under ideal conditions, but may take half an hour if it is cool or humid. If it is extremely cool and humid, it may never dry until conditions change.

Laying the Laminate

Once the contact cement is ready, the laminate is placed above it without being allowed to come in contact with the substrate. Once the two surfaces touch, they cannot be moved

or adjusted without damaging the laminate. In professional shops, sticks of smooth hardwood like maple or birch are used to keep the substrate and the laminate from touching. Make them ⅜ inch to ½-inch square, and break the sharp corners with sandpaper. If you coat them with paste wax, they will be less likely to pick up glue and will last longer. Dowels can be used, but they are costly to purchase, and tend to twist and warp. Dowels can also roll as you are placing the laminate, moving it where and when you don't want it to move. You can make a set of sticks out of scrap material. If someone tells you to use slats from old Venetian blinds or a sheet of Kraft paper for this purpose, smile politely, nod your head, and prepare your sticks.

When the glue is ready, place your sticks every 6 inches to 12 inches across the surface. Let at least one end of the sticks hang over the edge of the substrate by an inch or two so that you can grab them without moving the laminate (**Figure 328**). Place the laminate on top of the sticks as close to the position you want as possible (**Figure 329**). Be careful not to let it sag between any two sticks, or you will have it stuck prematurely. Check that the laminate is hanging over all the way around, and carefully remove the center stick, letting the laminate drop on to the surface of the substrate. Press the laminate down with your hand **(Figure 330).**

With the center adhered, you can now remove the remaining sticks. You can pull them out from beneath the laminate, but it's better to lift the edge of the laminate and pick up the sticks **(Figure 331).** Once the sticks are gone, drop the plastic into place. If there is a little bit of debris on a stick, and you pull it, it will likely end up on the surface of the substrate, forming a bump in the finished surface. This likely won't happen when you first start laminating, but as the work progresses, and you start to trim, things will get messy.

When all the sticks are removed, press the entire surface down with your hand. You want to press it into place and also feel if there is anything underneath the laminate that shouldn't be there. To permanently adhere the laminate you now need to roll it. A 3-inch wide rubber roller, called a J roller, is used. Press down as hard as you can with both hands on the roller. Start from the center and work out to the edges. Finish by going around the edges a second time. Don't let the roller run off the edge, or you will crack the plastic **(Figure 332).**

If you didn't get all of the substrate covered, or if you find a little piece of something between the laminate and the substrate, you can undo the work, but it is time-consuming and messy. Work a sharp knife into the glue line, and squirt some lacquer thinner or acetone into the glue line. Don't use a utility knife for this, as the blades are brittle, and likely to snap. Most cabinetmakers keep a glue bottle filled with solvent handy for general cleaning and for occasions such as this. As the solvent dissolves the glue, you

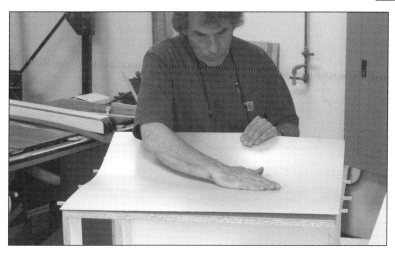

*Figure 330. **Pulling first stick**—After making sure the laminate overhangs the edges evenly, the first stick is removed, and the center of the laminate is pressed in place.*

*Figure 331. **Pulling remaining sticks**—After the laminate is adhered, lift an edge and remove the remaining sticks.*

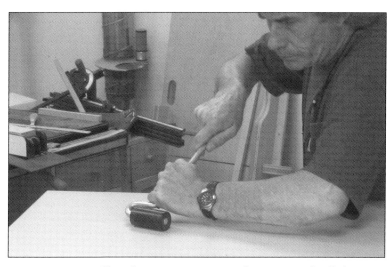

*Figure 332. **Rolling laminate**—Start in the center and roll the laminate out toward the edges. Be careful not to push the roller past the edge, as the laminate can crack.*

Figure 333. Bullet trimmer—*The single flute solid carbide bit cuts quickly, but should never be used against a finished edge.*

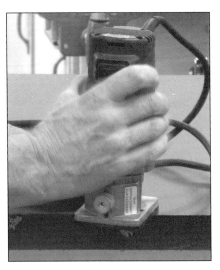

Figure 334. Bearing trimmer—*The ball bearing guide won't damage a finished edge as long as the bearing is free to turn. If glue builds up on the bearing, clean it immediately.*

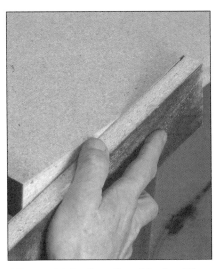

Figure 335. Sanding block—*The router will leave a small amount of material which should be sanded flush with a firm block.*

can begin to peel the sheet of laminate away from the substrate.

If you are trying to remove a foreign object, use as little solvent as possible. You can grind a hook in the end of a hacksaw blade or piece of steel strapping and try to catch the chip with it. Once the debris is removed and the solvent evaporates, you should be able to re-stick and re-roll the laminate. If it doesn't adhere, try heating the laminate with a clothes iron to set the adhesive. If it still doesn't adhere, you will need to remove the entire piece of plastic, let the solvent evaporate and roll on another coat of glue.

If you need to remove the entire piece, use as little solvent as possible. As the sheet comes off, you can reach in with a knife and cut through the glue. Remember that the solvent is flammable, and you will need to let it completely evaporate before you can glue the pieces again.

Trimming the Laminate

As soon as the laminate is rolled, it can and should be trimmed. The overhanging edges are fragile, and when they break, they tend to crack in to the finished surface. A small router is the weapon of choice for doing the trimming. A large router can be used, but a laminate trimmer is easier to handle, especially if you have many edges to be trimmed. There are two types of bits for trimming, and you really need to have both. When trimming against a raw edge, use a solid-carbide single-flute trimming bit. This bit does not have a ball bearing, it is guided by its bullet-shaped end below the cutting edge. This bit will cut much faster than a flush-trimming bit with a bearing. It also is less likely to pick up glue **(Figure 333).**

The time to use the bit with the ball bearing is when the edge being trimmed is against a surface that has already been laminated. The single-flute bit will burn this material, since the guide is spinning at the same rate as the bit itself. Make sure that the bearing spins freely, and clean any excess glue off the surface of the adjacent edge before trimming. If the bearing becomes clogged with glue while you are trimming, the bearing will start to spin along with the cutter and will burn the edge. The bearing will inevitably pick up some glue, and as the work proceeds, this should be removed. Avoid soaking the bearing with solvent to remove the glue. This will dry out the lubricant in the bearing, and shorten its life **(Figure 334).**

Flush-trimming bits should be called almost flush-trimming bits because they leave a tiny amount of the laminate hanging over the edge of the substrate. This must be removed. If it is a raw edge, it should be sanded with 80-grit sandpaper on a hard sanding block. Use an abrasive with the heaviest backing you can find, preferably cloth rather than paper. I make sanding blocks by cutting a scrap of particleboard or MDF 3 or 4 inches wide and gluing down half a belt from the belt sander with contact cement. This is more expensive than using sandpaper, but the sharp, hard edge of the laminate will destroy regular sandpaper quickly **(Figure 335).**

Hold the block flat on the edge, and rub the edge in long strokes until you can feel that the laminate and substrate are flush. If you have trimmed against another piece of laminate, you can't sand the edge without ruining the other piece of plastic. You need to bevel the edge slightly with a second router bit, and then file the edge flush.

The sequence in which the laminate is applied is important for the appearance of the finished work. Wherever the edge of the plastic is exposed, there will be a visible dark line. When you look at the finished work, you want to see as few of these lines as possible. You also don't want to leave an edge in a location where it is likely to catch on something if the substrate shrinks.

This means that the most visible surface is applied last, covering the edges of the other

pieces. In cabinets, the front edges of the box will be applied before a finished cabinet end. For cabinet doors, laminate the back, then the top and bottom, then the vertical edges, and finally the face. For countertops, start with the exposed end if there is one, then the front edge, and finally the top.

When trimming against a finished edge, the straight-cutting flush-trimming bit is followed by a similar bit that cuts a slight bevel. The greater the degree of bevel, the more of a black line you will see, so use the steepest one you can find.

A 7-degree or 8-degree bevel is preferred, as it will leave the best-looking edge. Take some time to set up this bit, because you want the lower edge of the cutter as close as possible to the bottom surface of the piece you are trimming. Anything that the trimmer doesn't take off will need to be removed by hand with a file.

If you set the bit too low, however, it will cut into the surface of the adjacent piece, exposing layers of paper below the surface and ruining the work. Because this can be a fussy setup, I keep one trimmer set up with a straight bit, and a second trimmer set up with a beveled bit. Some laminate trimmers have an edge guide and use a beveled bit without a bearing. These can be set closer, and reset as the carbide wears. They do a nice job, but if you don't have an extra trimmer to leave set up like this, you will spend much more time fussing with the trimmer than you will trimming.

There are also bits on the market that cut a bevel and a slight radius, called no-file bits. These come close to being accurately named when brand-new, but as the carbide wears, they are less effective.

Before running the trimmer with the bevel bit across the edge, clean any residual glue from the face of the edge. The cut from the

> When applying laminate to cabinets and countertops, cover the most visible surface last. This leaves the fewest black edge lines.

Figure 336. Bevel trimming—*A slight bevel removes the sharp corner. The steeper the bevel, the smaller the line at the edge of the laminate. Rout, then finish by hand-filing.*

Figure 337. File hand position—*Hold the file with both hands, and take care you don't file into the adjacent face.*

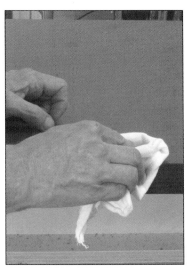

Figure 338.   Clean edge with thinner—*Remove excess glue with a rag dampened with solvent. Don't soak the joint.*

router should be as clean and as smooth as possible. Run the trimmer along the edge, pushing the bearing firmly against the edge. If you don't, the bearing can spin with the cutter, burning or scoring the edge.

File the Edge Flush

The final step is to use a file to bring the edge of the trimmed piece flush with the face of the other piece. Files made for this task are not expensive, and will be readily available from the plastic laminate supplier. I prefer one that has coarse teeth on one side, and fine teeth on the other, as seen in **Figure 336 & 337.** The teeth of the file point away from the handle or tang, and the tool should always be moved in this direction. The file should also be moved down from the face of the laminate. Sometimes it will be pushed, and sometimes it will be pulled.

The file should be moved in long strokes, at the same angle as the bevel on the trimming bit. As you file, you can see the chatter marks from the router bit disappear as the edge becomes smooth. After a few strokes with the file, feel the joint between the two pieces

of laminate with your finger. If you can feel the top piece sticking out, you're not done filing. Continue until the joint is smooth, checking with your finger more frequently as you near the end. If you go too far, and file into the face of the adjacent piece, there is no way to repair it. You will have to remove both pieces and start over. After the edge is brought flush, change the angle of the file and with a few strokes put a very slight bevel or radius on the corner of the laminate opposite the junction **(Figure 339)**.

Figure 339. Completed corner—*Round off sharp corners and the bottom edge with the file.*

16. COUNTERTOPS

While more exotic and more expensive materials are often used for countertops, plastic laminate is by far the most often-used material. This familiar material is easy to maintain, less expensive than other choices, and perfectly suited for the small-shop cabinetmaker.

In its simplest form, the countertop is one long slab, sitting on top of the base cabinets. The exposed edges at the front and end of the top may be self-edged with the same laminate as the top surface, or the edges may be solid wood. In most work, the substrate is ¾-inch thick particleboard, built up around the edges with two layers for a finished thickness of 1½ inches. In some parts of the country, 1¼-inch tops are commonly used. You can get particleboard 1¼ inches or 1½ inches thick, but building up the edges will make a better top, and it won't be ridiculously heavy.

Many people are dead set against particleboard under any circumstances, but countertops are the ideal place to use this material. The surface of particleboard will be much flatter than plywood, cost a lot less, and won't move around as much under the plastic laminate. If moisture makes you nervous about using particleboard, there is a moisture-resistant variety available. If you seal the edges around sink cutouts with silicone or acrylic latex caulking, you really don't need it.

If you want to use plywood, don't use construction-grade fir plywood. It is too inconsistent in thickness to make a good countertop. Look for something with many thin plies, no voids, and smooth faces.

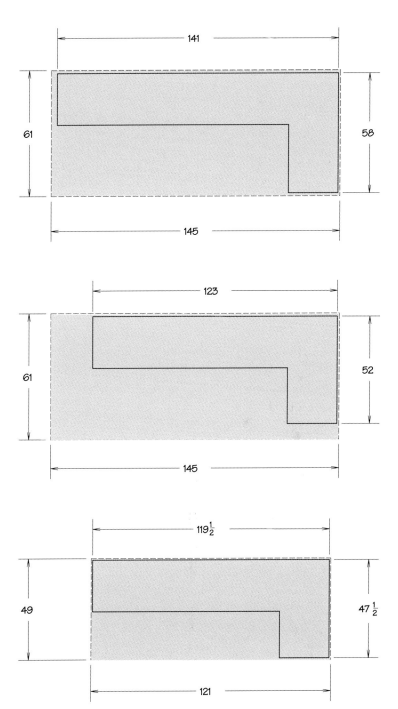

Figure 340. Plan countertops *to take advantage of standard sizes of sheet goods and laminates The two tops at the bottom vary by only a few inches, but the one in the middle will require purchasing as much material as the large countertop at the top of the page.*

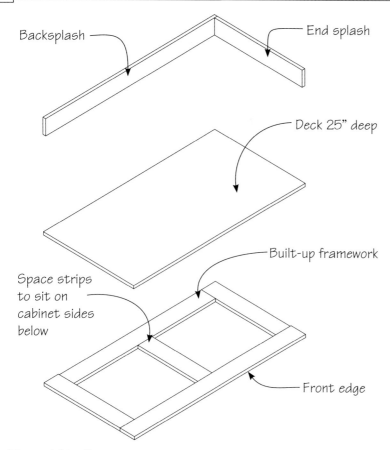

Figure 341. Countertop construction — *Since tops are 25 inches wide, you can't get two out of a sheet of particleboard or MDF that's only 48 inches wide. Saw the offcut into 4-inch strips for the backsplash and the built-up framework.*

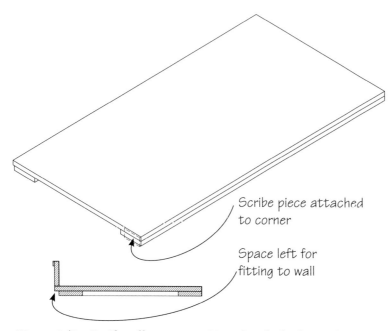

Figure 342. Scribe allowance — *Note that the built-up edge runs the full length of the front of the countertop, and the edges are flush. At the back, the build-up is inset ¼ inch to 1 inch, to allow for scribing.*

Layout

When laying out your project, keep in mind that the laminate is available in sheets up to 61 inches wide, and lengths of 97 inches, 121 inches and 145 inches. If at all possible, design the tops to fit close to, but not over, the standard sheet sizes. If your design calls for a 98-inch long top, you will need to buy the next largest sheet, and will likely waste the extra material. If your countertop turns a corner, and the short leg is less than 5 feet, you will be better off using one piece of laminate for the entire top rather than putting in a seam. The saving of labor and improved appearance over the life of the top will make up for the cost of the extra material (**Figure 340**).

Sheets of particleboard come about an inch oversize in each direction to allow you to trim off the factory edge. To apply a laminate or solid wood edge, you need a clean, flat surface, so be sure to saw all of the edges as you make the top. Particleboard also comes in various sheet sizes, ranging from 3 feet x 8 feet to 5 feet x 12 feet. If you have the space to handle and work with the material, you are better off making the substrate for the top out of one piece of material instead of piecing it together. When you are planning your material purchases, remember that the standard depth of a kitchen counter is 25 inches, and you won't be able to cut two pieces from a typical 4 x 8 sheet (**Figure 341**).

You will need extra material for building up the edges and making the backsplash. I rip the build-up pieces 4 inches wide. At the front edge, the build-up piece runs the entire length of the top, and the edges are flush (**Figure 343**). At exposed ends, the build-up runs from the back of the front build-up to the back of the top. At the back, and at ends that go against a wall, inset the edge of the build-up by ¼ inch to 1 inch from the edge of the counter (**Figure 342**).

There are several reasons for this. Perhaps the best reason is that it clearly defines which edges get finished and which edges don't. The second reason is in case the edge of the top needs to go against a crooked wall. If you need to scribe the edge of the top to make it fit, it is easier to only cut through one layer of material **(Figure 344).** If the walls of the room are really crooked, you might want to add a ¼-inch thick, 1½-inch wide piece a few inches long to the end of the finished edges. When you install the top, and cover the edges against the wall with the backsplash, the end points of the finished edges will be the only part that shows. The extra material at these points will allow you to keep the corner and back of the top away from the wall and still get a nice fit at the visible corners.

Once the build-up around the edges is complete, run additional strips from front to back, spacing them every 16 inches to 24 inches along the length. I space them so that they will straddle the edges of the cabinets below. Avoid putting them where the sink will be. With the particleboard for the top face-down on the bench, lay out and attach these pieces with yellow glue. I fasten them with 1¼ inch narrow-crown staples, but any fastener can be used.

Countertop Joints

If you need to make a counter longer than the available particleboard, or if you need to turn a corner, add a piece of particleboard at least 12 inches wide below the joint **(Figure 345),** if the joint is permanently put together in the shop. Use biscuits or a spline to line up the top surfaces. Pinch dogs are an effective way to pull the two parts together. Use glue and fasteners on the reinforcing plate, and be sure that the parts are level when they are put together.

If you need to make a joint that can be taken apart and re-assembled on installation, you

Figure 343. Deck fabrication—Working on the bottom surface, 4 inch wide material is glued and stapled to the edges and at regular intervals to make the top 1½ inches thick.

Figure 344. Back edges—Where the counter meets a wall, the edge build up is held back from the edge of the top.

need to provide a way to line up the two pieces, and pull them together. The top surfaces are prepared as for a permanent joint with biscuits or with splines. In place of one piece below the joint, two pieces are used, with one extending about an inch across the joint **(Figure 346).** Both pieces are routed to receive a special fastener, known in the trade as a dog bone.

This is a 1/4 x 20 cap-head machine screw with two flat pieces of steel attached. The flat piece nearest the head is not threaded,

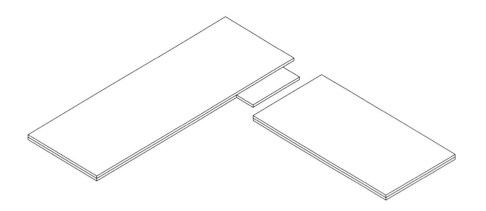

Figure 345. Joining countertops *— To make a top from two permanently connected sections, glue a wide piece of material below the seam to reinforce it.*

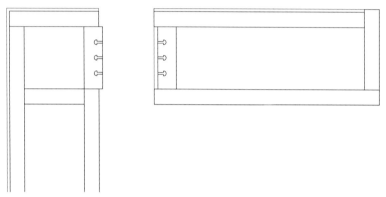

Figure 346. Joining countertops *— To make a top from two sections that can be disassembled and rejoined upon installation, use two bridge pieces and rout recesses for dog bone or flip bolt connectors.*

Figure 347. Flip bolt and template*—This simple template can be held to the bottom of the joint with screws. A guide collar locates the router bit.*

but the other piece is. To connect the field joint in the top, the two parts of the counter are placed together, and the dog bone is placed in the recess, with one of the flat pieces on each side of the top. A wrench is then used to tighten the fastener. A big improvement on the dog bone is the flip bolt, which can be tightened by hand and installed without using a wrench (**Figure 347).**

The recess is typically made with a router equipped with a straight bit and a template guide collar. A template is temporarily fastened to the connecting plates below the top, and the recess is cut with the router.

Joints in the countertop, whether field joints or permanent ones, are assembled and sanded flush before laminating. The easiest mistake to make is to assemble, smooth, and laminate a joint without ensuring that both surfaces are level and in the same plane. When the top is installed, the joint will gap.

If the top turns a corner, and must be tight to the wall on both legs, make certain to determine the exact angle of the corner, and the condition of the walls. The general rule in cabinetmaking is to make everything square, level, straight, and plumb, but this rule can be bent or broken when making an L-shaped or U-shaped top. It's often difficult to check a corner between two walls for square. There is usually a build-up of drywall mud close to the corner that won't be apparent at first glance. This can tilt the leg of a framing square and make thing appear worse (or better) than they really are. Measure 3 feet along one wall, 4 feet along the other, then measure between those two points. If it is 5 feet, then the corner is square.

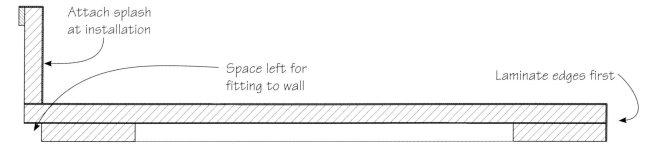

*Figure 348. **Section through countertop** — Arrange the edge build-up as shown, and leave scribe allowances at the wall. Attach the backsplash during installation, not in the shop.*

Countertop Template

The most foolproof (or fool-resistant) way to lay out the top is to make a template. If you are buying a granite or solid surface countertop, the suppliers will likely insist on coming out and making their own template before they will cut the top. If this is your first attempt at building a countertop, it would be good to follow their example. It's also a good idea to wait until you have the cabinets installed so that you can make the template at the exact height of the cabinets. This will add some time to your project, and it will be a little frustrating to have the cabinets installed without being able to use the kitchen. This is a better than bringing in a large L-shaped top and having one leg an inch away from the wall because you assumed the corner of the room was square.

A countertop template is essentially a story pole. Cardboard is frequently used, but I prefer strips of 1/4-inch thick plywood or Masonite, and usually use scraps of material from making cabinet backs. Lay them on top of the cabinets, and mark the extents of the top. If the corner is really tricky, I bring along my hot-melt glue gun, and fit pieces together rather than try to mark the angle.

It is possible to build and laminate the top in, or at least near, the finished and installed cabinets. This isn't an efficient way to do it if you're in business, but if you're building your own kitchen, and your shop is in the garage,

it's a reasonable method. Just cut the surface pieces for your tops bigger than you need them, place them on the cabinets, and mark out where they need to be trimmed. Once you are satisfied with how they fit, remove them from the cabinets, build up the edges, and do the laminate work. Be extremely careful when working around finished cabinets so that you don't damage them.

Laminate Edges First

Putting the laminate in place is the same process as has been outlined for laminating cabinets, but on a larger scale. The sequence of applying the plastic is to minimize the appearance of dark lines, and to prevent the catching of an edge in everyday use. The edges can be self-edged with plastic laminate, or a solid wood edge may be used. Before applying any of the edges, go over the edges of the particleboard or plywood substrate with a sanding block (**Figure 349, 350, 351, 352**). Any gaps, dips, or uneven areas will eventually de-laminate.

With self-edges, the end, or ends of the top are laminated and trimmed first. After they have been trimmed, the ends that will be covered by the front edge are sanded flush with the sanding block. Because the edges of the substrate are porous, apply two coats of contact cement to them, and one coat to the back of the laminate edge (**Figure 348**). The edge strips should not be cut with the

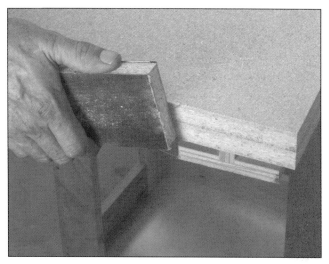

Figure 349. Sanding build up flush—*For the laminate to adhere properly, the edges must be perfectly flush. #80 grit sandpaper on a block will do this quickly.*

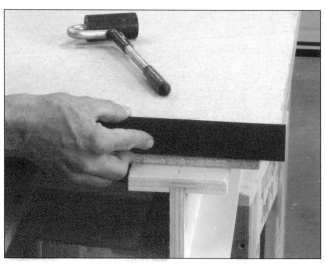

Figure 350. Sticking edge—*Starting at one end, put the laminate strip in place. The thumb and middle finger gauge the edges, while the index finger presses.*

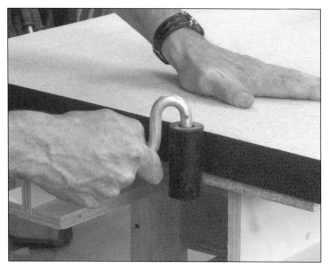

Figure 351. Rolling edges—*Contact cement is pressure sensitive, use a roller to adhere it to the substrate.*

Figure 352. Trimming edge—*A carbide bit with an integral bearing (bullet bit) trims the edge against the particleboard surface. Hold the trimmer base firmly against the laminate edge.*

table saw, as there is no good way to push pieces that thin safely past the blade. Use a laminate slitter instead, or cut the strip by clamping a straightedge to the bottom of the laminate, and making the cut with a router and a flush-cutting bit.

In the typical small shop, available space and cleanliness will likely be big issues. In addition to the space for the top, you will also need an equal amount of space for the laminate to sit while the contact cement dries.

You also need to prevent little chips of scrap and dirt from settling on the glued surfaces. Clean up after each round of trimming and sanding, and be sure that both the substrate and laminate are clean before you apply the cement, and once again before you put down the laminate. When you're cleaning, make sure that your clothing and hair are also clean. The chips from trimming can land anywhere, and the sneaky ones will hide in your beard so they will have a clean shot when they decide to jump onto the wet contact cement.

Once the laminate is on the edges and trimmed, the perimeter of the top should be sanded so that the laminate is perfectly flush with the top surface of the substrate. The safest way to do this is by hand with a sanding block, but that will take a while. A random-orbit sander or a belt sander will be much faster, but you run the risk of sanding a dip in the edge. If using the random-orbit sander, keep the disc flat on the surface, with most of the disc on the substrate during sanding. If you use a belt sander, keep the direction of the belt moving in toward the substrate, and keep as much of the platen of the sander flat on the substrate as you can.

Wood Edge

If you want a wood edge, you can apply it before you apply the top laminate, and laminate over it as seen in **Figure 353**. With this method, you cut the profile on the top corner of the wood and the plastic laminate at the same time. This saves you from having to sand the top surface of the wood against the finished surface of the laminate. The disadvantage is that it is hard to file a clean edge on the laminate itself. If you put a bevel on the edge of the wood, the dark line of the laminate can be filed, but it will appear to be very wide. If the wood is dark, you can get away with it, but with a light-colored wood, I wouldn't do it. There is also a chance that the wood might expand or contract, eventually breaking the glue bond at the edge of the countertop.

The alternative is to laminate the top surface first, trim and sand the edge flush, and then apply the wood edge **(Figure 354).** The edge trim should be as straight as possible, but it will likely need to be trimmed even with the top of the laminate. A shop-made router jig makes the cut with the bottom of a mortising bit, providing a clean cut with little risk of tearing out the wood. Its use is described in detail on **page 82**. After the

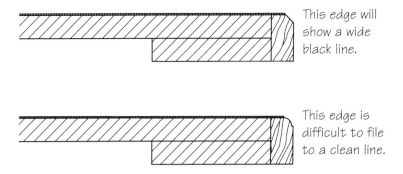

This edge will show a wide black line.

This edge is difficult to file to a clean line.

*Figure 353. **Wood edge first**— With these two treatments the wood edge is attached, then the top is laminated, and finally the decorative profile is routed.*

This wood edge must be carefully trimmed to the laminate.

*Figure 354. **Wood edge last** — With this treatment the top is laminated and the wood edge is then applied and trimmed flush.*

wood is trimmed, it should be sanded to remove marks left by the router bit. A short piece of scrap edging can be used to sand the top of the wood edge without damaging the laminate. Stick sandpaper to the edge of the scrap, and attach a second piece of scrap to serve as a fence. Because the scrap will be the same thickness as the edge, it won't sand into the laminate.

The wood edges will look best if the outside corners are mitered. Mill the stock wider than you need if you will be trimming it after application. If the wood is going on after the plastic laminate, remember that the overall thickness of the top will be greater than 1½ inches by the thickness of the laminate. The wood can be glued to the edge of the substrate, but biscuits every 12 inches will help to keep the edge of the wood flush with the top. Mask the laminate before staining or finishing. You can remove the finish from the laminate with lacquer thinner on a rag, but it will be difficult to obtain a clean edge.

Laminating the Countertop

Figure 355. *Preparation*—*Place sticks on the dry glue surface every 6 inches to 12 inches.*

Figure 356. *Placing the laminate*— *Put one edge of the plastic on the sticks, and then lower it into place.*

Figure 357. *Sticking the top*—*Press the laminate down between the two center sticks, and remove one.*

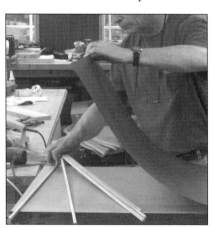

Figure 358. *Lifting end*—*Once the laminate is stuck in the center, lift one end off the sticks, remove the sticks, and let the plastic fall into place.*

Figure 359. *Rolling edge of top*—*The edge is most vulnerable. Put a second coat of contact cement around the perimeter, and be sure to roll the edges firmly.*

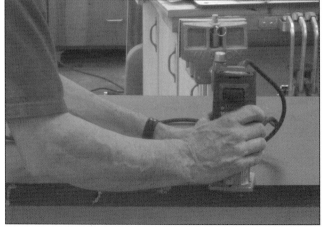

Figure 360. *Bearing trim*—*The trimming bit with a ball bearing will trim against the finished edge without damage-if you keep the bearing clean so it can spin freely.*

Laying the Top

In theory, you should also apply laminate to the bottom surface of the countertop. There is a special material called backer sheet made for this purpose. The backer sheet is the same paper and resin as in standard laminate, but without the decorative layer and protective coating. Without it, the particleboard can warp since it will lose and gain moisture more readily from the raw side of the board. In practice, it is rarely used, and as long as the countertop is attached solidly to the cabinets below, the chances of the top warping are very low. If you have an unsupported span longer than three feet, you should laminate the bottom side. Apply the backer as you would standard laminate, and put it on the underside before you build up the edges.

When you are ready to laminate the top of the counter, make sure to clean both the board and the bottom of the laminate just before you apply the contact cement. If you don't have a large, flat surface available to apply glue to the laminate, you can lay it face down on the counter itself to spread the glue. Move it to a safe location while you apply the contact cement to the top. The flat face of the top isn't as likely to delaminate as the edges, so a second coat of adhesive over the entire surface isn't necessary. I usually run the glue roller around the edges an extra time to be on the safe side, and if the top will have a sink cutout, I'll apply extra glue in that area.

When the glue has dried, run your hand over the surface to make sure there aren't any little chips on the surface. Place your sticks across the surface of the top no more than 12 inches apart **(Figure 355)**. When you pick up the laminate, carry it vertically by one edge if possible. It will tend to sag if carried horizontally. If the sheet is very long, you'll want to have some help to set it on the countertop. Carry it vertically, and rest one edge on the sticks near the edge of the

substrate. Gently lay the laminate down on the sticks, and slide it into position **(Figure 356)**. Make sure it is overhanging all the way around, and push it into place between the two centermost sticks **(Figure 357)**.

Lift one end at a time and remove the remaining sticks, then press the laminate onto the surface with your hand **(Figure 358)**. Roll it down, applying as much pressure as you can. Work from the middle out to the edges, and work the roller from front to back and side to side **(Figure 359)**. After rolling, run the palm of your hand over the surface to feel if there are any bumps in the surface. If there are, you likely have a chip left over from trimming between the board and the laminate. If it is near an edge, you might be able to work it out with a knife as described earlier **(page 191)**.

Seaming the Top

If a seam is required in the laminate, either for a permanent joint or for a field joint, both pieces need to be prepared before either is glued down. The joint should be prepared with the countertop assembled, face up and perfectly level. The first step is to determine the location of the seam, and mark it on the face of the substrate with a pencil and a framing square. If you need to put a seam in a top that has a sink, do not place the seam at or near the location of the sink. I know it's tempting, because right at the sink you will only have a few inches of counter exposed. But the seam is vulnerable to water and will eventually fail if located where it regularly gets wet.

Bring the two pieces to be joined to the line, and make sure that the substrate will be entirely covered. Cut the laminate pieces so that you have an inch or two extra length in case your first attempt at making the seam doesn't work. The trick is to cut both edges at the same time with a router and a straight-

Figure 361. Seaming jig—*By routing both halves of a seam at the same time, you can achieve a nearly invisible joint. The jig consists of two plywood strips fastened to a base, spaced apart by a hair more than the width of the router bit.*

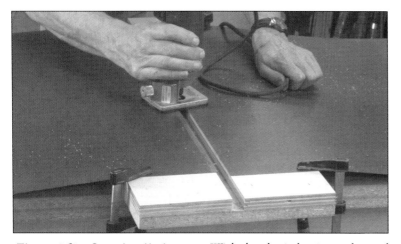

Figure 362. Seaming jig in use—*With the plastic laminate clamped to the jig, a flush trimming router bit is used to cut both mating edges at one time.*

Figure 363. Cleaning up seam joint—*Use the sanding block or a file to remove any burr on the back of the laminate.*

Figure 364. Fitting seam—*With one side glued, the second piece is put in place.*

edge. A seaming jig (**Figure 361**) is used along with a router with a flush-trimming bit. It doesn't matter if you use a bullet bit, or a bit with a bearing, but the bit should be sharp.

Place one piece on the layout line, and slide the other piece against it. After checking to be sure that the entire top will be covered, make four or five pencil marks across the joint. Slide the jig under the joint, with the gap in the jig under the joint. Line up the pencil marks on the two pieces of laminate. The two edges don't have to touch, but the gap between them must be even, and smaller than the diameter of the router bit. Clamp the two pieces to the jig. I do this right at the joint so I don't have to move the big sheets of laminate around. When everything is secure, run the router along the gap, pushing it firmly against the edge of the slot in the jig. Make one steady cut (**Figure 362**).

Remove the clamps and the jig, and with the sanding block remove any burr from the top and bottom of the plastic. Be careful that you only remove the burr (**Figure 363**), lest you damage the top surface, or change the thickness of the pieces. Lay one edge along the line and butt the other piece against it. The two pieces should match perfectly along the length of the joint. If there is a very slight gap, you might be able to sand the edges with the sanding block to get them to fit. If the joint doesn't fit after a few strokes with the sanding block, rout the joint again.

When you are satisfied with the fit, remove one of the pieces of laminate, and with the edge of the other piece along the layout line, continue the witness marks from the laminate onto the face of the substrate. This is so you can position the first piece you glue down exactly where you want it. If you stick it down too far to one side, there is a good chance that the second piece will not cover all of the board.

Apply the contact cement to all of the countertop, and to the back of both pieces of laminate. When the glue is dry to the touch, put the sticks on the substrate and position the first piece of plastic on the sticks. Slide the laminate on the sticks until the edge is in position on the layout line, with the witness marks on the board aligned with the marks on the face of the laminate. Stick the edge of the laminate on the line, remove the nearest stick, and push the laminate down to the surface of the board. Remove the rest of the sticks, then press and roll the entire piece of laminate.

Place the sticks in position and lay the second piece of plastic on them, adjusting the position of the plastic until the edges and the witness marks all line up. Carefully press the edge down against the board and the adjoining edge **(Figure 364).** Remove the first stick, and press down the first few inches of the laminate. If the seam is tight, proceed to remove the rest of the sticks, and when you roll, roll first toward the seam. If there is a bit of a gap, leave the next two sticks in place. Press the laminate down just past them and remove the sticks from that point to the end, and press the laminate down to the board. Pull out the remaining sticks. You should have a hump in the laminate near the seam. Working carefully toward the seam, push the laminate down to the substrate with your hands. This will force the end of the plastic into the seam and close the gap.

Backsplash

The back and end splashes are simply 4-inch wide pieces of substrate covered with plastic laminate on the face, top edge, and any exposed end or ends. A ¼-inch wide scribe strip can be added to the back edges where they meet the walls of the room, but this is rarely done. The backsplash will be fairly flexible, and standard practice is to glue it to the wall with construction adhesive, bending it

to conform. If you use a combination of hot glue and construction adhesive, you won't have to hold the splash in place while the adhesive dries. The junction of the edge of the splash and the wall is filled with acrylic latex caulking, which can fill gaps up to ⅛ inch.

Installation

When installing the countertop, remember that the backsplash will cover the junction between the top and the wall, so if you have a slight gap, you won't need to scribe the top. If you do need to trim the top, use a jigsaw with a reverse cutting blade like a Bosch T101BR. These blades have the teeth pointing in the opposite direction of a normal blade, and won't chip the top of the laminate.

When trimming, or when making a cutout in the top for the sink, you want to make sure that the base of the jigsaw doesn't scratch the laminate. It is often recommended to cover the bottom of the jigsaw's base with masking tape, but this doesn't last very long, and eventually creates a sticky mess that keeps the saw from maneuvering. Sand the base plate smooth if it is rough or scratched, and if you feel you need to cover it with something, attach a scrap of plastic laminate to it with double-faced tape.

If the cabinets are installed level, the counter should not require any additional leveling when set in place. If portions of the top are resting on cleats, as in a dead corner, the cleats should be installed level with the line of the cabinets. The counter should be attached to the cabinet rails, front and back, with 1¼-inch long screws. In places where you can't reach from underneath to set screws, a bead of construction adhesive will hold the top permanently in place.

17. CABINET BASES

In most of the drawings in this book, and in most of the cabinets I make, I build a separate base for the base cabinets to sit on. While this may seem like a lot of extra work, it saves time in the long run, improves the quality of the finished project, and reduces the chances of the cabinets sustaining damage from water.

Cabinets are often built with the sides of the cabinets extending completely to the floor. When installed, the cabinets need to be level both side to side and front to back. The problem with cabinets with full-height sides is that there is always at least one back corner, and often two or more, that you can't reach to put a shim in. What most installers will do in this situation is pull up on the back rail of the cabinet box, and screw the box to the wall studs. This does get the cabinet level, if the installer can hold it level with one hand and drive the screw with the other. Instead of sitting solidly on its bottom edges, most of the weight of the cabinet is now hanging on a couple of screws **(Figure 365).**

Instead of building the bases, adjustable plastic feet are available, and these are a reasonable alternative. My preference for building a base out of wood or plywood is partly practical and partly old habit. When the plastic legs first became available, they were on the expensive side. The other reason is that to adjust the legs at the back of the cabinet, you need to crawl into the cabinet with a level and a screwdriver to adjust them through the cabinet bottom. Because you need to level from inside the cabinet, it can be difficult to tell if the cabinet you are working on is too high or too low compared to the next cabinet in line.

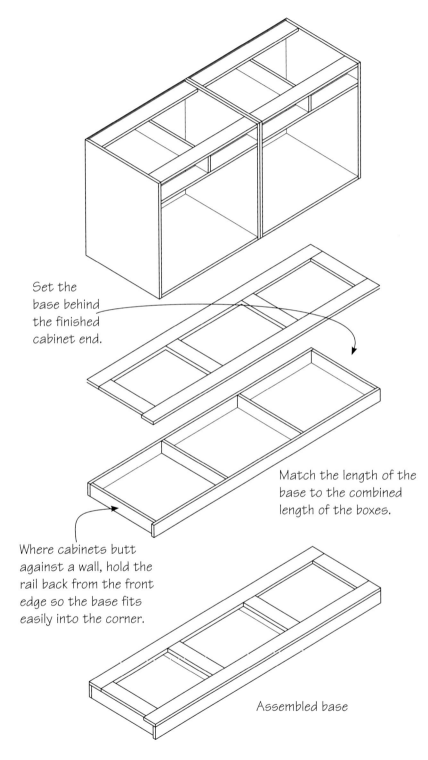

Set the base behind the finished cabinet end.

Match the length of the base to the combined length of the boxes.

Where cabinets butt against a wall, hold the rail back from the front edge so the base fits easily into the corner.

Assembled base

Figure 365. The cabinets sit on a two-part base that incorporates the kick space. Leveling the base on the floor automatically levels the tops of the cabinets, and thus the countertop.

The main advantage of the separate wood base is that it can be built to hold several cabinets, usually an entire elevation. It can be set in place and leveled from above, without any obstructions. I build the base either from 3¼-inch wide pieces ripped from a sheet of exterior grade plywood, or from whatever solid wood I am using for a secondary wood, usually poplar. For a normal 24-inch deep base cabinet, the assembled base will be 21 inches deep. The long front piece is cut to the length of the elevation. If the elevation is longer than the plywood, I will make an 8-foot length, and a second base the additional length needed.

The lower part of the base resembles a stud wall, and I place the short cross-pieces so that they land under the joints where two cabinets meet. With this part of the base standing on edge, the remaining pieces are laid flat, the edges of the long pieces and the short pieces at each end flush with the edges. The short pieces in between are centered on the edges of the pieces below. Glue and narrow-crown staples are sufficient to hold the base together, but if you don't have a stapler, or don't trust staples, you can hold the base together with nails or screws.

Constructed in this way, the base is a rigid structure that shouldn't sag or bend under a reasonable load. Leveling the base is easier than trying to level separate cabinets, especially if you need to insert shims, or remove any material at the back of the cabinet. When installing, the base is set in place, and a level line drawn on the wall where the top edges of the cabinets should be. Measure down from this benchmark to locate the top edge of the base.

With a 4-foot level running the long direction, and a 2-foot level the short way, it's a simple task to get the base leveled. If there are any high spots in the floor, the base will likely rock. Shims, either scrap cedar shingles or thin scraps from the shop, are placed under the base at the low points. You may need to cut or scribe any high spots from the bottom edge of the base.

Once the base is level, it can be attached to the floor with ¾-inch square cleats, or by driving screws at an angle through the base and into the floor. In cases where the floor is more than ¼ inch out of level, it may be necessary to trim some material off the bottom edge of the base, by marking it with a compass or an Accu-scribe, and cutting off the waste with a jigsaw. With the base level, the cabinets should be easy to install. Attach the boxes to the base with 1¼ inch screws in the corner and back.

18. FINISHING

The size and scope of a typical kitchen project will push the limits of your finishing capabilities.

A book like this really can't teach you everything you need to know about finishing wood. There simply isn't room to cover the subject thoroughly. What I will do is point you to some good resources, and cover the special challenges of finishing a kitchen full of cabinets, and the differences between a project like this, and smaller finishing projects.

Bob Flexner's book *Understanding Wood Finishing* has been recently revised and updated, and I recommend it. He explains the chemistry behind finishes, solves some mysteries and debunks many myths. Reading can't replace practical experience, but this will give you a good start, and enough information to make intelligent decisions on your own.

Other excellent resources are the many woodworking forums on the Internet. Chances are good that you can quickly get an answer from a fellow woodworker that has faced the same situation, and come out the other end with work to be proud of.

The size and scope of a typical kitchen project will likely push the limits of your finishing capabilities, especially if you are working from a small basement or garage shop. All the doors to be finished may not seem so bad when they are sitting nicely in a pile, but when you spread them out for finishing they can claim all of the horizontal territory you have available.

The cabinets, once assembled, will also take a lot of space. You may be able to fit them in the space, but will you be able to get to (and see) all the surfaces that need to be finished? Can you adequately ventilate the space to remove fumes, and will it be warm enough or cool enough or dry enough for the finish to cure properly?

So the first question to resolve will be where to do the finishing, and how much of the project actually requires finishing? Actually, that's two questions. If you are pressed for space, one of the best ways to deal with the problem is to use materials that don't need finishing after assembly, or finishing what parts you can while they are still manageable flat pieces.

With the advent of Melamine board, and factory-finished plywood, you can reduce your finishing workload considerably by using these materials. Even large commercial shops with well-equipped spray booths tend to use these materials when they can. The savings in labor gained from not having to sand, seal, sand, and topcoat the inside of a set of cabinets will more than make up for the higher material cost. Finishing the insides of cabinets is one of the most tedious, thankless tasks known to man.

The insides of the cabinets don't need to match the outsides of the cabinets, unless there are glass doors that leave the interiors exposed. The light color of pre-finished plywood or Melamine board makes it easier to see what's in the cabinets, and these finishes are more durable and easier to clean than any finish the amateur woodworker can apply. You're better off concentrating your efforts on the exposed parts of the cabinets. There will still be a lot of work, and you'll do a better job on the exteriors if you're not burned out and frustrated from doing the interiors.

Finish Before Assembly

If this hasn't convinced you, and you are determined to do you own finishing on the interiors of your cabinets, consider finishing the parts before you assemble the cabinets. If you're using biscuit joints, or rabbets for your joints, you can either cut them after the finish is dry, or mask off the areas that will need to be glued.

Setting up a flat surface for applying the finish, and some racks for drying will be much more manageable than crawling around trying to reach all of the surfaces that need finished on the inside of the cabinet boxes.

If you do finish the inside of the cabinets, do as much of the sanding as possible before you put the boxes together. Be careful when cleaning up any glue squeeze-out inside the cabinets. Don't use a lot of water, or you will need to sand again at the inside corners. Leave the backs off the cabinets until the interiors and the backs are finished, particularly if you are using a spray gun to apply the finish.

Finish After Installation

If your shop space is small, you might be better off waiting until the cabinets are installed, and finishing them in place. There are some distinct advantages in doing this. If there is a significant amount of trim in the room that also must be finished in place, doing the cabinets at the same time will provide a better match between the cabinets and the trim.

Another big advantage for finishing after installation is that any nail holes from the installation can be filled before the finish goes on. These will be less obvious than filling already finished cabinets. It's also an insurance policy against the inevitable dents and dings that will likely occur during the installation. With all the cabinets in position, you will have more control over staining than you would with the cabinets scattered in your shop. If you stain the cabinets in random order, you could end up with some color variations that won't be noticeable until the cabinets are next to each other.

With the cabinets installed, you won't be as cramped for space as you might be in your shop, and you will avoid any confusion regarding which surfaces will be exposed.

The down side to finishing after installation is mainly controlling the dust and eliminating the fumes. If this is new construction, or an empty house being remodeled this isn't

Finishing the insides of assembled cabinets is one of the most thankless, tedious tasks known to man.

a big problem. If however, you, your wife, your kid, dog, cat, bird and fish are trying to live in the house, finishing can present some real problems.

Sanding

Before you can finish, everything will need to be sanded smooth. How far to take the sanding is partly dependent on what type of finish is to be used. Many people make the mistake of going too far with the sanding; leaving the wood in a polished condition that won't let the wood absorb the stain. If you get the wood smooth enough that you can't see the sanding scratches you should be ready to stain. Wiping the raw wood with a rag dampened with mineral spirits will give you an indication of how the wood will appear under the finish.

If you are using an open grained wood like oak, the final sanding can be with #120 or #150 grit. Smooth grained woods like maple or cherry should be sanded to one grit higher, #150 or #180 grit. If you're using a water based finish, the first coat of finish will raise the grain, leaving you with a coarser surface. Overcome this by raising the grain deliberately after the final sanding. Wipe all the surfaces with a rag that has been dampened with water, preferably distilled water. Allow the surface to dry thoroughly, and then lightly sand with #220 or #240 grit sandpaper.

In commercial shops, the finish room is usually a separate space from the rest of the shop. If you're going to be finishing in the same area where the cabinets are cut and assembled, you will need to clean the space completely before you begin finishing. If you will be spraying, you will need to achieve a nearly dust free environment if you want the finish to look good. Once in a garage shop, I cleaned everything, and sprayed finish on a bunch of doors. Satisfied with the work, I closed the overhead door, only to see all the

dust from the back of the door drift down onto the wet surfaces.

After everything has been sanded, and is ready to be finished, remove as much dust as you can from the cabinets and surrounding surfaces. The best way to remove it is with a vacuum cleaner. You can blow the dust off with compressed air, but unless you have a way to remove the dust, this will likely only rearrange it.

Staining

If your work will be stained, prepare a sample, and check it's appearance in the room before making a final decision. Fluorescent lights in the shop can make colors appear differently than natural daylight or incandescent lights. If you have raised panels in the project, stain the panels before assembling them. The panels will often shrink enough to expose bare wood after the cabinets are installed.

Try to stain parts that will be next to each other at the same time. Variations in temperature, humidity, or your technique can cause the stain to be a different tone. Check parts as you go against your sample to be sure you aren't straying too far from the desired finish.

Topcoat

Most commercial shops choose a topcoat that offers good protection while drying quickly. Ordinary lacquer that is used for furniture offers marginal protection against the drips, spills and cleaners found in the average kitchen. The other concern with lacquer is its flammability. It is highly volatile in a liquid state, as is the sanding dust and overspray. In commercial shops, it is sprayed in an enclosed booth with good exhaust fans. It really isn't suitable for a home shop.

Vacuum up the sanding dust, otherwise you will only be rearranging it to float onto your finish.

Shellac dries quickly, but isn't durable enough for use in kitchen cabinets. Oil finishes also aren't suitable for the kitchen. They look nice, but don't build enough of a film to be durable. Oil based polyurethanes, and other varnishes are durable enough, but take too long to dry.

Water based polyurethanes offer good protection, and dry relatively quickly. They don't have the depth or clarity of lacquer or shellac, but if carefully applied, look good enough for a typical set of cabinets. This is the finish I would recommend to the amateur woodworker.

Brush or Spray?

Once you have decided where the finishing will take place, and what finish to use, you need to decide on a method for application. The choices are to brush on the finish, or to apply it with a spray gun. Both of these techniques take some practice to master, it can't really be said that one is easier than the other.

Spraying is much faster, but some expensive equipment is required, and the waste from the overspray needs to be considered as added material costs, and as a safety issue when using flammable finishes. Overspray also gets everywhere. If you're spraying in the same shop you work in, cover your machines before you begin. High Volume Low Pressure (HVLP) systems produce less overspray than conventional spray guns, but you still need an exhaust fan. If there is a significant amount of overspray in the room where the cabinets are finished, it will settle on the finish as it dries, leaving the surfaces grainy and rough.

I would only spray in a detached garage with an HVLP system and an adequate exhaust fan. I wouldn't spray at all in a basement shop or other part of an occupied house.

Spraying finishes is very efficient in a commercial setting, but I don't think the home worker will gain much in using them.

A large part of the boost in productivity commercial shops enjoy comes from having a dedicated area for finishing. You don't need to clean sawdust out of a spray booth before you begin because it never gets in. You don't have to worry about covering anything you don't want overspray on, because it is all in another room. You don't have to worry about overspray settling on the finish and ruining it because there is a large exhaust fan. And you don't have to worry about killing the parrot with fumes, or having the pilot light from the water heater burn your house down. The woodworker trying to apply a spray finish at home will have to deal with all of these issues.

Brushing will take a little longer than spraying, but if you factor in all of the cleanup, both before and after, associated with spraying, I think it's the best alternative if you don't have a dedicated finishing space.

The biggest equipment investment will be for a decent brush. The quality of the brush used will make a tremendous difference in both the quality of the work, and the ease and speed of application. Practice your techniques before you are knee deep in a large project.

Most finishing mistakes are from rushing the work, or not understanding the properties of the materials being used. A good finish will make average work look special, and good work look amazing. As with all the other aspects of cabinetmaking, take your time to get it right before trying to be fast.

Brushing is the best way to finish in the small shop, and a good brush is the best investment.

19. INSTALLATION

Install efficiently. People living on frozen food warmed in the microwave tend to be impatient, particularly if they can see their new kitchen, but can't use it.

Although installation is the last step to take place, it must be considered at the very beginning of the project. This is the point where oversights and bad decisions become apparent. Good planning can overcome the physical shortcomings of the room. If you know before you build the cabinets that a wall is out of plumb or a corner is out of square you can accommodate that during construction, or at least leave yourself some options. If these things are a surprise when you put the cabinets in, the chances of a graceful solution are greatly reduced.

Installation can also make or break the appearance of the project. Good cabinets can look awful if not installed correctly, and for cabinet doors and drawers to function properly, the cabinets must be level, square and plumb. This is the first rule of installation; no matter what the conditions of the room are, the cabinets are built and installed level and plumb. If you try to match the idiosyncrasies (or defects) of the room when building or installing the cabinets, the job will never look right.

On one of the first installations I worked on the boss told me, "The goal is to get home as fast as we can." He didn't mean that we should rush or do a sloppy job, he meant that we had to work as efficiently as we could. It's easy to get bogged down or be caught unprepared and have the install take far longer than it should. In addition to that, there is always a customer waiting anxiously for the job to be completed. This is especially true of kitchens. People living on frozen food warmed in the microwave tend to be impatient, particularly if they can see their new kitchen, but can't use it.

Establish Benchmarks

Before you begin fastening cabinets to the walls, you need to establish some benchmarks, and make some decisions. Don't bring the cabinets into the room until this has been accomplished. You need to get to know the space, and you will need some room to maneuver. The first thing to do is find the high point of the floor, and establish level horizontal lines for the top of the base cabinets, and the bottom of the wall cabinets.

Lay a four-foot level on the floor, in various locations and in different directions. You need to find out which way the floor slopes, both from left to right when facing the wall, and away from or towards the wall. I never expect the floor to be level-if it is, it's a nice surprise. Don't make a quick decision based on surveying a small area. There will often be high and low spots throughout the room and you can paint yourself in a corner by making a hasty decision.

The reason for working from the highest point is that it is much easier to shim up from the low points than it is to cut down from the high points. Once you have found the high point, measure up from the floor and establish a level line around the room. I like to mark a line at the top of base cabinets (34½ inches in most cases) and put a second benchmark at 54 inches (the bottom of the wall cabinets). You can also use some arbitrary distance in between, four feet for example.

It is possible to draw the horizontal line with a level, but a laser level on a tripod will be more accurate. If using a level, a four-foot or longer level will increase the chances of getting a good straight line. Make sure the level is accurate by placing it on a horizontal surface and flipping it end for end. If the bubble reads the same both ways, the level is accurate.

While you are laying out your horizontal benchmark, pay attention to the condition of the walls. Be aware of any places where the wall goes in and out. A wall may look nice and flat when viewed head-on, but low spots will show up as gaps behind the straight edge of the level, and the level will rock on high spots. You can also find peaks and valleys by sighting along the wall from one end.

As with the floor you want to work from the high spots. A gap at one of the low spots won't be a big problem. If you happen to start fastening cabinets at a low spot, however, when you get to a high point, you will lose the straight line at the front of the cabinets. This isn't the best way to find the high points. The only real solution if this happens is to go back, loosen the boxes you've just put in and start over.

You also need to know if the wall is plumb, if it leans in or out, or if it has a bow in it. When the cabinets are installed, the faces need to be plumb, so if the wall leans back, the tops of the cabinet boxes will need to be shimmed away from the wall. This is an easy fix for the base cabinets, but difficult for the uppers. If the wall leans forward, the bottoms of the cabinets will need to be shimmed—not a real problem to solve for the wall cabinets, but difficult with the base cabinets.

At this point, it may look like you're just fooling around, avoiding the actual installation, but the more you know about the conditions of the room, the better off you will be. The goal is to get it right the first time so you want to be sure before you start.

Corner Installation

If the cabinets only go against one wall, you're about ready, but if they turn one or more corners, you still have some surveying work to do. The cabinet, or cabinets at the corner are the most difficult to install, and they need to go in first. The lines of the corner cabinets will establish the lines for the rest of the cabinets in both directions. If you try to work into the corner instead of away from it, the chances are very high that something will happen to make you start over.

Take a good look at the corner and determine the relationship of the two walls to each other, as well as the relationship of each

Find the high spot on the floor and start from that. It is much easier to shim the low spots than to cut down the high ones.

The cabinet, or cabinets, at the corner are the most difficult to install and they need to go in first.

of the walls to the floor and ceiling. No matter how out of whack the walls, floor and ceiling are, the faces of each run of cabinets coming out of the corner need to be in the same vertical plane. If the walls are not square to each other, you usually will want to adjust the angle at the intersection of the cabinets to follow the lines of the walls. If they don't, the gap between the back of the cabinets and the face of the wall at the end of the run of cabinets away from the corner can be quite noticeable.

While examining the corner, check to see how much drywall joint compound is in the corner. Usually there is a build up in the corner that can hide the actual conditions of the two walls. Rather than placing a framing square in the corner, and basing your decision on that, measure three feet from the corner in one direction, and four feet from the corner in the other. If the walls are square, the distance across the two points will be five feet.

Locate the Studs

By now, you will have a good idea of what you will be up against when installing the cabinet boxes. Keep in mind whether the floor rises or falls in each direction, which way the walls lean, and if the corner is more or less than 90 degrees. With an understanding of how the cabinets will need to be placed, you need to know what they will be fastened to—you need to locate and mark the studs within the walls.

If you have a helper, this is a good way to keep him from eating all the donuts while you are establishing your benchmarks. Electronic stud finders are helpful, and if the walls haven't had their final coat of paint, I go ahead and make vertical pencil lines at each stud location around the room. If the walls are finished, make a small mark along the horizontal benchmarks. These lines will

be hidden by the cabinets, counter top and backsplash.

Ideally, the last coat of paint on the walls will come after the installation of the cabinets. This makes life a little more difficult for the painter, but there is likely to be some damage to the walls while installing the cabinets, and it will be an easier installation if you have the freedom to make some marks and poke some holes in the walls. If the room is new construction, it's also a good idea to take some pictures of the walls before the drywall is hung. I like to take digital pictures if I can so that a reference is available of exactly what is behind the walls, and where it is.

Wall Cabinets First

The next decision to make is which cabinets to hang first, the wall or the base cabinets. The argument for putting the base cabinets in first is that it gives you something to rest the wall cabinets on. You can put a box or jack on the top of the base cabinets to set the height so you don't have to hold them in place. This has some merit, but I prefer to set the wall cabinets first.

If the base cabinets are installed first, you really have to lean over them to reach inside the wall cabinets to drive the fastening screws. There is also quite a risk of damaging the base cabinets while installing the wall cabinets, either from something falling, or from something banging up against the face of the base cabinets. The only down side of putting the wall cabinets in first is that you might bump your head on one of them when working on the base cabinets.

Before putting the wall cabinets in place, I run a narrow strip of wood across the wall studs for the bottoms of the cabinets to rest on during installation. This establishes a level bottom line for the cabinets. It also makes it much easier to hold them in position before

> Ideally, the last coat of paint will go on the walls after the installation of the cabinets.

running the screws. If the doors of the cabinets can be removed, take them off and set them in a safe location, preferably in another room to keep them from being damaged.

How to deal with the corner depends on what type of cabinet or cabinets are located there. A single cabinet needs to be set carefully, as it establishes the lines for the remaining cabinets in each direction. If two cabinets meet at the corner, the intersection between the cabinets also comes into consideration. If the cabinets aren't too big, and the intersection of the walls is close to square, the cabinets can be attached to each other, and installed as one unit.

Upper cabinets can be installed by one person, but it is much better to have a helper. After the cabinets have been lifted and set on the ledger strip, they must be checked for level and plumb, and this can be quite tricky if you are attempting to hold the cabinet up by yourself. I use two levels, a small torpedo level inside the cabinet to check the bottom of the box front to back and side to side. I also use a two-foot level outside the cabinet to check that the sides and front are plumb. Having both levels handy means that you can be sure that the cabinet is level in all directions.

Transfer the location of the wall studs to the cabinets, and drill holes through the rails before lifting the cabinets in place. If there are any electrical outlets, or vent ducts that penetrate the cabinet back, mark the locations and cut the cabinet back with a jig saw before lifting the cabinet in place. Depending on the amount of room available, you may need to work from either the inside or outside of the cabinet. It's easier to transfer your measurements from the outside, just make sure that you are cutting in the right location, and that your saw blade doesn't tear up the finished surfaces on the inside of the cabinet box. Jigsaw blades are available in up-cut and down cut or reverse

tooth profiles. Use the reverse profile when the base of the saw will be riding on a finished surface.

Screws for Installation

Remember that the screw that holds the cabinet to the wall needs to go through the back rails and back of the cabinet and the drywall before it reaches the wall stud. All of the weight of the cabinet will be carried by the screws, so they need to be thick enough and long enough. Installation screws should be #10 x 3 inches or 3½ inches. Drywall screws can be obtained in that length, but they are too small in diameter, and too brittle to be safely used.

Pan head installation screws are an ideal fastener, although countersink head screws can be used. The advantage of the pan head is that the cabinet can be shifted slightly without damaging the cabinet rail. With a countersink screw, tightening the screw will tend to pull the cabinet back to its original location. Some people will object to seeing the screw head on the inside of the cabinet, but once the cabinet is in use, these aren't noticeable. There are self-adhesive covers for screw heads available in wood tones and to match common Melamine colors. You can also paint the screw heads after the cabinets are in place.

I like to get the cabinet in position on the wall, and hold it with a couple of screws driven snug, but not completely tight. As adjacent cabinets are placed on the wall, the cabinets need to be fastened to each other as well as to the wall. It's helpful to be able to shift the cabinets to align the front edges without going back and loosening screws.

Frameless and face-frame cabinets mount to the wall the same way, but there are some differences in attaching the cabinets to each other. Some installers prefer to put several

> All of the weight of the wall cabinet will be carried by the screws, so they need to be thick enough and long enough.

cabinets together before lifting them in place, but I think this makes lifting too difficult, and with a careful installation, isn't necessary. I hang the cabinets one at a time, fastening them to the wall and then aligning the adjacent front edges. If the edges won't line up, the problem will be at the back of the cabinets, at the wall. A cabinet pulled in to a low spot can be brought out a bit by loosening the screws that hold it to the wall.

This is the reason for leaving the screws a little loose until all the cabinets in the row are in place. When the edges of the cabinets are in line, I clamp them to each other, using either small wooden hand screws, or small "F" style clamps. With the edges in line and clamped, the cabinets can be fastened together, usually with a 1¼ inch long screw through the adjacent cabinet sides. Again, some people don't like to see fasteners inside the cabinet, but I don't think it's objectionable if the screws are discretely placed.

With face frame cabinets, the screws can often be placed directly behind the frame where they won't be easily seen. With frameless cabinets, the screws can go behind the hinge plates and won't be obvious. If you want the fasteners completely hidden in frameless cabinets, you can place the screws under the hinge plates. This creates more work than necessary, but it will allow for hidden fastening.

When all the cabinets in the run are fastened together, the screws holding them to the wall can be completely tightened, checking as you go that they aren't being pulled out of plumb. If this happens, you need to determine which screws are pulling in too far. If there are enough fasteners holding the cabinet to the surface of the wall, the few that pull too tight can be left snug but not tight. If there aren't enough fasteners to hold securely, the cabinet may need to be taken down, and some shims placed in these locations.

> If you want the fasteners completely hidden in frameless cabinets, you can place the screws under the hinge plates.

Soffits and Finished Ends

If there are cabinets with finished ends at both ends of an elevation, the installation should be started in the middle of the run, leaving equal amounts of wall space at each end. Where the back of a finished end meets the wall, this junction should be scribed. Scribing is a process of trimming the cabinet material to match the wall. This will be described in more detail later on.

If the run of cabinets starts at the wall, the edge that meets the wall will need to be scribed before the rest of the cabinets can be put in place. This requires putting up and taking down the first cabinet a few times, but that is preferable to placing all of the cabinets and then taking them all down to move them over ¼ inch or ½ inch.

If there is a soffit, the juncture of the cabinet tops and the soffit will present another complication. If there is to be a molding covering the intersection, make sure before beginning that there is enough room to fit the cabinets between the bottom of the soffit and the planned line for the bottom of the cabinets. You can cheat the bottom of the cabinets down ¼ inch or ½ inch without getting into trouble, but you shouldn't go further than that. Make sure that moving the cabinets down slightly won't leave a gap between the molding and ceiling or molding and cabinets. Run some screws from the inside top of the cabinets into the framing of the soffit, shimming where needed for a firm connection without distorting the top of the cabinet.

If the top of the wall cabinets needs to be scribed to the soffit, or to the ceiling, find the low point before beginning and scribe the tops as the cabinets are installed. The whole idea is to get them in place correctly the first time. Spending extra time at the start will always save time in the long run, try to eliminate the chance of doing something twice.

Base Cabinets

Base cabinets also start at a corner, and the designs shown earlier in this book allow room for adjustment in the corner. Work from the planned face of the cabinets, and not from the corner of the walls if you can. The corner you establish for the cabinet faces will be more true and reliable than the building walls. The complicated part of installing the base cabinets is usually allowing enough room in the right places for appliances, plumbing and electrical connections.

If the cabinets are to be placed on a separate base platform, getting the cabinets level will be relatively easy. The big advantage of the separate base is that you can reach the back if you need to. If you're installing cabinets with an integral base, and need to raise the back of a cabinet in the middle of a run you have to either pull the cabinets out, place shims and put the cabinet back or lift the cabinet from the back and let it hang from the screws through the back rail.

When I install base cabinets, I mark the locations of the cabinet ends on the horizontal benchmark to be sure that the base is located in the right place. When the location is accurately determined, the base is leveled. If the base is long enough, I use a four-foot level parallel to the wall, and a two-foot level in the other direction. Using a molding chisel or small crowbar, the low points are raised and shims are placed between the floor and the bottom of the base.

When the base is level in all directions, double-check the location before fastening it to the floor and wall. If there is a gap of more than ¼ inch between the floor and the bottom of the base, it will be easier to attach the base to the floor with cleats made from scrap 2x2 or 2x4 material.

If the floor is plywood, or hardwood, the cleats can be screwed into the floor. If you're working on a concrete slab, you will need to use Tap-Con fasteners as anchors. The base should also be connected to the wall. Usually you can go through the lower part of the base and into the bottom plate of the wall, eliminating the need to hit a stud.

Floor or Cabinets First?

One of the ongoing debates in building is whether or not to install the cabinets before the finished floor. Flooring contractors always want to go first, and so do cabinet installers. Of course the cabinet installers are correct in this matter.

The argument for putting the finished floor in first is that if the cabinets are ever rearranged, the flooring will be there, and it won't need to be replaced. The problem with this is that there will be holes in the finished floor everywhere a pipe or wire comes through, and everywhere the cabinets are fastened down. If the floor is hardwood, linoleum, or vinyl, the exposed areas will have faded to a different color, and be subject to wear and tear. In most cases cabinets stay in place until a major remodeling takes place, which will likely include replacing the flooring. Putting the flooring in first makes life easier for the flooring installer, and requires a significant amount of material that will never be seen.

Placing the cabinets first lets them be connected firmly to the sub floor, and prevents any damage to the floor from occurring during the cabinet installation. The thickness of the finished floor should be taken into account so that the tops of the cabinets are at the right distance from the floor, when the floor is in place.

If the base is sitting level, and securely fastened, the remaining work in installing the base cabinets should proceed very quickly.

Flooring contractors always want to go first, and so do cabinet installers. Of course the cabinet installers are correct...

Because they will be sitting on a level platform, the cabinets will only need to be put in position and fastened to each other and then to the wall. Each individual cabinet won't need to be leveled and adjusted.

Holes will need to be cut for pipes in sink bases, and there may need to be some cutouts made for electrical access. Once the location of the sink base has been established side to side, you can slide the cabinet back against the pipe stubs and reach over the back of the cabinet to mark their location without any measuring. With a small diameter bit, drill a hole from the back side of the cabinet. Then drill the correct size hole for the pipes from the inside with a hole saw. This keeps the hole saw from tearing out the finished back of the cabinet as it comes through.

When the cabinets are in place, they should be fastened to the studs through the back rails. Even though you don't have to worry about base cabinets falling, as you do with wall cabinets, the connections should be secure. Base cabinets can get bumped as appliances are put in place, and may shift as the building settles. The extra effort of running a screw to each stud will keep the cabinets looking good for a long time. Place a shim between the wall and cabinet rail, to keep the screw from bending the rail.

The boxes should also be fastened down to the base. I use 1¼ inch long screws located as close to the inside corners of the cabinet as I can reach. Again this is a place where a few people object to seeing a screw head, but it's better to have the cabinet securely attached to the building structure. FastCaps can be used to cover the screw heads if their appearance is objectionable.

Scribing to walls

When the back or front edge of a cabinet meets a wall the straight edge of the cabinet should be cut to match the line of the wall. This process is known as "scribing" the cabinet, and if done well will greatly improve the appearance of the installation. In the construction sections of this book, I describe where and how to leave extra material on the cabinet for this purpose.

The cabinet to be scribed is put in position, as close as possible to its final location. It is also critical that the cabinet be level, with its face parallel to adjacent cabinets and to the wall. Once in place, the outline of the wall is marked on the edge of the cabinet to be trimmed. The traditional tool for this is a compass, set to the distance to be removed. The leg without the pencil is moved down the surface of the wall, and the pencil transfers the mark to the cabinet. A big improvement over the compass is the "Accu-Scribe". With two legs opposite the pencil, this is easier to keep in position as the lines are drawn.

If just a single cabinet is being scribed, you only need to worry about matching the outline of the wall. If the cabinet to be scribed is at the end of a run of cabinets, the outline of the wall needs to be matched while maintaining the correct alignment at the opposite corner of the box, where it mates with another cabinet. If there is only one cabinet, it doesn't matter how far back the cabinet actually moves, so the distance between the pencil point and the sharp point of the compass is set to the biggest visible gap.

If you need to match the face of an adjacent cabinet, however, set the dividers to the distance that the two cabinet faces are offset, when the cabinet is in place and touching the wall. This is the distance that the cabinet needs to move toward the wall. Remember that the cabinet needs to be level, and parallel to its final location. This is often neglected with wall cabinets. If the cabinet is shoved against a wall that is out of plumb, the marks scribed will make the cabinet tight to the wall, but will prevent it from being leveled without a gap.

If the cabinet has a dark finish, the pencil lines can be hard to see. A strip of masking tape on the edge of the cabinet lets the lines show, and will keep the edges from splintering as the cuts are made. The actual cutting can be done in a number of ways; the weapon of choice is often determined by what's available on the job site. I use a jigsaw with a down cutting blade to make the initial cuts, and a block plane to smooth the cut lines. If only a small amount of material is to be removed, the block plane can do the entire job.

Belt sanders and powered planes are also commonly used, but are harder to control, noisy and messy. Some cabinetmakers like to put a bevel or a rabbet on the back of the edge to be trimmed, the theory being that this makes the process easier, because there is less material to be removed. This makes some sense if you are scribing entirely by hand, but if you're using a power tool, the thickness of the edge being trimmed won't make a significant difference.

With some practice, the scribe can be cut correctly on the first attempt. Marking with the cabinet level, and carefully cutting to the line should do it. It often takes a few tries to get it to what is commonly called "caulking distance."

One man's "caulking distance" can be another man's Grand Canyon, so you will need to decide how close is acceptable to you. I think it should be ⅟₁₆ inch or less, but many people are happy with ⅛ inch or ¼ inch. On really good days, the fit will be close enough that caulking isn't needed at all.

After the cabinets are scribed, they are fastened to the adjacent cabinets and then to the wall. Fastening the cabinet to the wall will often close any remaining slight gaps. If

gaps remain, they can be filled with a bead of paintable caulking. On commercial jobsites there is often an argument over whether the cabinetmaker or the painter is responsible for this. If you're working for yourself you'll be stuck with it.

Installing the Countertop

Installing the countertop should come next, although the temptation is strong to put the doors and drawers back in the cabinets. The steps that follow apply for installing plastic laminate or butcher-block counters. If your tops are solid surface material or natural stone, the connection between cabinets and counter is slightly different. Follow the manufacturer or fabricator's recommendations if you are installing these tops.

A one-piece straight countertop is the easiest to install. Before placing the top, go along the line of base cabinets and drill holes in the top rails or corner blocks of each cabinet. If part of the counter rests on cleats, mark a level line on the wall at the top of the cabinets. If you previously drew a benchmark at this location, make sure that it is still in line with the cabinets.

Place the counter on the cabinets and make sure that it is the right size. Check the fit of the counter where it meets the wall. At the back, you shouldn't need to scribe if the gaps are small enough to be covered by the backsplash. At the front of the counter, the distance from the front edge of the counter to the front face of the cabinets should be consistent. If one of the front edges meets the wall, check the fit at both the edge, and on the top. A gap on the top will likely be covered by the splash, but the front edge should meet the wall.

If you do need to scribe the top, mark the edges to be trimmed the same way the cabinets were marked. Again, be careful that the

One man's "caulking distance" can be another man's Grand Canyon...

front edge of the counter is parallel to the front face of the cabinets before marking. To make the cuts, remove the counter from the cabinets and place it on sawhorses. Don't turn the counter around to use the cabinets as a workbench or use an adjacent run of cabinets as a bench. You want to cut the edges of the counter, not the fronts of the finished cabinets.

I use a jigsaw with a down cutting blade to make the cuts without chipping the surface of the laminate. A strip of masking tape along the edge will help you see your pencil lines on a dark colored top, and will help prevent chipping. After the cuts are made, check the fit, and scribe a second time if you need to.

With the top scribed, you can now locate and make cuts for the sink if you need to. Layout the cut from the cabinet, so the sink will be centered in it. Remove the top and work in another location to prevent damaging the cabinets. The raw edge of the cut should be sealed; a bead of silicone caulking, smeared around the edge with a finger will accomplish this quickly.

If the counter is L shaped or U shaped, it will require more fitting than a straight top, and may include a field joint. Put the field joint together if you can before fitting the top to the walls. The appearance of the joint will be more visible than the condition of the top at the walls.

With the top scribed and ready to be fastened, the first thing to do is to make sure that all of the screws you will be using are the right length. You will be lying on your back, inside the cabinets, reaching for screws. The last thing you want is to grab one that is so long it comes through the surface of the top. Fastening the top will be much easier if there are two people, one to drive the screws from below while the other holds the top down and in place. The guy on top is allowed to

joke "did you mean for that screw to come through?" but only once.

Backsplash

Backsplashes can be scribed where the top edge meets the wall, but if they are ¾ inch thick material they can usually be bent slightly to conform to the wall. That edge will be caulked anyway, so gaps up to ⅛ inch can be easily covered by the caulking. There are a variety of clips and fasteners to hold the splash in place, but I think gluing them in with construction adhesive is a better method. Some adhesives can act a lot like contact cement if you push the parts together, then pull them apart and wait a few minutes. Pushing them together again usually lets the adhesive grab and hold the splash to the wall. If not, a combination of hot-melt glue and construction adhesive works well. Lay down a bead of adhesive, then quickly put some dabs of hot-melt on the splash and push it to the wall.

Handles and Pulls

With the counters in, take some time to clean up the insides of the cabinets before replacing the doors and drawers. If the cabinets are sitting level, there shouldn't be many adjustments to make to the doors and the drawers. Step back and look at the entire elevation of cabinets, and make sure that everything lines up and functions as it should. If the cabinets have been finished in the shop, touch up any nicks or dings, and install the handles or pulls.

When attaching the top, be very sure all the screws are the correct length...

INDEX

Index (continued)

Index (continued)

More Great Books from Bob Lang

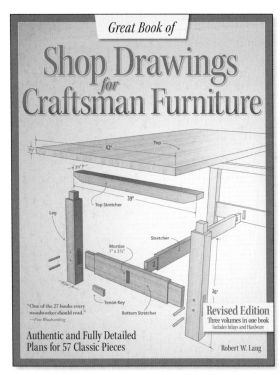

Great Book of Shop Drawings for Craftsman Furniture, Revised Edition
ISBN 978-1-56523-812-1 **$29.99**

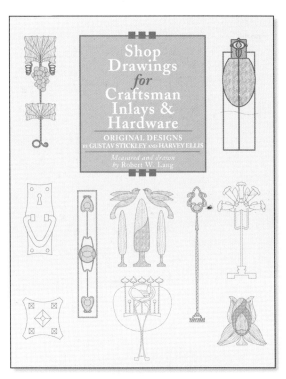

Shop Drawings for Craftsman Inlays & Hardware
ISBN 978-1-892836-20-5 **$19.95**

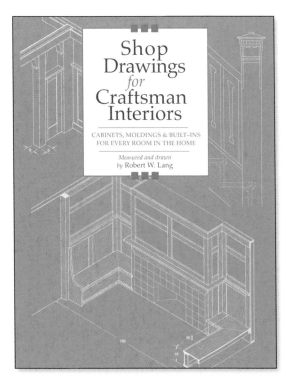

Shop Drawings for Craftsman Interiors
ISBN 978-1-892836-16-8 **$24.95**

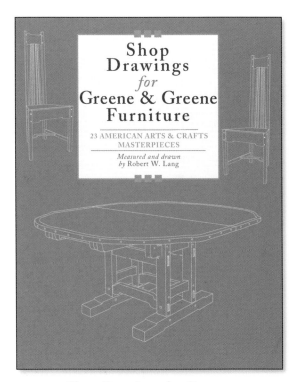

Shop Drawings for Greene & Greene Furniture
ISBN 978-1-892836-29-8 **$22.95**